a century of stories from Asia and the Pacific

Born in 1947 Russell Darnley had grandparents who were children at Federation, lived through World War I and struggled as parents through the Great Depression. His parents had their first jobs as World War II broke out. Growing up in Sydney with a seafaring father gave him an interest in what lay beyond. His childhood saw the birth of multicultural Australia, which he embraced, and ended with Conscription and the Vietnam War, both of which he resisted. As a young adult he travelled the world and discovered that his interests lay in South East Asia.

Working respectively as teacher, administrator, researcher, director of a field study centre in Indonesia, consultant to the Australia Indonesia Institute, educational writer and digital education pioneer he was awarded the OAM for his voluntary work after the 2002 Bali Bombings. Russell's outlook is eclectic and interdisciplinary, passionately scientific, yet profoundly spiritual.

Glass House Books

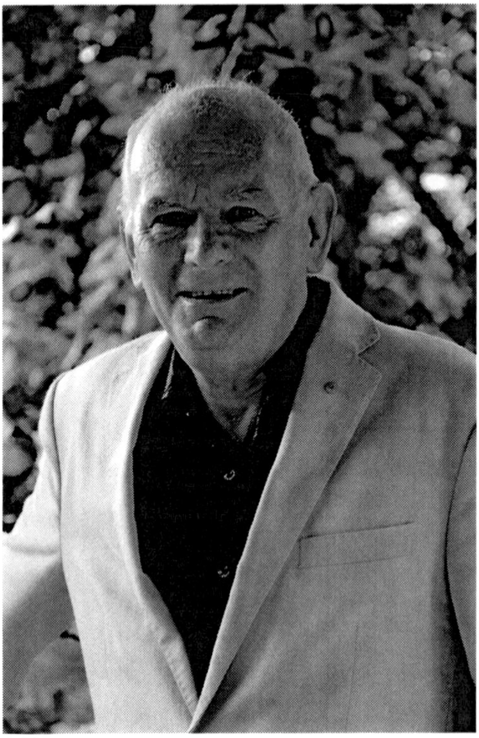

Seen and Unseen:
a century of stories from Asia and the Pacific

Russell Darnley OAM

Glass House Books

Seen and Unseen

Glass House Books
an imprint of IP (Interactive Publications Pty Ltd)
Treetop Studio • 9 Kuhler Court
Carindale, Queensland, Australia 4152
sales@ipoz.biz
ipoz.biz/IP/IP.htm

First published by IP in 2015
© Russell Darnley OAM, 2015

All rights reserved. Without limiting the rights under copyright reserved above, no part of this publication may be reproduced, stored in or introduced into a retrieval system, or transmitted, in any form or by any means (electronic, mechanical, photocopying, recording or otherwise), without the prior written permission of the copyright owner and the publisher of this book.

Printed in 12 pt Book Antiqua on 14 pt Avenir Medium.

National Library of Australia
Cataloguing-in-Publication entry:

Creator:	Darnley, Russell, author.
Title:	Seen and unseen : a century of stories from Asia and the Pacific / Russell Darnley OAM.
ISBN:	9781925231182 (paperback)

Subjects: Australians--Asia. Australians--Melanesia. Interpersonal communication and culture--Asia. Interpersonal communication and culture--Melanesia. Asia--Civilization--20th century. Asia--History--20th century. Melanesia--Civilization--20th century. Melanesia--History--20th century.

Dewey Number: 306

This work is dedicated to James, Jackson, Lachlan, Sava, Milos, Anja and Cruz Dominic

Acknowledgements

Book and cover design: David P. Reiter

Images: Russell Darnley

Acknowledgements to Paul Arbon, Dachlan Chandradinata, David Chaplin, Lauren Daniels, Caroline Elwood, Randal Grayson, Steve Jarick, Asri Kerthayasa, Henky Kurniawan, Ray Long, Rochayah Machali, Helen Metlenko, Nita Noor, Kim Patra, Matina Pentes with thanks for years of collaboration, Margaret Sbrocchi, Steve Storey, Nyoman Suradnya, Melanie Templer, Adrienne Truelove and Tony Wallace. Finally, special thanks are due to my wife Catherine for her loving support and constructive criticism.

Disclaimer: This is a work of creative non-fiction in which the author has recreated events, locales and conversations from his memories of them. To protect their anonymity he has, in some instances, changed the names of individuals and places, and some identifying characteristics and details such as physical properties, occupations and places of residence.

Contents

Sid Thompson and D Company	1
Red Poppies and Janur	12
Camphor Silk and Ivory	21
Made in Japan	30
Joss Sticks and Cracker Night	41
An Encounter with White Australia	47
Surviving the Sixties	52
First Landfall	63
From the Sublime to the Horrific	76
The Dream	90
The Thief and the Angels	98
Magic, Polygamy and Triangles	105
Beyond Bhoma's Powers	116
Balikpapan: Looking Backwards and Forwards	124
The River Guide	133
Siberut and the Simple Life	146
The Pig and the Cockfight	159
Kanda Empat: The Four Siblings	169
A Day of Departures	175
Kampanye – The Campaign Procession	179
Pemilihan Umum – The General Election	190
Unspoken Realities	199
An Unusual Kind of Thunder	207
In the Charnel House	223
Baby Boomers and Japan	245
My Second Meeting with Jonathan	257
Singapore 43 Years on	263
Vietnam: A War Revisited	275
Headland	286

Sid Thompson and D Company

From Coogee's northern headland, the view sweeps over the beach to the next point now dominated by Wylie's baths. Beyond and unseen is a place of my childhood where my grandfather, Sid Thompson, often visited in the 1950s. Here a dramatic embayment, a spectacular sandstone overhang and a small waterfall cascading from swampy land combine to create something unique a place infused with a special energy.

"Let's go'n look at the lions, Rusty," he'd say, capturing my imagination. Then off we set down Neptune Street, the smell of the sea enticing as we made for the old Batty Mansion. Here on the hill above the overhang, impassive stone lions gazed to the north and to the south.

On another day, Sid said, "Come'n, I'll show y'the coral," and we scrambled down beside the waterfall at low tide and stepped amongst squirting cunjevois to explore the pools and bogey holes, gouged along the lower parts of the rock by the action of waves.

"Have a look here in that pool," Sid pointed. "See the colour? Soft coral, that is. A long way from here, where the water's warmer, it grows with branches like plants' n lots of other shapes too."

I peered into the pool fascinated by the blues, mauves and pinks; the starfish, whelks, anemones, limpets, sea urchins and crabs. Further on, beneath the massive overhang, waves surged against stone except when tides ebbed to their lowest. Here the display reached beyond the pools, clinging to the rock shelf and fallen boulders. Shadows, salt spray and seepage created a sombre space in a child's mind. In this place of primal energies, Sid was in his element.

All these years later, I still hear his voice. Perhaps I should say I feel his presence when I step back upon that tidal zone where sea and stone meet: a nuance, a flow of ideas and a sense of his reactions, his meanings. Most manifest in that primal space we visited, his presence enriches my thought. We spoke of so many things back then, and sometimes, I even catch glimpses of him.

The sea was calm when I found Sid there again after 50 years. He had scrambled up onto one of the large boulders and sat relaxed, gazing seaward and drawing on his pipe.

"Sid, can you hear me?" I called.

He turned, that serious look on his face that he so often wore.

"Rusty! What are you doing here?"

"I often come here, ever since you first brought me."

"Is that so? So you like this place?"

"How did you find it?"

He drew on his pipe, watching a flock of sea gulls diving on baitfish off shore. At first there was no reply. Then he removed his pipe and looked at me. "I loved the sea. It runs in the family, y'know. M'dad was a sailor from Jersey. Loved the coast, he did, and like him, I enjoyed long coastal strolls'n fossickin around. Sometimes I'd throw in a line. If the tide was right I'd have a dip in a bogey hole. That's how I found this special place."

He continued, as he drew up his legs and squatted. "I like sittin here looking out to the east. There's a deep channel runnin just off shore n'sometimes in the spring y'can see whales passin."

I looked at my watch as I scrambled onto the boulder beside him. We had an hour or so before the tide blocked my retreat. Here in this shady place his incorporal presence was so intense. It seemed like a good a time to listen to what he was prepared to tell me and I hoped he would tell me about his war experience. Over the years, I'd often wondered how he must have felt, when right after the move to Bondi, he picked up the *Sydney Morning Herald* one morning only to read:

> Great Britain's position in relation to Germany has now been clearly defined. Since the neutrality of Belgium has been violated by the latter Power, Britain is at war, and that is now the condition into which the Empire has been flung. For good or ill, we are engaged with the mother country in fighting for liberty and peace. It is no war of aggression upon which Britons have entered, but one in defence of small nations threatened with humiliation and absorption, if not with extinction; and above and beyond everything our armies will fight for British honour.

And so I asked him: "Sid, how did you feel when right after the move from Summer Hill the war broke out and you were called on to fight?"

"I loved Australia, y'know," he replied, gazing out to sea. "I wasn't so fussed about protectin' Britain, the Motherland' as they called it, but I didn't like the Prussian militarists'n I knew there were German colonies on the islands up north. Livin' at Bondi made me think about the importance of our sea trade. I knew anythin' interferin' with that trade well 'n truly threatened our prosperity, our freedom. I had some skills from the 39th militia 'n there was that young man's sense of adventure. I'd just left home 'n the world was a splendid and excitin' place. They called for volunteers so I enlisted."

For Sid, like many other Australians, war in Europe must have seemed remote but when the British War Office called for Australian support in seizing the German colonies in New Guinea, New Britain and New Ireland the response was prompt. German wireless stations on New Britain were critical to the operational effectiveness of the Imperial German Navy's East Asiatic Squadron linking it

Seen and Unseen

with German naval head quarters in Kiau Chau[1] China and back to Germany. Such links made sea-lanes between Australia and the Middle East vulnerable and afforded the German squadron great freedom of movement in Asia and the Pacific.

Sid continued, "They called for volunteers for a special Naval' n Military Expeditionary Force almost immediately. ANMEF they called it. I was an ideal recruit. When I joined up, I was put in D Company, Tropical Unit 1st Battalion."

"I knew you went to New Guinea, Sid, but I don't know much about it."

"Well, I'll tell y'the story. Leavin Sydney was a big event. Crowds of people linin' the streets callin out 'Hooroo', 'Good luck', 'Give it to em, boys' or singin 'God Save the King' 'n 'Rule, Britannia!' Marchin' down Macquarie Street on our way to the Man o'War Steps, this beautiful well-dressed woman ran out 'n grabbed her son's arm. Suddenly there was a bloke with a big camera takin a photo."

"That photo! It's iconic! It's in lots of children's history books. Funny thing, you know it's seldom associated with ANMEF. Usually with Gallipoli."

"Ah yeah, pretty awful Gallipoli, the first of many tragedies. I won't say our lot was easier but it was simpler."

Within a fortnight of war's declaration, the ANMEF consisting of 1,000 infantry plus 500 naval reservists and former Royal Navy seaman set sail for Palm Island off the coast of Queensland.

"I'll never forget goin' to the tropics for the first time," said Sid. "I'd never been in that sticky heat before. We had two weeks trainin for the exercise'n it was bloody hard yakka in that heat. We knew sorta where we were headed but officially it was secret. We knew it was well

---

[1] Now known as Qingdao (青岛) and located on the The Shāndōng Peninsula (山东半岛).

n' truly on when the battleship *Australia* arrived. Things moved pretty fast after that. We left Palm Island with a naval escort 'n these new submarines called HMAS AE1 'n AE2. Steamin' for four days through the Coral Sea there was no sight of the Kaiser's navy. Then early one mornin', we stood off New Britain. We went ashore in boats. One group landed at a place called Kabakaul 'n made straight for a radio transmitter at Bitapaka. Our group landed at Herbertshöhe. We reckoned we'd find a radio transmitter but there was naught. We didn't encounter any resistance either."

On the road to Bitapaka, ANMEF came under fire from snipers in trees and trenches set beside on the verges. Resistance was aided by the road's narrowness and dense lowland rainforest forest laced with thorny rattan palms. With vision limited to less than a dozen paces along sections of the road contact was intense but short. German resistance quickly overwhelmed; Bitapaka was taken by 7pm. Within days, the acting governor surrendered German New Guinea.

All further operations in Bougainville and on the mainland of New Guinea were unopposed. Total losses in action amounted to six servicemen. The only substantial loss of the campaign was submarine *HMAS AE1*, which disappeared without trace, probably striking an uncharted reef off the Gazelle Peninsula and sinking with all 35 hands.

"No one knows much about ANMEF," Sid observed. "Gallipoli and the Western Front were really crook 'n it's what they remember. I reckon people don't even know much about the German colonies."

"They don't," I said, "but I see the action up there as having a different significance. It flagged the emergence of an embryonic strategic regional engagement. For me, looking back, this event had a geopolitical significance.

As you say, it was dwarfed by the scale and gravity of the losses in the Middle East and on the Western Front but these were more directly serving British interests. To my mind, your operation highlights what was just outside the consciousness of most Australians at the time. In fact, it revealed forces that continue to shape our culture and our region. Our ally Japan, for one, was very put out that it wasn't involved in this action or in the carving up of territories later."

"'Struth, I've buckley's of understandin' that, Russ. We were just tryn'te survive. The Germans were easy to beat but there were other dangers things ya couldn't see. For starters, we lost that submarine, then we had ta get through the wet season. It started rainin' in late October'n by December, Hughie was sendin' it down in buckets." He laughed, using the old Australian phrase for God throwing down the rain, then he continued, "Lucky I'd been promoted to lance corporal'n was workin on the telephone switchboard. It was no bludge but it was mostly out of the rain."

"What was Rabaul like in those days, Sid? It was badly damaged by a volcanic eruption in 1994. I can't imagine it before that."

"It was beaut back then, with wide streets n'nice colonial buildins. A lot of the houses were on piles surrounded by verandahs 'n hedges at the front. Down the middle of the roads there were flame trees, acacia n' she-oaks. Kitchens were out the back of the houses in case of fire, so the servants were out the back too. Yeah, 'n another thing: Rabaul even had a cinema 'n botanic gardens."

"Sounds like you were comfortably accommodated, Sid."

"It was oright, comfortable, plenty of fresh fish, prawns 'n mud crabs. It helped havin' lots of Chinese in Rabaul."

"Yeah, the Chinese. They were visiting and settling

in places all the way from New Britain to Sumatra as far back as the Ming Dynasty."

"Looked like they'd been around for a while. By the time we came, they were plenty. Most worked in the copra industry, some worked for the Germans 'n some had gone out on their own buyin 'n sellin copra. Big money in copra, y'know. Maybe there were 500 in town and maybe another 1000 livin' about. There was a Chinatown runnin' along the main street near the Tolai markets. Me 'n me mates enjoyed a Chinese feed. We ate at a Chinese restaurant called The Asiatic."

"That's amazing. I had no idea."

"Oh yeah, the Chinese were well organised 'n good at doin business with the Tolai –better than the Germans or us. We all respected their business skills. They got the go-ahead to build The Asiatic. Good tucker it was. There was a 'big man' behind it all. If I remember rightly his name was Ah Tam."

"What sort of businesses did he run in Rabaul? Were they legitimate?"

"Ah Tam'd been in Rabaul for a while. A drivin' force behind Chinatown, he was. Apart from the restaurant, he recruited 'n managed carpenters, cooks and coolies, a finger in many pies. Then there was his license to import opium. I reckon he was runnin' the gambling 'n rumour has it he imported 'n ran 20 to 30 Japanese prostitutes. As the telephone operator, I picked up on a lot of this."

"So this was Rabaul, 1914. None of this comes out in the newspapers of the time. Reports back to Australia just announced the ANMEF victory. I'd always assumed there was little for you to do other than wait out the wet season."

"In a way, our victory wasn't real," Sid reflected. "Just when we thought everythin' was apples, the real enemies got organised. We didn't see 'em at first. They moved

Seen and Unseen

through our ranks very quietly. Expert in camouflage, they were, n' chose their targets well. They used all sorts of tricks like fallen palm fronds, coconut shells, boats, tin cans 'n tarpaulins. Comin' right in among us'n we didn't realise they were dangerous. Then out on the edge of the town in low lyin' 'n swampy areas there was another lot gatherin' strength. They were even more dangerous. I reckon y'd know them better as dengue[2] fever' n malaria[3] these days."

What Sid described is well documented. Medical reports from the time tell us that two varieties of malaria, *Plasmodium vivax* and *Plasmodium falciparum*, were common in the area and that in ANMEF's case immunity was the key to the problem. Then it must have been most disquieting. Few if any would have known about these dangers and fewer still would have had any degree of immunity.

Sid continued, "Apart from a few marines who'd served time in India or the Malay States, few of us had ever been exposed to anythin' like this. Our medical officer requisitioned quinine but for some it was useless. It was only good for one sort of malaria; the other sort killed the boys pretty quickly, but we lined up for quinine

---

[2] Dengue is a virus spread by the *Aedes aegypti* mosquito. It causes an acute viral fever often with symptoms such as headaches, bone and muscular pain, rash and a lower than normal white blood cell count.

[3] Malaria is a far more dangerous condition produced by one of four protozoan parasites of the genus *Plasmodium*. Carried by female *anopheline* mosquito, its resistance to treatment varies, depending on the parasite involved. Its life cycle is complex. Both *Plasmodium vivax* and *Plasmodium falciparum* were common in the area. *Vivax* tends to recur in three day cycles causing high fevers alternating with chills, profuse sweating, sever headaches and extreme weakness. It is particularly debilitating because it destroys red blood cells. It commonly recurs and relapses may occur years after infection. *Falciparum* malaria is far graver and if left untreated, amongst people without immunity, is often fatal within three to four weeks.

when it arrived."

"Yeah, that deadly one is *Falciparum*, and quinine's no use with it."

In Sid's time, the doctor probably didn't know much about the epidemiology of malaria or that Melanesian people of New Guinea and the Bismarck Archipelago had a degree of immunity to it. Though death rates amongst children were high, the Tolai had learned to live with it. In coastal areas where it was endemic, constant reinfection stimulated and maintained an immune response to *vivax*. Mosquitos, parasites and humans lived in a type of environmental balance but the sudden appearance of a large alien population had significant ecological implications. It created a new ecological space, increasing the number of opportunities for the plasmodium parasites to flourish unconstrained by the problem of immunity. Amongst the ANMEF men, there was a parasitic population explosion and accelerating rates of transmission.

"Sometime durin' the wet season I caught vivax malaria," Sid continued. "I kept havin these bouts of high fever'n chills, intense sweats, thumpin headaches'n I felt as weak as a bloody kitten. I couldn't get off me bunk. Later they told me it destroys red blood cells. I got what they called anaemia. I felt like the wreck of the Hesperus."

"So that was the ANMEF story but what about the Chinese? How were they dealing with it and what about the Germans?"

"I don't know much about the Germans but seems the Chinese had their own medicines. Of course it was all unofficial 'n our medical officer didn't want to know about it."

"So he didn't go looking for answers?"

"No, it was like out of sight out of mind, but the cook at The Asiatic was a very clever man. He saw I had malaria 'n he took me over to the Tolai markets. He knew Ah Tam

Seen and Unseen

was growin' plants for Chinese medicine on a big patch of land just outside Rabaul. Some of this was sold through the markets. Ah Tam also imported a lot from China. It was expensive but I managed to get enough Black Cardamom 'n a fruit that he called Ya tan tzu. Later on I found the fruit was called Java Brucea fruit in English. Both of these did me a lot of good. They eased the effects of the malaria."

Certainly there's no evidence that ANMEF did anything more than issue quinine tablets to the troops, yet alternative treatments like these must have been everywhere but unseen to ANMEF's leaders. Agus, an old friend from Jakarta, knowledgeable in traditional medicine, confirmed this with me when he said: "Sid's right. There are many alternatives in Indonesia and Melanesia, simple things like a ginger known as tsaoko fruit[4] and the widely available Java brucea fruit. There is also an herb imported from China called sweet wormwood. It's widely used in Chinese medicine as an anti-malarial. It's more effective than quinine in treating *vivax*."

"The tides are comin' in, Rusty," said Sid. "You'd better be movin'."

"Yeah, I'd better, but tell me about the malaria," I asked, wanting to get to the end of the story.

"I had bouts of it for years 'n I'm sure it contributed to me death in 1952."

"But the Chinese medicine helped, did it?"

"Yeah for sure," Sid confirmed. "I'd have been much worse off without it. After the war I used to pick it up in Chinatown, down in Dixon Street."

Sid's confidence in traditional Chinese medicine was unusual for people of his background. In the last months of his life, he was receiving treatment from a Chinese <u>herbalist. How</u> effective it was for him then is unclear

---

[4] *Amomum costatum*, 草果; also known as Black Cardamom, a member of the ginger family.

because his heart was the main problem towards the end of his life, but he confirmed that it helped with the malaria.

"Come on, Rusty, time to go. I'll come along for a ways. Y'know, I've been thinkin' of old Colonel Holmes, the CO of ANMEF. He understood our effort. When he came back from the Western Front, he said, 'While they hadn't undergone all the risks and hardships of other overseas forces, when looking at the casualty lists from malaria, their lot was not an enviable one.'"

Sid stopped along the rocks as I continued. He said: "There's no point 'n bein' bitter about war. The point is what we do to remember the sacrifice of the many 'n what we do to prevent future wars."

His response to the tragedy was remarkably adaptive. He sought neither glory nor compensation. He understood and felt the sacrifices of war yet I can't remember him having much to say about war at all. As an adult I often wondered how he must have felt when 27 years later a militia unit, bearing the same name as his old unit, fought the Japanese advance along the Kokoda Track sustaining massive casualties from the unseen enemy, malaria.

Red Poppies and Janur

Shortly before his death in 1952, Sid Thompson built at timber cottage in Bargo, south of Sydney. One quiet afternoon after my chat with him by the sea, I imagined him sitting by the substantial fireplace, hardwood logs emitting a glowing ambiance. A large gilt framed image of a Romanesque cathedral hung above the mantle piece. Porcelain horses galloped towards it from one side and a fine Japanese vase sat sedately on the other. The smell of fresh sawn timber and a faint scent of eucalyptus filled the warm air.

"I've been researching the ANMEF, Sid."

"You're back, Rusty!" Sid looked up from his seat by the fire, "Have a pew. So what do you know?"

"Not as much as I'd like to, Sid. Would you tell me a bit more? I mean, why don't people talk much about ANMEF?"

"A few reasons. When I got back to Sydney in the autumn of 1915, the news was full of Gallipoli, Palestine and the Western Front. This was grabbin' people's attention. I was pretty crook with the malaria so I wasn't talkin' much either."

"Reading the history," I said to him, "I see ANMEF's contribution was remembered for several incidents. What was going on in Rabaul? The story about the military police being gaoled and the officers pillaging German homes: what was all that about?"

"As the telephone operator, I had a fair idea what was goin' on," he replied. "You see, enlisted men were barred from Chinatown 'n the military coppers did the rounds to make sure we weren't there."

"I guess you went there anyway, Sid, eh?"

"I knew when not to go. So, four coppers were convicted of raidin' Ah Tam's opium den and stealin money. They got three or four years in Goulburn Gaol. Fair dinkum, they were just actin' as coppers did in those days, tryin' to take a commission from the opium business. Just like cops back home – on the take."

He leaned forward over the hearth and tapped his pipe ash into flames that danced around hardwood logs then he sat back unscrewed his tobacco tin and pressed fresh tobacco into the pipe. Lighting up, he settled back into his comfortable armchair. Eventually he spoke.

"All the while this was goin' on, a team of officers had their own operation runnin'. Colonel Paton, Lieutenant Davidson and two other officers were busy takin' silver spoons, medals and other small items, even women's clothin', from the homes of German officers and settlers. Oddly, an enquiry went very light on them. I think it found they had 'no felonious intent'. I s'pose this is the sort of thing that happens when there's little else to do. Maybe they saw themselves as souvenirin'. Like stamp collectin', eh?"

Sid's story reminded me that one set of rules applied to officers and another to enlisted men and non-commissioned officers. The Labor member for Bourke, Mr Anstey, argued against the harshness of the punishment metred out to the military police. He said:

> It took 24 hours to condemn men by court-martial to three and four years' penal servitude, but the inquiry into the other affair had been going on for three months, and there appeared to be no prospect of anything being done. The offences of the men could not be compared with those of the officers, who, on unquestionable evidence, had been guilty of wholesale rape and looting, yet the officers had the audacity to sit upon the court-martial and condemn the rank and file.[5]

---

[5] Mr. Anstey, Labour member for Bourke in the House of Representatives

"Was ANMEF under a cloud because of the looting?" I asked. "Was this guilt by association for you? Was it an embarrassment? I heard that on the whole you avoided ANZAC Day marches. Was that why?"

"Not really. I thought about it . . . a lot. My military service was easy. Sure, I was sick but those blokes at the Gallipoli and even more the ones on Western Front . . . they faced horrors 'n calamities beyond imaginin'. Some were even left with doubts about what it is to be human."

His facial lines deepened, his image always clearest to me when we considered serious matters.

"I read something along those lines," I said, "but was there more to it than this?"

"Yeah, for me there was. See, after the war, cenotaphs were built to commemorate the fallen," he said, waving his pipe stem like a pointer, as if counting out the objects. "One side had an inscription 'Lest We Forget', the other side read 'To Our Glorious Dead'. In truth, I don't know whether the fallen are glorious. Who can say? The way I see it's between the fallen and God."

"Maybe its origin is in the old idea that the monarch was God's appointed," I said. "So if soldiers die serving the king, they were acting according to God's will and this makes their deaths glorious."

Sid raised his pipe, drew deeply and released a cloud of smoke. He gazed up into the smoke as if the answer might lie somewhere in its midst. "If the dead are glorious, they must have died servin' the divine but who says so? Kings? Politicians? There's no guarantee of glory," he said. "Best for us to honour their sacrifice, I prefer 'Lest We Forget'."

---

as reported in *The Argus*, Friday April 23, 1915, p. 8. 'AUSTRALIANS IN RABAUL. SERIOUS ALLEGATIONS. CHARGES AGAINST OFFICERS "LOOT, PLUNDER, AND RAPINE."'

I noticed the lines on his face, deepening with his intensity.

"Directly after the war," he continued, "I didn't think much about this. For me, though not for everyone mind you, life was easy up to the crash in 1929. I had a war service home, then I won the lottery in 1925, sold the home and bought a new brick cottage on Alison Road, Coogee."

"What was it like around Coogee in those days?"

"It was very pleasant. Lots of new flats and cottages were bein' built. There was plenty of money around. My new house was close to the Coach 'n Horses Pub and walking distance from the beach and Coogee Sports Club. In those days I was runnin' a book. I'd take almost any bet; it was just more fruit for the sideboard and with all the cash flowin in, I became a mike."

"What's a mike?"

He raised his brow as if it was something I should already know. "Someone who lends money to bookies. It was a bad move financially. When the stock market crashed, no one could settle his debts. We lost the house and I was out of work."

"Tough times."

"Right 'u are on that. At first, I picked up a little work diggin' out the ponds at Centennial Park. This was Jack Lang's response. Spend money on the unemployed so the economy didn't die completely even if it meant borrowin'. It cushioned the worst effects of the crash."

"Lang was a little ahead of his time, I reckon."

"I wouldn't know," Sid smiled. "It didn't put butter on the table mind you but it kept our heads above water. I had to go lookin' for somethin else. Eventually I found work in the bookstore at Central Railway Station. It was a bloody solid walk though: an eight mile round trip everyday without the tram fare."

Sid's determination walking some 56 miles a week is a testimony to his strength. When I wandered around old Central Station, I saw that much of the station's architectural grandeur was retained and it was easy to imagine Sid walking the railway concourse.

"Workin' at the station's bookstore was just servin' customers, stockin' shelves 'n keepin' the accounts. My closest work mate was a woman from Tumut, Sophia Mowbray."

I'd long wondered how Sid came to know Sophia or Crossie as we came to call her. "I didn't know any of that, Sid. What did Sophia's family do in Tumut?"

"She was an orphan, y'know, raised by people called Mowbray. They were missionaries on an Aboriginal settlement near the town."

Sid's comment reminded me of my recent trip through Tumut on the way back from Melbourne. It's changed a lot since Sophia's day. Back then it was a multicultural centre at the convergence of the Ngunawal, Walgalu and Wiradjuri nations. It had a Chinese community comprising people who settled there after the Kiandra Goldfields petered out and the usual mix of settlers from England, Ireland, Scotland and Wales.

"Why did she move to Sydney? What drew here, the bright lights?"

"No, she wanted to help with the war effort. She also did a lot of voluntary work with TPIs, Totally and Permanently Incapacitated Soldiers. She used to visit one particular bloke, an Englishman called Horace Crosby."

"So that's the story. I've heard a bit about that. What was Horace doing in Australia? Did he come here after the war?"

"No, he came from Bristol just before the war. Some say his wife died, others that she was German and went back to Germany. Either way, he left his daughter, Marion, behind. He was workin' as an accountant out in Nyngan when he enlisted."

I thought of that era and how difficult it must have been for Horace going to work in an isolated, hot and arid place like Nyngan. Sure people would have spoken his language but he must have faced great isolation and sadness. I wondered about Marion as well. How she must have felt facing a double loss.

Sid continued, "When Horace joined up in December 1915, he was 42 years old. So as well as wantin' to fight for king and country, he was keen to see England again and visit Marion. Unfortunately he'd already been injured in the Boer War; he was a member of Kitchener's Horse, you know."

"No, this is all new to me but go on."

"Well, fightin' on the Western Front, he aggravated old injuries and was medically discharged. Untreatable hernia, he had."

"So Sophia met Horace through her voluntary work?"

"Actually I got them together; well, not directly. Horace lived in Randwick straight after the war. He was just up the road from me. We often met at the Coach 'n Horses. He'd get a neighbour to push him there in his wheelchair. As I was makin' a book, I'd take a few bets there. Round that time, he and some other returned diggers were talkin' about settin' up a Chinese tea import business. Well, it caught my attention. It was a good idea but money was their problem. Horace had the skills, the rest were just a bunch of mates so it didn't go anywhere. I should've put some money in."

"Yeah maybe," I said, "but there's many a slip twixt cup and lip. Did he find something he could do?"

"He did. In 1922, he saw an opportunity that didn't need much cash and was a guaranteed market. It was makin' red crepe paper poppies for Armistice Day. So he took the leap."

Seen and Unseen

I'd never considered how this well established part of our culture began but I learned that for the commemoration of Armistice Day in 1921, the Australian Returned Soldiers and Sailors Imperial League, later the RSL, imported one million silk poppies made in French orphanages. It was a noble and charitable act, but the flowers were so expensive, they were hard to sell. Not to be deterred, they called for people willing to make poppies and simple laurel wreaths with purple ribbon bearing the words 'Lest We Forget'.

"Are you saying that Horace started this off, Sid?"

"Horace was one of the first but soon he needed more permanent care so he moved to a new soldiers' home at Punchbowl. When I met Sophia I suggested she visit him."

"It's a long way from the city to Punchbowl. It must have been the outer edge of Sydney in those days, almost the bush: well beyond the trams."

"Yeah, it was, but it's on the railway line, remember."

"Oh yeah, of course it is."

"He was almost old enough to be her father and I knew he missed Marion. I thought he could do with the company and besides he needed a little help with his business, just carryin' and cartin' mind you, nothing heavy. Then blow me down if they didn't marry."

"So it was a surprise, eh?"

"Yep, it was. Then 18 months later he died. It was a bad year that year. I'd just lost my eldest daughter to diphtheria, your Aunty Enid. She was a beautiful girl barely 12 years old. We were devastated, particularly your mother Betty. I don't think she ever got over it."

I remembered the incident. Mum often spoke of her sister Enid. Sometimes we'd visit her grave in the old cemetery at South Coogee. I played there as a child and kept a special relationship with Enid often making quiet personal pilgrimages to her graveside.

"There was little time for mourning then," Sid said. "We

bore our grief silently with survival our main concern." His stoic expression gave little away as he continued, "Sophia took on the business and in this sad time, invited me to work with her. Soon your Nana Doris was drawn into this work as well."

"So that's how it all started?"

"Yep, from a simple beginnin'," he replied. "Now that Horace was dead, we began callin' Sophia, Crossie in recognition of her loss and she became very active in Legacy. She thought of herself as a war widow even though Horace died more than a decade after the war. She felt cheated because the war prevented them from consummatin' the marriage. In that sense, she was a widow but she channelled any negative feelings into charity."

As I reflected on Sid's words, I realised that only as an adult was I able to gain a sense of the loss, separation, bereavement, grief, tenacity and endurance that formed this generation's experience before they had even reached their 40th year.

I remembered the days and evenings spent sitting around a card table cutting up petal shapes using a metal template; stretching each petal so it assumed a concave shape reminiscent of a poppy's petal; gathering clusters of petals about a button set at the end of green bound wire; and, tying all together with a few more deft twists. As a final touch, a small 'Lest We Forget' tag was glued to the stem. As a child it seemed that between Crossie's place and ours, most if not all of the poppies for Remembrance Day were created.

"Your team must have had a virtual monopoly on poppy and wreath production," I said.

"We did, I'm sure."

"You know, it became so commonplace to spend time immersed in this cottage industry, I rarely mentioned it outside the home. Yet on reflection, it marked our family and connected us in an almost devotional way."

"That was our purpose," said Sid.

"As I became older, I realised that making each poppy was an act of commemoration in itself. I remember hearing conversations about the young who'd sacrificed their lives for our freedom. No one took this for granted. We acknowledged and honoured the sacrifice."

"Yes, we did," Sid nodded in agreement.

"Later I learned of the Japanese girl Sadako folding paper cranes for peace. I know in your case it was born of the need to earn a living but it had a far deeper significance approaching the mystical."

Sid offered no comment. I continued regardless. "No other family I knew was engaged in such a way. Each ANZAC Day or on any special anniversary when wreaths were laid at cenotaphs or places of commemoration for the fallen dead I knew those were our wreaths being laid. In a sense it placed us at the centre of things. We had an unseen connection. Other young people either weren't interested or didn't believe me if I mentioned this. It felt like important yet strange work."

When Sid died in 1952, Doris and Crossie continued the business employing people on a piece rate basis and roping in any competent passing relative.

Years later, sitting with Balinese friends as they spent hours preparing delicate *janur* (palm leaf offerings) for temple festivals, I realised just how unusual my childhood had been.

All over Indonesia, there are similar forms of *janur*. In Bali, as the day of a major festival approaches, women in particular sit in groups folding, weaving and plaiting palm leave to create *janur*. If I ever speak of my own childhood of the boxes of red paper and the days and evenings spent fashioning red flowers, Balinese friends understand. It's not strange work after all.

Camphor Silk and Ivory

Immersed in a five year old's sense of grief at Sid's passing and dad's long sea voyages, I slept uncomfortably as driving rain and strong wind swept down the narrow passage. Loose corrugated iron rattled, trees swayed and high-tension wires droned. Disturbed by the sounds, I woke sitting up and peering out into the passageway. An amber coloured face hovered in space, unmoving, unsmiling. I blinked it remained. In a state of terror, I recognised it as the Tiki from the sail of Thor Heyerdahl's raft.

"Mum, there's a face at the window!" I screamed. "Please make it go away!" Warm arms gathered me, yet the face remained. "It's still there!" I cried.

"Hush, darling. There's nothing, just the wind and the rain."

"No, I saw the face! The face from the raft in the huge waves."

"It's gone, darling. Quiet now. Don't wake your sister."

When storms raged or tropical cyclones tracked out their unpredictable paths through the Coral Sea, I often woke at night wondering if my seafaring father was safe. A mother's obvious concern drove the feelings, my fears rendered more vivid by the startling cover picture on his copy of Thor Heyerdahl's *The Kon Tiki Expedition*. Pitching down the face of a huge Pacific wave, Thor's balsa wood raft seemed tiny and helpless.

Families with fathers who go to sea on ships are challenged by their comings and goings. Family dynamics change with the demands of shipping while for those at sea life is a confrontation with elemental powers so aptly described in the words of this psalm:

Seen and Unseen

> Those who go down to the sea in ships,
> Who do business in many waters,
> These see the works of the Lord,
> And His wonders in the deep.
> He spoke, and a stormy wind arose,
> And its waves were lifted up.
> They mount up to the heavens,
> And descend into the deep;[6]

When, as a boy, I asked my father how he decided to go to sea, he said, "I'll tell you this, son: I didn't have much choice. My dad left when I was young so I had to start work early. I needed a reliable trade and picked up an apprenticeship in Fitting and Turning at Cockatoo Island. I'd done my time by 1944 with some extra studies in steam engine maintenance and operation. I was qualified to join the Merchant Navy then but they wouldn't let me go because I was working in a strategic industry. Cockatoo was the largest dockyard in the southern hemisphere."

"I didn't know that, Dad."

"Yeah, I finally got a posting in May 1945 as an engineer on the Taroona bound New Britain."

Reading through my father's meticulous shipping records after his death, I came across his description of the vessel. He wrote:

> *Taroona* was an ocean going passenger ferry, a twin screw, oil burning express turbine steamer. During the war, she was requisitioned and refitted as a carrier of troops and general cargo. Her refit involved the mounting of a 4" anti-submarine gun on the stern and anti-aircraft guns on the upper decks. Heavy armour was placed around the guns and the bridge, consequently she was very tender, and inclined to pitch and roll excessively in rough seas. Despite these modifications she could still manage 18 knots top speed although was restricted to about 16 knots.

---
[6] 'Psalm 106' from the text of the *St Athanasius Academy Septuagint*.

Gleaning details of Dad's merchant naval history from his papers was difficult. He talked about the sea, ships he sailed on, ports he visited and people he met but not a lot about the work he did. Gaining a sense of his working life was easiest when he met up with his old sea mates like Barney.

Barney lived in an apartment at Kings Cross. It was full of the signs of the sea, coral, cowrie and nautilus shells, starfish, ships in bottles, paintings of foreign ports and all manner of unusual objects. When we visited him, I loved playing with his wind up elephant all decked out in the finery of the British Raj. I also sat on the edge of conversations in that space where adults often forgot children were present. They reminisced about the ships they served on, the peculiarities of different vessels and the men they worked with. *Taroona* often came up in conversation.

"Allen," I remember Barney saying to my father, "if my recollection serves me well, before the war, *Taroona* was on the Bass Strait run between Port Melbourne and Launceston, right?"

"Yeah that's it, Barney."

"So it was early on in the war, she had a refit for carrying troops and cargo up to New Guinea, right?"

"Right and as you know I joined her towards the end. We arrived at Wewak during late May 1945."

"How did you manage to unload, by the way? I guess there were plenty of our boys around. Were they drafted to help?"

"We used captured Japanese troops to unload onto lighters. Despite what's said about Japanese soldiers never surrendering, this lot seemed very happy to be out of the action. We could still hear the sounds of battle in the distance."

Seen and Unseen

My father often spoke of that first voyage and the distant sounds of battle as the AIF 6th Division pursued elements of the Japanese XVII Army through the Torricelli Mountains between between Wewak and Aitape. In its rugged terrain some 13,000 Japanese troops managed to keep up a limited action but without supplies they soon surrendered.

"That was the closest you came to the action then?" Barney asked as he set a glass before Dad and poured out a generous shot of rum without any comment. As they both settled into Barney's sumptuous armchairs, I reasoned that this must be what they often did.

"Apart from a close call," Dad said, "and I mean inches, with a Japanese mine in the Coral Sea, it was turning out to be a quiet war for me, but then God strike me pink, I had a serious fall while topping up piston rod sealing oil in the refrigeration compressor."

"How'd you manage that, Allen?" asked Barney.

"Well, it was forward in the bow and the sea was rough. We were on the edge of a tropical cyclone."

"That explains it then. Bastards of things those cyclones!" Barney exclaimed.

"Yeah, bloody hell! It laid me up for a few days but you know how it is youth triumphs over pain. It's only in later life it counts against us."

"I did a few voyages up that way after the war," Barney added. "I liked working into the eastern parts of Melanesia, New Britain, New Ireland, the Solomons and the New Hebrides. Luxuriant, exotic, the people are very warm and friendly."

"Yes, I like the people. Can't say my Pidgin's very good though, Barney. How's yours?"

"I'm getting there."

Apart from all the technical information and commentaries along with the brief character sketches of crewmembers from skippers to stokers, time spent on the edge of such conversations opened up a wider world for me. Ports are full of conversations like this and port cities usually outward looking, the antithesis of insularity, a wellspring of tolerance and worldliness. It was a privilege to grow up in this milieu.

My father was an assiduous collector of anything that caught his eye. On his immediate post war voyages through Melanesia, his knowledge of the region broadened. When we heard his footsteps in the passage and glimpsed his form through the translucent panels of the front door, we kids peered at his abstraction hoping to see how much he was carrying. When the door finally opened and after a simple "Hello Dad," formalities were cast aside. "What have you brought back this time, Dad?" we asked.

Within our family, Melanesian artefacts, particularly those from the Solomon Islands, made frequent appearances. Fine tightly woven pandas mats; baskets and containers were a feature of our picnics. Numerous other artefacts even tanned crocodile skins were playthings.

Dad never did master Pidgin and, in a joke at his own expense, often told us of one trip through the Solomon Sea en route to Rabaul back in 1948: "I was amazed to see Bougainville's Bagana volcano in full-throated explosive display. I stood on the deck in the evening watching blasts and surges from the cinder cone. There was a man standing nearby, a Melanesian."

"Him make big noise," I said, hopeful of a response.

"Yes, the volcano is atypically active this evening," came the erudite and patient reply.

"I felt quite stupid," he said, grinning. Insufficiently educated in details of local culture, uncertain of the man's status and unaware of the intellectual traditions of the Tolai people, he tried to communicate in his own version of Pidgin English and it went pear-shaped. He told and retold this story as if to expel his residual feelings of discomfort.

In the early 1950s, my father eased into coastal shipping but was sent to Hong Kong to bring a vessel back after a refit in 1953. This was a change for all of us. Until then he'd coped well with the challenge of malaria in Melanesia. Now he confronted a different array of microorganisms.

Back then, smallpox and typhoid vaccinations were compulsory for Hong Kong and Chinese ports. Both inoculations can have quite dramatic effects on a person and he experienced painfully adverse effects from both.

Going on seven, I remember him saying: "My God, I barely know what day it is. I can't move my arm. I have a fever and I feel like death warmed up," he complained. "If I'd known it was going to be like this I'd have given the whole flamin' thing a very wide berth." Bursting into tears he slumped over the table.

I'd never seen a man cry before. Noticing the huge abscess on his arm, I remember thinking it was very serious but I could do nothing to help.

"Imagine what it would be like to be covered in these. I can see why smallpox was a killer in the old days," he said, wrestling with the pain.

Smallpox was still a world health issue at that time. Almost 25% of people inoculated suffered fevers and a third became too sick to work but the contract to join the ship as Chief Engineer was already signed so the next day, he boarded the plane for Hong Kong.

A telegram announced his return and soon after, a squeaking front gate and familiar footsteps marked his arrival.

"Hi, Dad, what did you bring this time?"

"Nothing. Just me," amazement filled small faces,

my little sister's reaction drifting into puzzlement then grinning he said, "Nothing yet. Russell tomorrow you'll come with me to the ship to collect our cargo."

"Great, Dad. The ship, wow! Did the crew come with you from China?"

"No, son, it's an Australian crew; the Chinese crew stayed there."

Next day we caught a taxi to Walsh Bay and climbed a steep gangway onto the ship. In a few paces, we stepped through a doorway arriving at the head of a companionway that dropped steeply into darkness. Below something very powerful emitted a constant rumble. It smelled of oily kerosene.

"Stay close behind me, son, and hold onto the rails."

"It's hot, Dad. Why do those pipes have bandages? What's that black thing, hanging on the peg, it looks like a witch? Why is it so hot? What's that rumbling noise? There's water down there, is the ship going to sink? Are we safe?"

"It's all fine, son. This is just the engine room. That rumbling noise is the diesel engine; it makes the electricity when we're in port. There are no witches and the water down there is the bilge, it helps us balance the ship."

"It's noisy down here, Dad."

He tapped a dial and said something to a man wearing a greasy boiler suit who appeared from behind a tangle of bandaged pipes.

"Let's go up to my cabin. I've checked the engine room."

We climbed back into the light and in a few more steps entered his cabin.

"It's not very big, Dad, only about as big as our bathroom."

"Cabins are small, son."

My eyes caught a Gilbey's Gin bottle full of threepences and sixpences.

Seen and Unseen

"That Dragon on the bottle reminds me of the one on the Viking boat in the picture," I observed, just hoping he might say, "Take the bottle; it's yours," but he had other plans.

Gesturing towards the far end of the cabin, he drew my attention away from the horde, "Here's the treasure chest."

A carved wooden chest sat inviting investigation.

Eyes wide, I pleaded, "Can we open it? Can we open it, Dad?"

"We can have a quick look," he teased with authority.

Its lock was a mysterious etched brass device that he slid open with a strange 'L' shaped key. An amazing bouquet filled the room, a little like eucalyptus something like mothballs yet different and subtler.

"This is a camphor wood chest, son," he said. Then, in a practical tone he added, "It will be ideal for storing our winter clothes through the summer."

"What are all the carvings?"

"There are Chinese men and women, great trading junks and dragons. Wait till we get home and you can have a closer look."

"Is it a pirate's chest, Dad?"

"Maybe it is. Now wait here while I call the taxi truck to move it."

Once home, the chest yielded a wonderful horde of silk and ivory, handcrafted table clothes and serviettes and numerous small artefacts, the scent of camphor transforming our small flat into a part of China.

Intrigued by the deep carvings and the remarkable lock I asked, "Can you show me how to open the lock, please, Dad?"

"Of course. Place the key into this small slot at the base," he said demonstrating. "Press in till it clicks then pull the lock apart. Easy see. You try."

Camphor Silk and Ivory

For hours I played with the lock and key mechanism fascinated by its simplicity and amazed by its difference though what really engaged me were the deep carvings. They challenged my aesthetic reference points. I tried relating it to the Willow Pattern plates we had, to the romantic story of the lovers becoming doves. There was a connection and but these figures were robust, deeply incised and most unusual. Dragons lurked in those deep recesses and spread across the brass lock plate. Powerful human figures radiated strength and intent. I was drawn to the chest's power and audacity.

"I like this chest, Dad; it's beautiful. Can you tell me the story?"

"I can't really, son. Chinese civilisation is ancient and complicated. This is just a small part like a window."

"I thought Japan and China were almost the same but the boxes are very different."

"Which boxes, son?" Dad asked.

"You know, the Japanese pilot's earplug box from the war – it's different."

I reached across to the bookcase next to the camphor wood chest and I picked up the small carefully crafted box. Its finely finished pale pinewood unadorned save for a few characters etched onto its surface. A minimalist small clip fastening it shut. Two neatly crafted earplugs nestled inside.

"Where's the pilot who wore them?"

"He's gone, son."

"Gone where?"

"Just gone."

Thinking about the pilot, unknown and unseen, imbued this object with a ghostly presence. It was a difficult feeling. It was much easier to think about the camphor wood chest.

Made in Japan

Mervyn Costello was an Irish Australian neighbour with rooms in an old Coogee mansion just down the road. As an eleven year old, I was developing my own relationships with local characters like Merv and we often chatted over his front gate. He worked as a shipwright through WWII but the drink got the better of him after the war. Now he worked as a tally clerk on the wharves. In between benders, he was an erudite commentator on Australia's maritime history, particularly the war years.

One elbow on the front gate and an open bottle of beer sitting on a ledge behind the gatepost, Merv held forth in a well-lubricated voice. "Y'know, they didn't tell the truth about how close the Japs came in the war. There was a lot'a Jap 'n even some German naval activity along the coast here."

"Really, Merv?" I responded, pretty certain he wasn't just boozed up. "I know they managed to attack Sydney Harbour with midget submarines and sink a ferry but I thought that was all."

"Be told. Don't look so bloody skeptical; the Japs mounted far more attacks than that. At least 30 merchant vessels were sunk in Australian waters 'n scores more attacked. There must'a been over 600 killed."

"Okay. I've just never heard that before."

"War time censorship, mate, that was the reason. Your dad would'a known workin' at Cockatoo," Merv assured me. "After Pearl Harbour 'n the Allied fleet's defeat in the battle of the Java Sea there was little to stop the Jap navy comin' into Australian waters. People were on edge. Old Fred Mauger over the road tells me when the midget subs attacked he heard explosions 'n thought a Jap invasion 'd begun so he ran down the beach with his .22 rifle."

"I've heard that story. Reg Mauger told me, but then Reg tells a lot of stories."

"No, I think this one's true. Mind ya a .22 wouldn'a done im much good."

"No, only good for shooting rabbits, eh Merv?"

"Yeah, for sure, mate. Y'know people feared a Japanese attack in 1942. Remember, Darwin'd been bombed 'n if people'd realised how serious the damage was, fears would'a been worse. Anyone who could afford to move out'a Coogee did that's why I'm livin here. Lots'a old mansions and larger properties were subdivided 'n people from the industrial areas like Balmain 'n Pyrmont moved in."

"So you've been living here that long, Merv. Since the olden days." I smiled.

"Ya cheeky boy," he muttered through the corner of his mouth feigning displeasure. "Yeah, well I was comin' and goin' from port but the feelin' back here was pretty damn dark. Even when we defeated the Japs that year in Milne Bay, there was still a lot'a fear."

At war's end, a baby boom began transforming Coogee, then through the 1950s the suburb acquired social and cultural diversity. Cheap apartments and flats drew waves of migrants, many from Central Europe, yet its dominant culture expressed through beach life, club, pub, horse racing and rugby remained a solid British Irish mix.

It was an idyllic place for children. The ocean was vast and mostly benign behind the protective barrier of Wedding Cake Island. A rocky sandstone coastline, rolling foreshore parks and access to large private spaces surrounding the sumptuous mansions of another era enabled luxurious opportunities for play.

In winter during school holidays, we would play touch football from early morning till sunset on a wide sweep of parkland at the top of Grant Reserve just south of the beach. My friend, Ian, was first on the scene in the mornings. He lived opposite the park. Often we would wave to Ian's father Phil as he walked down to the bus stop near the beach. In the afternoons he always took a bus that arrived on the hill above his house. His habit was always to walk down.

"Ian, why does your dad never walk uphill?" I asked once.

"He hasn't recovered from the war. He's still sick." Ian replied.

"How do you mean? I asked. "What's the matter with him?"

"Well, I don't know for sure. He won't say much about what happened in the war. All I know is he was a prisoner of the Japs."

"In Japan?"

"No," Ian replied. "He was in Changi in Singapore."

"I've heard of Changi. It was a bad place wasn't it?"

"Dad said there were thousands in that place and a lot died."

"All I know is there were lots of Australians there and the Japs were very cruel."

Later when I mentioned my conversation with Ian to Mum, her reaction was strong and passionate. "What those men went through in Changi and on the Burma Railway. . ." her voice trembled with emotion, "they were like skeletons when they came back with all sorts of rashes and tropical ulcers. I remember Phil saying to me, 'Cruel people, those Japanese, Betty. The conditions our boys faced were inhuman.' When I think what those Japanese did to our boys I…" She paused on the verge of tears, struggling with memories of young men lost from her life.

Made in Japan

"Are you all right, Mum?" I asked, concerned that I'd drawn out painful memories.

"Yes dear, yes. I often think about them . . . before they went, fine chaps, strong and healthy. Men I knew from the beach, lifesavers doing surf patrol. Handsome men." She took a deep sighing breath as tears welled. "They came back sick and damaged. I'm sorry, son, but . . . I cry when I think about it . . . when I think of them."

Above all else, she was a Coogee girl. Swimming was like walking to her. She was part of a group whose life centred on the beach in the pre-war years. They swam, surfed, dived, danced and pushed the remnant edges of the Victorian morality. She was one of the first to wear a two-piece swimming costume and like her young male counterparts was fit and healthy with few cares, beach and coastal life allowing them some respite from the tough years of the Great Depression.

Worried I'd provoked painful thoughts I said, "It's okay, Mum. Thankfully the war is over now."

"It is, yet I think of the ones who didn't come back and all the suffering they must have gone through and I think of the boys who did come back, so many of them never talk about it. They're changed men. They drink a lot. Who knows what they're thinking."

"It's hard to understand that. I wonder why a lot of them won't talk about the war?" I asked, not expecting an answer.

"Just the pain and the tragedy of it I suppose," she replied. "Phil was badly affected. Others had different experiences. Some like Ray Kelly helped even the score on the Kokoda Track. He doesn't talk about things; real heroes seldom do. Just a small man, he is. You've met him. He lives in the flats at the end of Havelock Avenue. We stopped and spoke to him last week when we were walking past."

Seen and Unseen

"I remember. He's not very tall," I said, a little puzzled as I expected a war hero would be some big strapping man.

"It was often those little chaps that emerged as the real heroes and survivors," she observed. "He was involved in a lot of hand to hand fighting and was also part of a final assault on the Japanese up on the north coast of New Guinea."

Years later, as a more serious history student, I learned that Australian forces were relentless in their attacks on the Nankai Shitai[7] as it was violently reduced to strings of shallow jungle graves along the Track and the northern beaches. Maybe this explained why even as a child, I'd recognised Ray's somber demeanor a brooding quality, a suppressed anger and a tendency to isolate. I couldn't identify anything particularly heroic about him at the time. He was quite scary but Mum's certainty assured me that this must be what war does to people.

Not everyone was as intense as Ray or as unresolved and emotional as Mum. Some veterans like our neighbour, Ted, were much warmer, forgiving characters. He too was in New Guinea working as a medic. Unlike Ray, he was an assiduous collector of war souvenirs and would often trot out his collection.

Holding up a mortar round its metal casing now replaced with turned wood Ted said, "On the Track we used these mortars at very close quarters against the Japs." Then he'd say, "Who'd like to see a Japanese finger?"

We didn't have a choice as he produced a small wooden box, flicking open the lid to reveal a grey cotton wool couched finger within.

"Go on, touch it," he said.

---

[7] The Nankai Shitai was a regiment numbering about 5,586 elite troops, veterans of earlier campaigns. Carrying little food they hoped to live off the land or captured supplies. They were equipped with large amounts of ammunition, heavy mortars, heavy machine guns and mountain artillery.

At the slightest touch the disembodied finger began to move in the box. It was a macabre joke: his finger inserted through a hole at the side and covered with powder.

A child's world is one of play unless confronted by violence. Playing with toys labeled 'Made in Japan' was a frequent pastime for many children in the post war years. Japanese toys were cheaper and flimsier than their British equivalents but even when they broke, they revealed ingenuity in conception. I marveled at their simple elegant mechanisms. My father's aunts had finely painted wooden Japanese dolls and my grandparent's first acquisition in married life had been an elegantly crafted Japanese vase. What I saw of Japanese art was delicate, precise and sensitive conveying a refined concern for detail.

Stories of war and Japanese brutality were true but there was another reality still obscured by the pain of war. The story was incomplete. Japan remained an enigma, but not for long.

Harry Jensen was a family friend through the Labor Party. A local man, Lord Mayor of Sydney, and an enterprising businessman with interests straddling the electrical and footwear trades, he showed an early interest in trade with Japan.

"Betty," he called to my mother one day as we stood by the pool at Coogee Beach, "I'd like to invite you to a civic reception for Japanese Prime Minister Kishi."

"Thank you. I . . .I'm very busy with the children. When will it be? Not in the evening, I hope."

"No, Betty it's an afternoon event. I hope you can make it. Kishi has been a big help in post war reconstruction. He has already been active in promoting businesses and he wants to broaden Japan's trading relations."

"What are his politics, Harry?" she asked.

"He's anti-Communist but from the centre. You'll receive an invitation shortly."

"Thanks Harry, I'll look out for it."

She looked uncomfortable and said to me when he'd left: "I can't go to that. I know Harry wants to put the war behind him but I couldn't shake Kishi's hand. I don't like them. They are cruel people."

I was quietly disappointed in my mother. She didn't usually discriminate against people and I knew then it was unresolved anger. Even as a boy, I knew it was important that people like Harry were taking an initiative. His role was instrumental in changing post-war attitudes towards Japan, yet the plight of the Japanese people remained unseen. While a tangible emotional connection with their suffering was still outside the perception of most Australians, it was about to change.

Iri Maruki arrived in Hiroshima on 9 August 1945, three days after the atomic bomb was dropped. Reading newspaper reports of the bombing and concerned to help family members, he made his way to Hiroshima arriving at night. His first encounter with the scale of devastation was incapacitating. Like a sleepwalker, he staggered through the darkness still eerily illuminated by fires. Compounding his disorientation was an uninterrupted panorama of Hiroshima Bay and the islands of the Inland Sea. Buildings no longer blocked the view.

"Two kilometers from the center of the explosion, the family house was still standing," Iri recounted.

When I first read his words I was surprised. I'd always imagined that everything for many kilometres around had been blown away with no signs of habitation much less human life remaining.

Iri's explanations dispelled many myths. He said of the house, "The roof and roof tiles were mostly gone, windows had been blown out, and even the pans, dishes, and chopsticks had been blasted out of their places in the kitchen. In what was left of the burned structure, rescued bomb victims were gathered together and lay on the floor from wall to wall until it was full."

Iri was not a rescue or relief worker, he was an artist. Soon joined by his wife Toshiko, they worked providing relief to anyone in need. He recounted, "We carried the injured, cremated the dead, searched for food, and found scorched sheets of tin to patch the roof. With the stench of death and the flies and the maggots all around us, we wandered about in the same manner as those who had experienced the Bomb."

Healing the scars of nuclear inferno seared into their own psyches was also important work for them. Later in pursuit of that healing, they turned their efforts to the creation of eight 6 x 24ft panoramas, each comprising eight panels and depicting the impact of the bomb on the lives of ordinary people. For eight years, they toiled with the simplest of materials, rice paper, charcoal and vermillion only able to guess at the final effect as their small studio was too small to assemble a complete panorama.

In 1958, the panels reached Australia, creating a watershed in Australian attitudes towards the Japanese. Perhaps no single event had a greater influence on the emotional state of post war Australia. The panels left their mark on me as a child and later I learned much more about them.

Australian author and essayist, Vance Palmer wrote of them in the exhibition catalogue:

> These eight Hiroshima Panels have come out of a deep emotion that has been restrained and shaped by the discipline of art. And so they do not merely affect the nerves but awaken basic feelings – pity, love, compassion, and a sense of the oneness of human beings in the face of suffering. Finally, they compel those who see them to vow that such diabolic visitations shall not occur again.

When the panels were exhibited in Adelaide, they drew the largest crowds ever to attend an art exhibition in the city. Some 10,000 people viewed them in less than four days. Just five days after the exhibition opened in Sydney, police were called as 15,000 visitors crammed the New South Wales Art Gallery overflowing into a jostling crowd outside in their efforts to catch a glimpse.

Such a public response also echoed through the print media. The influential *Australian Women's Weekly* carried a full page spread on the panels observing that, "Their choice of materials – Indian ink, vermillion, and rice paper – was largely due to their poverty, but there is no poverty in the conception of their work."

With emotions still raw, debate raged in the press, and while most praised the works some critics were reluctant to concede an opportunity for Iri and Toshiko to tell of their people's tragedy.

An art critic for the tabloid newspaper *The Mirror* wrote, 'Abject poverty of thought and expression emphasised by stale repetition of motif, characterises the 'Hiroshima Panels.' Continuing she added, 'The imagination of every intelligent visitor will certainly recoil at being required to regard mere multiplicity of bare backsides as Art, however many roods of rice paper it covers.

'Such a display – if I should sink to its level by adopting Carlyle's phrase – 'merely feeds the art lovers belly with the east wind.' She went on to claim that '. . .they possessed about as much asthetic value as a cartload of tripe.'

Playing the nationalist card, she added, 'I protest very vigorously against the work of top ranking Australian painters being ousted from the gallery wall by these depraved doodlings of tenth rate Japanese cartoonists, so far removed from the true spirit of Japanese art.'

Replying to *The Mirror*'s critic, Lloyd Rees, Senior Lecturer in the Faculty of Architecture at the University of Sydney was certain on the merit and importance of the panels. He wrote:

> Having had long experience in the Academic tradition, I say, without hesitation, that the works which you compare with a 'Cart load of Tripe', have drawings of the human figures so sensitive and powerful as to be beyond the reach of any artist in Australia, with the possible exception of William Dobell.

While as an adult, it's easy for me to reflect on the transformational experience these offered; as a child of eleven I was confronted and challenged by the panels, by the tensions inherent in the work. The human forms, most naked, their clothing burned or blown away, were both realistic and iconic. Stark and uncompromising, I remember them to this day.

On reflection, the *Sydney Morning Herald*'s art critic came closest to understanding the body of work when he wrote:

> If these panels have something of the basis of a modern Calvary – through an agony of fire, smoke, and water the torn bodies struggle forward – we are left with no answer of faith but only despair. The panels, monumental in size, are brilliant realisations by the artists Iri Maruki and his wife, Toshiko Akamatsu.
>
> Through the tenseness of the slow moving rhythms and acid bite of the firm contours they establish a poetic realism – a mixture of Eastern and Western art.
>
> If the realism states with precision and in an almost illustrative manner the wounds and suppurations of the dead and maimed, the means of expression – by the quality of its poetic inflection – almost opposes one's response to the events. The oppositions quite produce the feeling that beneath the protest is something of acceptance – of 'Oriental' fatalism.
> It takes an exhibition like this to break our sense of isolation. Mankind, it seems, needs such promptings.

Seen and Unseen

One returned prisoner of war, Harry Evans, summed up the panel's effect when he said, "After seeing the Panels I wouldn't wish that bomb to fall anywhere, even though the Japanese gave me a rough time."

Mum had much less to say about the war after that. I think we came to understand that whatever the atrocities committed by Japanese soldiers, they were no worse than the bombing of Hiroshima and Nagasaki. The true atrocity lay in war itself, in the chaos and cruelty it unleashed.

While the discourse of the time was beyond me as a child, the Hiroshima Panels became a touchstone in my life, infusing me with an opposition to war and nuclear madness. The deeper significance they would assume for me, however, was as yet to be seen.

Joss Sticks and Cracker Night

Perceptions of Asia in post-war Australia were determined by the war against Japan and refracted through a pervasive sense of Britishness. Amongst ordinary folk across the country, there was scant knowledge of Asia. Whether Japanese or Chinese, the 'little yellow man' was considered inferior.

Queen Victoria's birthday on May 24 was a particular celebration and affirmation of this Anglo-centric cultural dimension. Empire Day, as it was known, was directed mainly at school children. In Coogee, the school morning involved a march to the local RSL hall followed by addresses from dignitaries, members of Parliament, the Anglican minister and perhaps some other denominations, but not Catholic priests or rabbis.

'Kipling's Recessional' and 'God Save the Queen' were sung at this event and homage was also paid to our great land with the singing of 'Advance Australia Fair'. The original second verse always included and expressing a strident anglophile dimension.

> When gallant Cook from Albion sailed,
> To trace wide oceans o'er,
> True British courage bore him on,
> Til he landed on our shore.
> Then here he raised Old England's flag,
> The standard of the brave;
> With all her faults we love her still
> Britannia rules the waves
> In joyful strains then let us sing
> Advance Australia fair.

Speeches were infused with invocations of the civilising importance of Empire following which we were all granted a half-day holiday and presented with a polished red Jonathon apple. Red was the colour of the British Empire and even at this late hour, though Indian independence had dimmed its power and Suez all but extinguished it, there was a lingering imperial twilight. Fortunately, once out of the hall we could get on with the real business of the day.

"See ya down the chook yard this arvo," Reggie called, racing out into Byron Street.

"Yeah, see ya later. I know where there's some great tyres. We can put'em on the top," I shouted as he ran on ahead.

"Should be a great one. Weeks'a work on this one," called Reggie, barely glancing back.

Through the May School Holidays, we gathered fuel for our bonfires. Some were enormous. Now it was time for these piles of accumulated rubbish to have their finishing touches. Sometimes we started even before the May holidays but this was the most active time.

Still following the habits of summer in May, we often went barefooted. It was a reassuring sign of the approaching season when late in the day, after working tirelessly on our bonfires, our unclad feet felt the autumn chill. A grounding, delightful feeling, the chill of our feet confirmed our hard day's work and the promise that soon it would be Cracker Night.

The chook yard wedged between the back fences of properties with frontages on two streets was our bonfire site. Reggie, Donnie and the twinies, Graeme and John, were there when I arrived.

"Reggie says ya know where there's some tyres, Russ. Do ya?" asked Donnie.

"Yeah, I do. Ya know Mr Bradley's garage next to Crawford's on Alexander Street? I saw three old tyres there."

Joss Sticks and Cracker Night

"Great, let's go and get'em," said Reggie. "We can roll em round the block and down the twinies' side passage." He and the twins headed off to the garage.

Recycling things like cars tyres was rudimentary in the 1950s, so they were easy to get and prized for producing our aim of excellent flames and masses of black, acrid smoke. They also helped ignite all of the other combustibles and illuminated the chookyard.

An archetypal bonfire was built around a centre post with car tyres stacked like donuts. Around this, we set almost anything that would burn. As a finishing touch, old fibro[8] sheets were popular. These were best dropped down around the centre post and while they didn't burn, they crackled and exploded when the fire was hot. I now wince at the environmental vandalism of it all.

"It'll be hard to get'em on the top," cautioned Donnie as the tyres came bouncing down the side passage a few minutes later.

"There's enough of that post sticking out to hold'em," said Graeme, his tyre slamming into the side of the bonfire.

"…on top of the ones already inside," added his twin brother John as his tyre thumped in alongside the other.

"Watch out!" called Reggie as his tyre came tearing down the twinnies' backyard, missing the bonfire and slamming into Campbell's back fence.

"We need a Guy Fawkes on top," said Graeme. "Anyone got any old clothes for the body. We can stuff'em with newspaper."

"Yeah, I'll make the Guy Fawkes," I answered. "Mum said I could have some old clothes."

Tyres in place and the Guy Fawkes sorted, conversation turned to more important matters.

"Have a look at this," said Reggie. Opening a shoebox pulled out from its hiding place under an old piece of

---

[8] Asbestos and cement sheets.

galvanised iron, he revealed an impressive hoard of crackers. "I've got everything from Tom Thumbs to tuppeny bungers. What have you got?"

"I've got some Roman Candles," I answered, "about four Golden Rain, a couple of Catherine Wheels, a Mount Vesuvius and six Sky Rockets. Oh yeah, jumping jacks too."

"Jumping Jacks aren't pretty ones and the rest of 'em are for little kids," Reggie added. "Why've y'got those?"

"I like 'em and Meg likes 'em, so does Donnie's little sister Joanne," I said. "I always get some. My skyrockets are British Standard brand, the best."

British Standard fireworks and the Australia equivalent Globe were beautiful, reliable, well made and somewhat expensive compared with the Chinese alternatives. As we grew older however, the Chinese fireworks became most prized. Penny Bungers, Tuppeny Bungers and sometimes even bigger ones hit the market. Double Happys and Tom Thumbs were also worth buying. Unimpressive as a single retort, they guaranteed a machine gun like blaze of sound if left in their woven strings.

"How we gonna light 'em tonight?" asked Donnie.

"I think Ray Long's coming. Dad spoke to him last night," chimed in Billy who had just scampered up the extension ladder connecting his backyard to the chook yard.

"Great! Is he bringing the lighters?" asked John.

"I think so," Billy replied.

"Anyone got matches?" asked Reggie

"Yeah, here's some." Donnie handed him a box.

"I'll do a Penny Bunger," he replied reaching into his shoebox and producing one. Holding it between thumb and index finger, he handed me the matchbox saying, "Here, you light it, Russ."

"Okay, here goes," I said, striking the match.

"Don't look at it!" shouted Graeme.

"Turn your head away!" chimed John.

His head turned well to the side he held on as the bunger exploded, his fingers unscathed.

"The trick is to hold it just between y'finger tips," said Reggie.

Cracker Nights always had their casualties. It was quite a dangerous event by contemporary standards. Risky behaviours were synonymous with the night and weeks leading up to it. At first we experimented holding Tom Thumbs as they exploded, then progressed to Double Happy's and then developed the art of holding Penny Bungers ever so gingerly as Reggie demonstrated.

Sunset was at 4.57pm on 24 May. Darkness fell rapidly and by 6.00pm the bonfire was alight. Each year we waited for the special visitor. He was a close friend of Billy's father, Dr McKenzie. When his presence was detected word spread quickly.

"Ray's here!" one of the McKenzie kids shouted.

We waited as he climbed up the extension ladder onto the chook yard.

"Hi Ray, did you bring the Joss sticks?" someone asked.

Beaming, he'd answer, "Of course, here you are." Handing one over as word spread and all the children flocked around him.

Ray Long was a Chinese Australian Engineer. The Joss Stick was his great contribution to Cracker Night.

"Ah, smell that! It's beautiful," said Donnie's little sister Joanne.

Once Ray arrived, our celebrations acquired a bouquet of burning sandalwood, the smell of joss drawn towards the bonfire as intense heat lifted flame and smoke, driving any odours of burning rubbish high into the night sky.

Seen and Unseen

Pyrotechnically speaking, the hardest thing to do was to light fireworks safely and reliably. Accidental ignition of someone's entire cache of fireworks was the most dangerous event. While this seldom happened, when it did, pandemonium erupted. People scattered in all directions in a spectacular confusion of explosions and whizzing balls of sodium, magnesium and phosphorus, then came the disappointment, the regret, the blame.

Matches were difficult to manage and cigarette lighters had to be filled with expensive lighter fuel. A Joss Stick was a sort of mini fire stick and so much easier but on reflection, Ray's contribution was much subtler.

Ray only brought Tom Thumbs, Double Happys and Bungers. I enjoyed watching him yell with delight at the deafening explosions. Above all, what Ray brought to Cracker Night was his great generosity. He succeeded in transforming the event not by attempting to control the outcome but in the act of giving, he created something new.

Though too young to appreciate Ray's kindness in its fullness, he was a special man radiating good humour, an adult incarnation of the joyful children that adorned the packets of Chinese fireworks so common in those days. Like a laughing Buddha, he was the 'god' of Cracker Night radiating a joyful simplicity bringing another reality, a face of China, a glimpse of the Tao.

"There'll be no ghosts left around here tonight," Ray beamed as he lit a string of Double Happies. "

"Are there really ghosts, Ray?" I asked.

"I don't see any at all," he chortled, beaming with that smile I hadn't seen since the year before.

An Encounter with White Australia

Friday was Crossie's day, her visits always fondly anticipated. Invariably, she took up her position at then end of a table in the kitchen, often declining to remove her hat. She projected a countrified formality, speaking slowly and deliberately as many a countrywomen did in the early 1960s before television began to transform our language into more standard forms.

Now that Sid and Doris, our Pa and Nanna, had gone, she was our remaining contact with the generation born in the last decade of the 19th century. Her devotion to us, her constant interest and attention, provided a valuable intergenerational link and Crossie extended her own critical brand of love and caring. Though judgmental at times, she held a special status in our family; her long connection with us grown in the ceaseless production of all those red crepe paper poppies

Sitting at the kitchen table, she said to me, "I have tickets for the military tattoo at the show ground for next Saturday if you'd like to come, Russell."

"You beaut! Sure would, Crossie!"

"I'll pop over by cab. We can catch the tram from here."

"What's on this year?"

"There'll be a program at the show ground. They ran out of programs at my Legacy group meeting."

"The fireworks last year were great. It's such good fun."

"Yes, it is, but we must remember what our armed forces have done for us. It's most important to respect them and recognise their work. They have endured great sacrifices for Australia's freedom."

"Yes, I do, Crossie."

Attracted to the pageantry, the military technology, the blank small arms and artillery fire, I was also skeptical about the point of war and I wondered what Pa would have to say.

Crossie continued, "The Americans helped us a lot during the war but we must never forget England. Without the British traditions, this country wouldn't have amounted to much and thank heavens for the monarchy." She spoke with the authority of her years. "King George was a great leader for us all during the war and just as well because if it had been left to that good-for-nothing brother of his, we'd have had all sorts of trouble. George was a model of service and dedication. Without the monarchy we'd have ended up like the Americans. Look at all the problems they have now."

Crossie taught me much about the Australian heritage and her view of history's passage. She was nationalistic and one eyed, an archetypal, conservative, Anglo-centric Aussie. Yet in the cultural settings of the 1950s, her views had relevance and authenticity.

Still in the shadow of war, conversation often turned to Changi, Kokoda and Tubruk. War documentaries frequently played on television. Military drill and marching characterised the daily management of children in schools and Boy Scout rallies festooned with flags and symbols took on a character reminiscent of Nuremberg 1939. As younger kids, we played war games, digging foxholes and shelters, raining barrages of rocks down on one another. We were fascinated by what remained of the artillery emplacement at Clovelly, the camouflaged observation post at South Coogee and the extensive underground bunker system and gun emplacements behind the rifle range at Long Bay the ultimate playground. We'd even sneak behind the targets while the red flags were raised thrilled by the sound of wide shots ricocheting off bare sandstone.

Arriving home from school one Friday sometime in 1962, I greeted Crossie at her place by the kitchen table. Moments later, my sister and her friend Pat arrived. As they entered the kitchen, past Crossie's special spot, she was heard to say, "She's black."

I noticed the strained look on Mum's face as she beckoned me to follow her into the living room.

"I'm sorry you had to hear that, dear. Crossie's a bit prejudiced against people she considers non-white."

"Why? Why say that about Pat?"

"Her mother is Burmese and I think her father might be what we call Anglo-Indian."

"Yeah, I thought she was Indian because her mother sometimes wears Indian clothes."

"Well, they're neighbouring countries. Maybe there are lots of Indians in Burma."

What Mum was saying was completely foreign. I knew the people from New Guinea and the Solomon Islands were dark. Dad had pictures of them in his encyclopaedia and I'd seen a man from Africa once but I couldn't relate any of these very significant differences to Pat.

"So, I don't get it. Pat's lovely, friendly and happy. I suppose she is a bit darker than most. Why's that a problem for Crossie?"

"Crossie grew up on a mission. She helped her mother patch-up Aboriginal women who had been beaten-up by their husbands. I think this is where it started."

"It's nonsense. If she helped the women, how could she dislike people with darker skin?"

"I know, but that's how she is."

"We've been to the Aborigines Advancement League events at Paddington Town Hall. You taught us not to discriminate."

"I know, son. Crossie's from a different time."

After the initial surprise, I let it pass. I knew Mum genuinely believed in the notion of 'a fair go' so I understood her response. It seemed an odd way to react to Pat, and such a superficial feature to seize upon. To me, Pat was most beautiful; more than that, she was totally gorgeous to my puberty driven perception. I loved her looks. I also knew her brother Les who was a little shy. I liked them both.

From that day on, I realised Crossie saw the world differently than I did. I began to set small tests for her to check her attitudes and measure those differences.

"What would you think if I married a Greek or an Italian, Crossie?"

"You're too young to think about that sort of thing."

"Yes, I'm too young to marry, but what if?"

"Each to their own kind. There's no point in making life more complicated than it needs to be," she responded.

Then at another time, "Crossie, my friend Tom is Jewish, and he doesn't believe in Jesus as Christ. What do you think about that?"

"It's not his fault that he hasn't been properly educated."

"He knows about Jesus, though," I stressed to see what more I could elicit.

"I'm sure he does. After all, it was his people who killed Jesus."

"Yeah, I asked Tom about that. He says he had nothing to do with it and that Jesus was crucified by the Romans."

"Does he? Well you can't believe everyone," she said with a familiar tone that meant the conversation would go no further.

On another occasion, I raised the still sensitive issue of the Catholic-Protestant divide.

"Mum is a Catholic and Dad is a Presbyterian and Free

Mason. Which one do you think is right?"

"It's not for us to judge. I have my own beliefs. It's best we just focus on taking care of one another."

Replies like this last one showed an unwillingness to judge despite her rigidity and welded on opinions. There was no way I could choose either. I just stepped back from the question of religion.

All that my testing questions did was confirm what an enigma Crossie was. Her formality and her propensity for ritualistic behaviour marked her apart, yet was probably just indicative of a woman who lived alone and was set in her ways. Her racism, well, I still hadn't understood this. It just seemed like an eccentricity. In so many ways, she reflected and espoused typical British cultural values and common rural Australian patterns of speech and style. So I began to look and listen more closely and something came into focus; physically she was unlike my family.

About this time one of the tabloids did a special feature on Crossie still turning out vast quantities of red crepe paper poppies; she was a pioneer in the industry of remembrance and still at it. The article featured a picture of her at work. She sat side on to the camera, her face turned towards the viewer. That was it why hadn't I ever noticed before? Crossie was Chinese!

Surviving the Sixties

Heng sat on the steps leading up into the barrack block that housed our fifth year classrooms. He was forever grooming himself it seemed.

"Heng," I asked, "is that rocker style?"

"What? What d'ya mean?"

"Ya flick the comb through your hair, back at the sides and rolled at the front."

"Yeah, that's the way I do it."

"But ya look like a rocker."

Heng kept combing his hair.

"Ya school uniform adds to it, stove piped trousers, sharp pointed black shoes. Y'd look the part down at Stones Milk Bar."

"Walau!" Heng said tersely, a Malaysian word meaning 'goodness!' "So what! It's Ipoh style." An engineer's son from Ipoh, Heng arrived in Australia under the Colombo Plan, bypassing the White Australia Policy.

Stylistically at least Heng was a rocker, the latest iteration of the bodgie, a 1950s word for a young man with greasy hair, tight jeans and a propensity for loutish or rowdy behaviour. Falling into that niche unwittingly, he seemed without any clue of its local tribal significance.

"Ya know Stones Milk Bar?" I enquired, trying to start a discussion about groups and gangs.

"That's the bell. Can't be late. Prentice'll be angry."

He didn't seem interested or maybe I was prying too much, I thought. Time to shut up.

"Yeah, let's go," I said, grabbing my very weighty school bag. "We're starting that unit on Asia. I wrote off to the Japanese and Indonesian embassies. I've got a whole lot of stuff. Maybe Prentice'll be interested."

Surviving the Sixties

Mr Prentice was a tweedy bushy browed, ex-RAF pilot. Fit, eccentric and a great raconteur. He was unquestioningly absorbed in the theme of Empire and Britain's civilising global role.

Our classroom was a former cloakroom at the convergence of four barrack block school wings. Aluminium panelled constructions, they were like ovens in summer and freezing in winter.

"Well, boys, so we begin. My own experience of Asia was during World War II. Stationed in Bengal, I flew bombing and strafing attacks on Japanese targets throughout Burma. Since the war the area has enjoyed a period of peace yet there are those who seek to disturb the Commonwealth. The present Indonesian policy of *Konfrontasi*, which means confrontation, is one such challenge."

I raised my hand.

"Yes?" he said, peering at me between bushy eyebrows and the reading glasses balanced on this nose.

"Mr Prentice, will we be studying Malaysia and Indonesia with you?"

"I'll come to that." He never used my name; it was as if as a person I wasn't fully manifest.

He continued. "Without the presence of British and Australian forces in Malaysia, *Konfrontasi* might succeed but thanks to them it will be easy enough to defend against. These people don't make matters easier. They are not inclined to hard work and this is made all the worse by the enervating tropical climate and associated tropical diseases."

"Bull, *haolian*!" Heng muttered quietly, calling him a smart alec while barely moving his lips.

"What was that? Yes, you boy. What did you say?"

Heng remained silent, avoiding eye contact but exuding discomfort.

"Don't bring those attitudes here. Leave them back where you come from."

Mr Prentice's imperial outlook and his apparent lack of regard for people such as Heng were far from alien in Australia at that time. The White Australia Policy still hung over the nation's approach to settlement.

Such behaviour from our teacher gave us something in common.

"Wow, he gave you a hard time, Heng," I said to him later. "He doesn't like me either. I reckon because I'm out spoken about politics. My family is Labor. My great grandfather was in the Labor Party."

"Labor? I don't know," he replied.

"It's politics. You know about other things, right?"

"Prentice, he should wake up his ideas," Heng replied in his special English idiom.

We were an unusual combination and according to the unspoken rules of the era, it wouldn't usually have followed that Heng and I would become friends. I was a rugby playing, surf club member and he an engineer's son from Ipoh, but the school was a melting pot. Besides, my interest in the Asian region and in Asian cultures was growing but what drew me to him was the discrimination he faced.

Ironically, apart from the opportunity to witness the implicit racism of our geography teacher in action, the major lesson Heng taught me was about consequences of sectarianism and inter-cultural conflict.

"Last year we got independence from Britain," Heng told me. "Before that, people like Prentice ran it. They told us what to do. Now the Malays run it. They don't like Chinese people and all Malays have special rights."

"Do they? I didn't know."

"Yeah, unfair," said Heng with a look of exasperation. "My people are from China more than 300 years back and going to Singapore, Malacca and Penang. We have old traditions."

"I know a little about China, Heng. I didn't know Chinese people were in Malaysia for so long."

"Yeah, our tradition is called Peranakan."

"I haven't heard that word before. What does it mean?"

"It means Straits Chinese, people from China who have lived for a long time along the Malacca Straits. We work hard and we just want to get on and do business and take care of our families."

Years later, after travelling in Malaysia and Sumatra, I realised that what Heng said made a lot of sense. There was much social and political tension following Malaysian independence. Throughout 1964, serious sectional violence broke out in Singapore and Tun Abdul Razak, Malaysian Deputy Prime Minister alleged it was caused by ethnic Indonesians and Communist Chinese agitators. Singapore's Prime Minister, Lee Kuan Yew, insisted that ultra nationalist elements within the United Malay National Organisation (UMNO) were to blame.

One day, as we waited for Mr Prentice, Heng kept muttering to himself, "Fight the Malays! Kill the Malays!"

"Heng, you can't say that," I insisted. "It won't help. Violence won't work. It's serious, I know, but what can you do?"

"Nothing!" he muttered. "Bloody Malays!"

Several weeks later, Heng disappeared, making a brief reappearance for the final examination before disappearing again.

Four years passed. I was living with a large eclectic student household in a Glebe terrace. It was an ideal location for students with open space at the side and rear, a small cliff at the back then a back lane and an even higher cliff behind. Opposite a single row of terraces stood between us and cluttered industrial land fringing Blackwattle Bay. We felt free to make a lot of noise.

Most of us were on scholarships: two were postgraduate biochemistry students, two were medical students and three of us arts students. Two had been on the 1965 Freedom Ride and three were draft resisters. A succession of friends and hangers-on could also be found passing through at any time. Life was about exploring the new in an academy of free enquiry; we experimented to see how far we could go. In a nutshell, we exchanged ideas and substances. Then early in 1968, the household began to polarise.

Through the many conversations, some balanced and attentive, some emotional and polemical, we mapped out our changing political personalities. Henry, in particular, became more consolidated on the revolutionary socialist left.

"Guevara is right," he said as he squatted by the record player and sorted through his latest consignment of the Cuban newspaper *Granma*. "We don't want just one Vietnam. The world needs many. This way, the military resources of the imperialists can be stretched so thinly they can't contain the world revolution."

"I understand, Henry, but war is horrendous," I replied, as I settled down on the lounge ready for a long debate. "A victory for the National Liberation front and the North Vietnamese forces would be a better outcome but because they're the lesser of two evils. Just how much napalm, Agent Orange, fragmentation bombs and white phosphorous can the Vietnamese people take? I wouldn't want to see this proliferated to every small country seeking self determination."

"Sure, Russ, but a few months ago you agreed with me. What's changed? You becoming a hippy? You certainly dress like one?"

"Just toying with the trappings. I like the idea of getting back to nature, questioning the Protestant ethic and capitalism."

"What you're saying's all very attractive but it's vague and becoming absorbed by the market system. Marcuse calls the process 'repressive tolerance'."

"True. A lot of the people saying we should 'turn on, tune in, drop-out' or just 'tune into the cosmic consciousness' are highly urbanised. Most of them are absolutely dependent on Western consumer society. It's all very well for them to call for a psychosocial revolution but there's a wave of unscrupulous charismatic carpetbaggers out there ready to make a buck out of this."

"Then you should be closer to my position," Henry insisted. "How much longer are you going to sit on the fence?"

"I'm realising that I've been indulging in a lot of theatricality. Even some of my understanding and advocacy of socialist politics have been experimentation with extremes. I have my posters of Lenin, Trotsky and Che Guevera, even have a copy of the *Little Red Book* autographed by Humphrey McQueen, but they're just collectables."

"So you're not a revolutionary socialist anymore. I guess now you'll just go off and lead a comfortable bourgeois professional life raising a family in the suburbs, eh?"

"That's a bit harsh, Henry," I replied, irritated by his response. I felt the need to explain myself in the face of his dogmatism. Standing I stepped across the room and took my copy of *The Eighteenth Brumaire of Louis Bonaparte* from the bookcase.

"I've learned a lot from reading Marx, particularly his historical works, but I've decided I'm not a Leninist," I said, gesturing with my book towards the Lenin portrait he had posted on the wall above the bookcase. "If I were to put a label on myself at the moment, I'd say I was an anarcho-marxist. I don't like big government and bureaucracy but I do recognise that we need governance provided it's democratic."

"I noticed you wrote that crazy slogan on the brick wall outside, 'Long live the untrammelled dynamic of the universal dialectic'. What on earth does that mean?"

"A few things. For starters it's a parody of Maoist sloganeering. It's meant to be theatrical. Don't you get it?"

"This is all beyond theatre, Russ," he said with a look of real concern. "Why are you being such a dilettante?"

"Yes, it is beyond theatre and there is a more serious side to this," I said as I settled back on the lounge. "If you must know, I was commenting on the importance of unfettered change in the natural world as well. I recognise that we humans need a softer touch in the way we managed our environment. It's time for reassessing the meaning of dominion."

"I get that, but the world needs to feed its people. There are some hard technological decisions to be made. It's all very well to experiment with a new politics based on the nascent theories of ecology and environmental science but the reality is unless small nations can free themselves from imperialism their resource bases are simply going to be exploited by powerful western countries."

"Sure, Henry, but we can make choices as consumers. We don't have to buy products that are ripped out of poor countries where workers or peasants are paid slave wages. Dropping out of formal studies this year has given me entre to a much broader range of disciplines than the average student."

"How does dropping out of university give you insight? You're not going to tell me you've discovered a guru who's helping you tune into the cosmic consciousness. After all you were just critiquing the hippies."

"Fair go, Henry. No, I'm not. Look, since I got the job as a television camera operator with the University Television Service I've been attending a huge variety of lectures. Sure it's from behind the camera but I'm getting a free education. I've already done most of the Physics I course."

"That's interesting. What else have you done?" Henry respected anyone who was attempting to learn and to investigate new fields. Despite his commitment to revolutionary Leninist politics, he was prepared to listen and seemed genuinely interested in my work.

"Fair hunks of archaeology, ancient history, architecture, biology, botany, drama, psychology and veterinary science. We also do a bit of medicine as well, correlation clinics they call them, and some anatomy. Working with cadavers can be confronting. I don't know what it's preparing me for. Maybe it's just character building." I grinned.

"Okay, Russ, I can see I'm not going to change your mind in one conversation. Must get to the union building before noon. I'll catch you later." He zipped up his bag, swung it over his shoulder and made for the door.

Nineteen sixty-eight was a year of great change. Conversations like these were common enough.

Apart from the ideological debates, music was also important, in my case, Eastern music. Discovering the musical form of the raga, played with sitar, tabla and tamboura, was a revelation offering a tangible pathway into other modes of understanding. Then one day, someone turned up with *Music from the Morning of the World*. The title was a reference to Pandit Nehru's description of the small island of Bali. This music was powerful and engaging, unfamiliar and pentatonic with unusual instruments, metallophones, gongs, bamboo flutes and elusive instruments that sounded like frogs, mixed with an extraordinary syncopated human voice performance called the 'Kecak Dance'. It was raw and energetic yet cooperative and grounded. Most of it was from Ubud, somewhere in the hills of Bali. Going to Bali, at some point, became an imperative.

Arriving home from uni in the afternoon, I found someone draped in towels lying asleep in the outside bathroom tub, spikey black hair all that was visible.

"Hello, who are you?" I asked.

Heng's head emerged from beneath the shroud of towels.

"Hi, Russ. I need somewhere to stay for a while."

"Heng! I haven't seen you for four years. Wow! It's great to see you! How did you find me? What's up?"

"I went to your old place in Coogee and your mother gave me this address. I'm working as a psych nurse at Callan Park now but I need a favour. Can I stay here for a while?"

"Yeah, sure. There's a spare bed for a few weeks. One of the guys is away. You look exhausted. Go and flake out on his bed now if you like. I'll tell the others we have a house guest."

"I'm hungry. I need to eat first. Let's go and get some food."

"We've got food here. Chops, some spuds and some onions."

"No, no! Let's go to the Malaya. You know it?"

"At Railway Square? Yeah I've been there. I've never seen you there though."

We spent several weeks eating at the old Malaya. Heng ordered *Hǎinán jī fàn*, Hainan chicken rice, every time. We didn't talk much and I didn't ask any more about his problem. I assumed it was an immigration issue and

Surviving the Sixties

thought it best to remain ignorant and provide him with a safe house.

Heng, however, was uncomfortable in the Glebe house. It was not his scene and there was something on his mind. He was furtive and wary. I thought Immigration was after him for sure and it gave me some satisfaction to know I was helping to keep him safe from the government.

One day after a meal at the Malaya, he insisted on us walking down to Dixon Street in Chinatown. Stopping in front of a restaurant he turned to go in.

"We've already eaten, Heng. Do you want more already?"

"No, just come through the restaurant," he urged.

"If you're just going to the toilet. I'll wait here."

"No, no, just follow me," he insisted.

Inside, it was familiar enough. Some laminated tables in the centre, a scattering of diners, benches and booths at the side and a few more diners revealed as we headed towards the kitchen at the rear. I was acquainted with the kitchens in Chinese restaurants along the Dixon Street strip as some of them kept urns of tea in an alcove just inside and I was forever going there to top up my tea. In others, the only toilet was out the back, which meant negotiating the kitchens. We moved through the usual kitchen clatter and then pressed on through another doorway entering a world I hadn't expected.

Fifty or so men and a few women sat playing cards and majong. As the door closed, kitchen noises were replaced with the subtler flutter of paying cards and clicking of majong chips. Heng nodded to a man, spoke with him briefly and I thought handed him something small and compact, but someone crossed my vision at the time so I couldn't be certain.

Heng's associate seemed to point towards a flight of stairs in the back corner, or was I imaging this?

Was that a look of mild panic creasing Heng's face?

Heng stepped away and moved towards me, saying with urgency, "We have to leave now, Russ." He made straight for the kitchen door and on through the restaurant.

Following him, I asked, "What's up Heng?"

"Nothing," he muttered as we stepped out into Dixon Street.

"Is there a problem?"

"No, no problem."

That afternoon, Heng packed up his few belongings and left. I never saw him again.

First Landfall

I'd arranged to meet Jo to reflect on some of our early journeys together. Since our divorce back in 1978, the compulsions, uncertainties and anxieties of early adulthood had mellowed into maturity ensuring that whenever we did meet, the conversation was usually rich and in a spirit of goodwill.

Her house is in one of those beautiful bushy valleys that are so much a feature of northern Sydney. As usual, the front door was open and I observed again that she was still less preoccupied with security than I was.

"Jo, are you there?" I called.

"Yes, just come through," she said in a welcoming voice. "I'm in the dining room."

The dog let out a half-hearted bark, letting me know that I was on her territory.

Jo and I exchanged affectionate kisses on the cheek and she said, "Have a seat at the table." She motioned to a spot. "Cup of tea?"

"Yes, thanks, Jo."

"So, where would you like to start?" she asked as she lit the gas under the kettle.

"Yes, where to start? I know. Remember the old cream Morris Minor with the clapped out engine?"

"I do. It belched out clouds of blue smoke every time we pushed the accelerator."

"These days it'd be off the road with a defect notice in no time. Back then it was tolerated. We should've overhauled the engine."

"I suppose we should have," she said, and then added, "but every spare cent went towards the trip."

"It wouldn't have made it to Fremantle. I had visions of a thin blue line of smoke across the Nullabor, the seals blowing oil squirting everywhere and us standing by a smoldering wreck in the middle of nowhere."

"The middle of nowhere?" Jo grinned. "If we learned one thing, it was just how relative nowhere is."

How could I forget that lesson? One never knows when an opportunity to learn will present itself. Perhaps its significance wasn't so obvious at the time but it illustrated a fundamental truth about Australia and its people.

"You're talking about the elderly Aboriginal man who boarded the bus in Port Augusta, are you?" I asked her.

"Yes, I am."

"It's stayed with me. I've thought about it for years."

Jo poured the tea and sat back looking at me.

"As I recall," I began, "we stopped at a roadhouse in Ceduna for dinner. It was just after six, around sunset. He stood outside alone. I thought he was reluctant to come inside so I went out to invite him in for a cuppa. Just as I stepped out he began making his own way in. He tried to open the door from the hinge side at first. I thought maybe he'd never lived in a place with doors."

"A pity we didn't ever get to meet him," Jo reflected.

"I've always regretted not striking up a conversation."

"Ships that pass in the night, eh?"

"Yeah, true."

Back on the bus, I watched the tops of low scrubby trees flashing past. Soon it was too dark to see anything. After a couple of hours the old man moved to the front, stopped the bus and walked off into the darkness. What he saw, how he knew where he was, puzzles me to this day. Looking at maps of the area, I think he was a Yalata man. He knew when he was home.

Sitting in Jo's sunny dining room reflectively sipping tea, our journey's beginning came easily to mind: 1972 was a time of transition in global travel. Some inexpensive sea journeys were still to be had but air travel from Australia in the new era jets like jets like the Boeing 707 and 747 remained expensive. There were cheap charter flights to Europe but these operated out of Asian ports like Singapore, Kuala Lumpur and Bangkok. So approaching Asia by sea and then picking up a charter flight was an economical and exciting prospect.

"In many ways, I regret we weren't part of that earlier generation, Jo. The long voyage to Europe was a romantic epic. Imagine crossing the equator, meeting King Neptune, stopping at Port Said and Suez, taking side trips to the Pyramids, then sailing on to Piraeus and Genoa before docking in Southampton."

"Yes, retracing the steps of the ancestors," said Jo with a touch of irony. "Leisurely returning to the Mother Country. What a Eurocentric notion! How undeniably part of the 50s culture!"

"I'd never say I was grateful for the Vietnam War."

"I should hope not," exclaimed Jo. "It was an appalling unleashing of military industrial might."

"It was, and gratitude would be a perverse response, but through all that tragedy, a generation was radicalised. Our attention was drawn to the immediate north; to the decolonising forces at work in Indonesia, Malaysia and Indo-China."

"Well the dominos didn't fall and it made us more aware of Asia. New cultural interests awakened. I ended up majoring in Indian history, remember?"

"Yeah, and India had a huge impact on music and fashion; I guess religion too in the sixties. It was sudden. I think the overland backpacker trail to Europe helped, and the Beatles, of course."

Jo chuckled. "*Sgt Pepper's Lonely Hearts Club Band*? You were rather preoccupied with the transcendental for a while there."

"In 1968, the year we met? A turbulent one for me, I think I read too much R.D. Lang."

"Is that what it was?" she laughed.

Her words triggered recollections of the pain sitting beneath the flamboyance of student demonstrations, of 'flower power' and the calls for 'revolution now'. It was that existential pain inherent in the struggle for adult identity, but it was taking place in such a protected environment. The Vietnam War and Conscription were threats to our safety and the sleuths of ASIO and other shadowy security agencies were busy documenting what they determined was our threat to national security, yet it was nothing compared with the struggles our peers in the developing world faced. We were the privileged beneficiaries of an affluent society.

"There were lots of distractions for me," I said. "I was attracted by the Taoist tradition at first. I reckon the childhood Chinese connections had a bit to do with it. Mao fascinated me. I saw him as an emperor. Then I started to think about that merging of cultures further south, the confluence of Indic and Chinese in South East Asia. It was a year of sorting things out for me. I knew there was something happening in Indo-China, Malaysia and Indonesia back then and I wanted to know about it."

"We weighed up the possibilities of hitchhiking to Darwin, if you remember."

"Then flying to Dili, slipping over the border into West Timor and island hopping through Indonesia to Singapore. I think the gamelan in Bali might have captured me, you know."

"It might have but given what emerged later in Singapore my health would have been at risk," Jo added with a somber resonance. "Besides I was keen to reach the Asian mainland quickly."

Our journey north on that trip was on the Austasia

Line's *SS Malaysia*. Our plan was to make landfall in Singapore then head north as far as Luang Prabang before returning to Kuala Lumpur for a charter flight to London. Singapore had the reputation for being a tough place. In effect, it was a one party state with very specific ideas about its future. Strict dress codes applied, long hair was out unless it had a religious basis. Post offices at the time displayed images of hippie hairstyles that would incur refusal of service or at least a long wait. Tales abounded of people arriving at Changi Airport and being refused entry until their hair was cut.

"What puzzled me," Jo reflected, "was the informality of immigration and customs when we arrived. It didn't seem to make sense, given Singapore's reputation."

"We did fill out some forms and handed them to the purser with our passports. Later on, we collected them from an immigration desk in the dining room."

"That's right," Jo affirmed. "I'd forgotten that bit, but then we were just left to wander out of the port. I expected a formal customs clearance, but we just walked out into Singapore. After the benign and friendly Chinese crew, I was very uncomfortable."

"Ports had their own unique intensity in those days, Jo. Visiting Dad's ships around Pyrmont and Walsh Bay, I experienced it but Keppel Harbour had a different edge. People's gaze underscored our place in the world, of our privileged status as cashed up, young Australian backpackers."

"Yes, it was a relief when that taxi appeared. We asked for the YMCA and he took us straight to the old Chinese YMCA just 500 metres away in Palmer Street. It was comfortable. Well, at least in my brief experience of it."

I saw the cloud cross her face.

Trying to make light of things, I said, "It had great air conditioning but dreadful breakfast sausages."

Jo didn't respond. So I continued.

"We pushed things too hard on that first day, ignoring heat and humidity just throwing ourselves into the challenge"

"We sure did," Jo affirmed. "We followed an aimless path at first then decided to head for the new Peoples' Park shopping complex in Chinatown."

"I think we were both a bit overwhelmed and disoriented. It was a case of information overload. Perhaps that's what explained the next event."

"What was that?"

"An embarrassing incident in the hawker centre at Peoples' Park."

"Oh, that one," she sighed. "We should have paid up front when we ordered. It was great food though. It was the first time we'd managed to sit down. Looking around I was still finding it hard to believe we were in a foreign country."

"Yeah, distracted all right, we were."

"So distracted that we wandered off without paying. Did you think I'd paid?" she asked.

"Maybe. All I remember was a small girl chasing after us with a look of alarm and righteousness. Despite our apologies, we weren't believed. We were cast as people trying to skip without paying the bill."

"Didn't we incur the ire of her father. . . " Jo said with regret.

"How could I forget that? They'd just sat down to a meal. 'Why don't you eat some of this food as well?' he said. This distrust can still be an undertone in Singapore. Recently I handed over a ten baht coin instead of a Singapore dollar and no amount of apology seemed to redress the situation. It was as if I'd done it on purpose."

Jo walked over to the window seat that she's transformed into a small indoor garden of carefully nurtured ferns. She stood with her back to me looking at their beauty in shafts of afternoon light.

"Then there was an intense pain. The last thing I expected was any sort of health problem during that trip."

"It was so sudden."

"Actually there was an encroaching discomfort and malaise but once the pain started, it was unbearable."

"You'd done a lot of walking. We'd walked from Chinatown to Raffles Place. I never know whether to say fortunately or unfortunately, but within moments we found that brass plaque announcing the presence of a specialist in obstetrics and gyneacology. That she was from Trinity College Dublin was incidental."

Jo turned towards me.

"The pill was toxic enough but had I known the dangers of IUDs, there's no way…" she fell silent.

This was a time of experimentation and innovation within the medical domain particularly in the management of fertility and contraception. Often the unsuspecting became guinea pigs in ongoing global research. Early birth control pills and several types of IUD were in wide circulation – their effectiveness and safety far from assured. Amongst the IUDs, the Dalkon Shield now stands out as having serious design flaws capable of introducing bacteria, leading to potential sepsis, injury, miscarriage, and even death. In Jo's case, it was a surprise pregnancy, with complications brought on by the device.

"How many days was I in hospital? I just remember sleeping a lot."

"Four, I think, Jo."

While Jo was in hospital, I wandered alone in a strange city with little sense of what to expect. To my eyes, everything seemed peaceful but I wondered about unseen dangers and street crime. Being alone and worrying about Jo intensified my uncertainty.

Somewhere in a guidebook was an enthusiastic description of a hawkers' market in the car park on Orchard Road. I caught a taxi there to find the atmosphere sensational. Bright lights, colour, busy sounds of people and food sizzling in woks were alluring, aromatic, seductive and confronting. Choosing what to eat was difficult, but in the end I ordered stir-fried squid and vegetables because I was standing closest to that hawker's stall.

Perhaps it was the exhilaration of finding the place and successfully ordering a meal, or the sense of mild disorientation accompanying this experience, that explained the decisions I made in the next strange part of the evening. I had only the sketchiest sense of the city's geography, so I set off down Orchard Road towards the city centre. After a short distance, a young man stepped from a doorway into my path.

"You want to buy *ganja*?" he asked.

"*Ganja*? Do you mean marijuana?" I said, startled that he was so brazenly touting his trade.

"Yes, number two Sumatran from Alas," he replied with the confidence of someone selling fresh vegetables in a market.

Shocked by his directness, I blurted out, "Ah, no thanks. This is Singapore; it's a serious crime."

This was Lee Kwan Yew's Singapore and not a place with the Sydney's liberal values and tolerance. Who is this young man anyway? I wondered. He's not Chinese or Indian.

Attempting to retain a polite yet dismissive tone I asked, "Where are you from?"

"I'm Malay from Perak."

"I'm from Australia and the only thing I want to buy in Singapore is a camera."

I'd mistakenly assumed that the *ganja* dealer would have little interest in cameras.

First Landfall

"You want a camera? I have a friend down on Bras Basah Road. He can give you a good deal."

"Do you? That's not much use to me. I'll need to spend time looking at equipment in the daylight. It's already late."

"Let me take you there now. It's just a short way from here. It's on this road. You can always come back tomorrow."

Unaware of the workings of the commission system and against my better judgment, I followed him apprehensively or, rather, he accompanied me as he seemed to be going in my direction. Soon we reached the Bee Loh photographic shop. Reasoning there was no commitment in looking, I went in.

"Welcome! Come in, sir," said the Chinese shop attendant.

My companion drifted into the background. No one greeted him or displayed the slightest recognition. There was no sense that he knew anyone; this made me a little wary.

"What are you looking for, sir?"

"Well, a camera, but I need time before making a decision."

"Certainly, sir. Do you prefer an SLR or large format camera? We have all the leading cameras and can give you a special price on most."

I had a sense that I wanted a half frame camera, a Pen FT. This was the first single-lens reflex half-frame camera and in the pre-digital days once an image was committed to cellulose it was irreversible, so doubling the shots was economical. I had an idea what they cost in Australia but not here.

"Do you stock Olympus?"

"Yes, both full and half frame models," he answered, turning in his chair to lift several Olympus cameras from the shelf behind the counter. My companion began to close in a little, perhaps sensing that I might buy on impulse.

"I need to research prices and compare them with Australia," I advised.

"Here, all are duty free. Pick a camera, tell me what you would pay in Australia and I will beat that price."

My companion was now standing right beside me. Feeling increasing pressure to buy, I paused, inhaled deeply then said, "No, thanks, not right now. I'll come back in the daytime." At that I turned and walked off as quickly as I could.

It was a warm balmy evening, a scent of blossom hung in the air. Carefree summer nights in Australia, infused with the smell of frangipani, came to mind. A comforting, familiar feeling accompanied me as I walked a block or two before realising I was alone again and lost. It was late, dark and unlike Singapore of today, there were no taxis to be seen.

Puzzling over my predicament, several plans emerged. I could walk back to the shop and then towards Orchard Road and attempt to find the route my taxi had taken into the area. No, not a good idea – it might involve a further encounter with the ganja seller. I could find the coastline and follow it till I reached the port. And I've no idea how far or how safe that might be. I'll catch the first public bus that comes, buy a ticket to the terminus and then negotiate my way back to the hotel from there.

The plan worked like a dream. It was unnecessary to go to the end of the line because the bus went right past my hotel's street.

My Tanjong Pagar hotel was central but had one problem – it was bland and it didn't feel like Asia, so I looked for other options. My guidebook mentioned cheap but comfortable Chinese hotels along Waterloo and

Bencoolen streets. Most were about eight to ten Singapore dollars and already full. One remained, the Kian Hua. There was a bar at the front, the hotel entrance at the side. A man sat behind a wooden desk animatedly chatting on the phone. He ended the call as I approached.

"Halo, you want room? Just twelf Singapore dollar one night. No breakfast."

His relaxed posture, disheveled clothing and features struck me as reminiscent of Bob Gould.

"You want room?"

"May I see it first?"

"Cheong!" he called.

A previously unnoticed boy rose from a low stool behind the desk casting his newspaper aside and motioning me to follow.

Inside was cool. Off a gloomy corridor we entered a large basic room. A single 40-watt light globe illuminated two double beds made up with sheets, pillows and bolsters. Several pairs of rubber thongs were arrayed under each bed. For a moment, I thought I must be displacing members of the family, feeling that awkward sense of my privileged place again. Where was this unseen family, I wondered? There was no immediate sign of them. Maybe the other kids were at school. Then came the realisation, the sandals were for me or anyone else staying in the room and the protocol was to remove one's footwear at the door. There was even a shoe rack.

"OK, thanks," I said as I returned to the manager's desk.

He was on the phone again and just as abruptly ended this call as well.

"You want room?"

"Yes. I'll pay for three days."

"If you stay one week you pay just eleven dollar, one night."

"I don't know how long I'll stay, but here's the money" I said, placing forty dollars on the desk.

Seen and Unseen

He slipped the money into a drawer, returning four crumpled well-used notes and adding, "You must write name, passport number, where you come from and where you go in this book."

While I filled out the book, he made yet another call and just as abruptly ended it as I gathered my bags to go to the room.

"No need you do that – he take it," he said gesturing at Cheong.

"Thanks. I have a question. Isn't it expensive making so many telephone calls?"

This was long before the era of digital exchanges, mobiles and discounted telephone calls. Back home people often kept a money tin beside their phone so that when the bill came it wasn't too much of a shock.

"No. No charge for Singapore call. Good business. Our government want us use telephone."

"Okay," I said as I moved off towards the room. "A good idea, makes it like two-way radio."

"Not radio, telephone."

"Like walkie-talkie, you know?" I tried to clarify.

He looked blankly then smiled, "Walkie-talkie? No, I sit here."

Having solved the mystery of the rubber sandals, one more remained. Where were the amenities? There was no shower or bathroom, just a washing area at the rear and some squat toilets. Squat toilets were no challenge to a young man but this was my first encounter with a *bak mandi* (a large tiled tub). Coming from the world's most arid inhabited continent, I carried hidden perceptions about water and waste. Even in the tropics, it seemed obscene to use such a large amount of water so I resisted the temptation to climb in before noticing the small plastic dipper. It didn't take long to work out the procedure. Strip, dowse yourself with water, soap up and then wash it off again taking care to keep the water in the tub clean and free of soapy residues. It was refreshing.

In the daylight, Bee Loh Photographics was at first unrecognisable, but it turned out to be a mere block away. Without the tout's help, and with minimal discussion, we settled on a fair price for a black-bodied Pen FT with additional wide angled lens. I rejected a second hand telephoto lens on offer and lived to regret it.

Seen and Unseen

From the Sublime to the Horrific

Several days after my move to the Kian Hua, Jo was discharged from Mt Alvernia Hospital, shaky, pregnant, and hardly ready for the road but keen to get going. Being parents wasn't part of the plan yet both of us accepted our unexpected travelling companion without question. So now we were three.

Jo's doctor advised taking things easy and as west Malaysia was bound to be the least challenging part of the planned itinerary, we headed north for Malacca and a new beginning.

Our Malacca connection was tenuous; Subramanian was a friend's friend who had returned a year earlier to teach history. We found him living with his Australian partner, Mary, in a place called Taman Muhibbah, a complex designed to house British troops and now available as a housing estate populated by teachers and civil servants.

Entering Subramanian's house felt secure and familiar. Reminiscent of Australian suburbia it came with verandah, sitting room, kitchen, bathroom, laundry and bedrooms. Initial introductions completed, we sat sipping tea and recounting our experiences so far. More by accident than design conversation turned from small talk to politics.

"Subramanian, what does Muhibbah mean?" I asked.

"Harmony. It's an invented word, Malaysia's national wish. Some say it exists only as a definition. Malaysia was granted independence, not like our neighbour Indonesia."

"Yes, I know something about that. Soekarno was very prominent in the Indonesian struggle. Then some years ago, the military staged a coup and purged anyone they considered a Communist or leftist side lining Soekarno."

"Struggles for national independence galvanise people around national symbols. In Indonesia's case, it was the secular nationalist doctrine summarised in the idea of Pancasila and the word *Merdeka* or independence."

"So there's no way it has the strength or national unity," said Jo. "Is that how it works?"

"Right, that's it. The hope is for unity as a nation but colonialism often just papers over important differences like traditional cultural boundaries and borders. It can also entrench certain privileges. Here, the Malays have special privileges and this makes unity difficult." His voice audibly dropped, conveying a concern someone might hear him. Mary looked uncomfortable.

"I know about Malay privileges," I said. "My school friend was a Chinese Malaysian from Ipoh. From what he said, the special status given to Malays is unfair."

Now speaking in quite hushed tones, Subramanian continued. "Here to be a Malay or Bumiputra is synonymous with being a Muslim. Although together Malaysians of Chinese and Indian descent outnumber the Malays, by virtue of Malay privileges Islam is the de facto official religion."

"My friend Heng was very unhappy about the privileges. He told me that a certain number of Malays had to be employed in enterprises whatever their skill level. I can't imagine this is very efficient."

"Well, here you see it in action. We aren't even meant to be having this conversation. Criticising Malay privileges is considered seditious. Let's do something more interesting," he added. "It's almost time to eat. I'm going to cook a fish curry. You two can have the first room on the left, just down the hall. Rest up while I'm cooking." He smiled and rose from his seat before disappearing into the small kitchen at the side of the house.

Throughout the entire conversation, Mary was silent.

With Subramanian's departure she retreated down the short hallway to a room at the end. Jo and I looked at one another as we gathered our backpacks and hand luggage.

"I think our stay must be brief," Jo whispered. "Despite Subramanian's hospitality, I have the distinct sense we aren't welcome."

"You're right. I was hoping you might have a few days rest but I don't see much option than for us to move on in the morning."

"Let's drop our bags in the room and sit out on the verandah for a while; it feels close in here," was Jo's only response.

Next morning, we took an early leave and soon picked up a public bus bound for Port Dickson just up the coast. It had a small port and fuel storage area but its redeeming features were its secluded Casurina lined beach and small but vibrant night market with friendly hawkers and welcoming patrons. Now it seemed we were beginning the journey we had planned.

In Malaysia of 1972, people travelling with backpacks like us were called hitchhikers. This applied whatever means of transport we chose and since we hadn't even tried hitchhiking, the persistent appellation convinced us it must be easy, so we decided to give it a go in the next leg of our trip to north.

Waiting under the shade of a tamarind tree and enjoying the cooler morning air, we watched as cars passed our outstretched thumbs.

"At last," I beamed. "Looks as though we might have a lift."

A pale blue Mercedes sedan slowed then increased speed and headed off again.

"They're not stopping. Perhaps they had second thoughts about loading our backpacks," said Jo. "I think we might as well catch a bus."

"Yeah. It was a nice idea. I'd like a bit more certainty anyway."

I too was having second thoughts not wanting to subject Jo to any unnecessary worries.

Minutes later as if on cue, a public bus appeared. I waved and it stopped for us. We paid a small fare and relaxed into our seats in anticipation of a comfortable trip to our next stop, Seremban.

Southern peninsula Malayasia seemed like one vast rubber and oil palm plantation. At first, boring grid plantings dominated our journey, offering scant respite from monotony. Just as their symmetrical passage became hypnotic, the road began to rise, winding through gentle hills and small timbered areas. As we rounded a bend, the road dropped into a small valley.

"Did I see what I just saw?" asked Jo in alarm.

"You mean the four bodies lying by the road?"

"Yes."

"Their heads were covered. They were lying beside the wreck of that blue Mercedes."

We'd flashed past. The adrenalin pumped. We both sat numbed, trembling, hearts beating fast. Slowly the adrenalin subsided.

"Glad we didn't get that lift, Jo."

"Me, too."

After our night in Seremban, a brief train trip saw us in Kuala Lumpur by the middle of the next day. Here we had a connection with wealthy Sikh, a client with Jo's father's export business. A providore selling bulk Indian spices, ghee and dry goods from a shop front business in the city, his home address on Jalan Ampang was prestigious and his house was palatial. Our accommodation was a special guest room near the front door. Wherever we went, we were chauffeured. Meal times were banquets. We ate heartily and the food was delicious. When we finished eating, we were pressed to eat more.

We were taken to the usual tourist sites, the zoo, Batu Caves with its many steps, the State Mosque, Parliament House and then as an added bonus to the mock Tudor complex of the KL Club.

While appreciative, we felt overwhelmed and out of synch with the values of our well-meaning host. His eldest son had moved out, worked as a gynaecologist and had married a woman from the United Kingdom. Another newly married son still lived there with the parents. He seemed dull, indulged and rather aimless by contrast with his wife, an intelligent pre-school teacher who, in the prevailing patriarchal system, was not allowed to work.

Jo approached the gynaecologist for assistance, hoping for a second opinion on how safe it might be to journey north. Unwilling to commit himself, however, he would only provide a list of medical contacts advising that we shouldn't travel rough.

After a few days, it was time to move on to Penang. We journeyed by train and finally by bus heading for Batu Feringgi on the island's north coast.

Batu Feringgi beach was a renowned hippie destination but long before we arrived, weariness and the site of a beautiful beach, its aquamarine sea and coconut palms protected by a small promontory invited us.

"Jo, I'm happy to settle for this place. By all appearances, it's quiet as well."

"Quick, press the button to stop the bus," she urged.

The bus came to a smooth stop outside the Eden Hotel.

"If it's no good there are several others along the road, all on the beach."

"I agree," said Jo. "Let's have a look."

There was a gentle sea breeze, taking the edge off the intensely hot day. After a quick survey of the accommodation, we chose a bungalow away from the main hotel. It had a shared sitting room, but was ten paces from the beach. After settling in we ambled down to the water.

White sand stretched for 800 metres to the west, where a small river flowed into the Straits of Malacca. To the east, a granite outcrop protected the beach. Here, its sand was littered with pottery shards bearing enigmatic characters and horseshoe crabs continuously emerged from the warm, gentle tide.

Jo threw a sarong over a shady stretch of sand near a huge granite tor and sank into its coolness. "Coming here and seeing this beauty," she said, scraping together a pile of sand as a head support. "I'm even more aware of how stressful everything has been. Even the hospitality in Kuala Lumpur was stressful. I felt as though we were always being evaluated."

"We were. Not so much in a judgmental way but more out of curiosity. They were very generous, the food was great, but I don't think I'll be able to face another chapatti for a while."

"Death by chapatti," Jo laughed.

In this sublime location, we sank into a relaxation, shedding the tensions of our journey. Intoxicating smells emanated from the kitchen; its specialty Kapitain King Prawn Curry was inexpensive and delicious. Straits Chinese cuisine, supplemented by a distinct taste of Padang and South Indian fare was the hotel's offering and made all the more pleasant by the polite, cordial and hospitable staff. Here we had everything we wanted. Eden was such a wonderful retreat and respite.

Penang Hill, where temperatures sit around 4°C cooler than at sea level, is an ideal setting for strolling through gardens and enjoying views. With time and space slipping by, there was no destination until Jo and I found ourselves on a slow descent first through gardens and then through rainforest arching above. Occasionally, noisy gibbons swung through the canopy, then all was quiet but for a soundscape of birdcalls.

Emerging at the foot of Kek Lok Si Pagoda, we found a sense of arriving at an intangible destination that opened opportunities to visit inner spaces, calmed and energised by the surroundings.

A Pond of Longevity hosted hundreds of turtles set free by devotees. Dominating the complex was a 30-metre pagoda tower and deeper within, a magnificent statue of the Goddess of Mercy, the feminised version of Buddha so often found in Chinese tradition. We gazed upwards through the branching corners of the pavilions, forming decorative vine-like pointers accentuating the austere yellow zone of formlessness painted at the top of the pagoda tower.

"Laos and the Mekong are calling," I said. "I have visions of elephants and jungle treks, riverboat journeys and exotic fruits, Jo."

"You've been looking at your Royal Lao tourist visa again; I saw you."

"Well, it is a very romantic notion but then again this space has a very special energy."

"It helps me feel stronger but Laos is a long way off. Let's just take things easy for a while."

"I can hear Luang Prabang calling now."

"Goodness me. Can you?" she laughed. "I see you want to get on the road again. If we can move at my pace, I'll try."

"Fine, Jo. I don't expect anything more."

Enthused and encouraged by the Kek Lok Si Pagoda

we set our departure for two days hence.

Outside Eden Hotel on the day before our departure for Thailand, two people appeared. We recognised Grant and Lucia from different social events in Sydney but didn't know them well, much less as a couple.
"Hey! I know you two!" called Grant.
"Friends of Paul's, aren't you?" Lucia added.
"Yeah, I remember you. Had no idea you were travelling together. You remember Grant and Lucia, Jo?"
"Yes, hi! How are you?"
"Ah that's a long story," said Grant. "You want to have a coffee with us?"
"Sure," I said, "let's go back into the Eden."
They had not long arrived from Lake Toba, in Sumatra, staying first at Batu Feringgi, then moving on to the Eden after a police or immigration raid. They weren't clear about which. Maybe they didn't know.
"Yeah man, you've gotta check out Sumatra," Grant said. "It's far out. I mean real volcanoes. Like you can walk right up to them. No kidding."
"So cool," added Lucia. "And the ganja in Lake Toba. Like, it's everywhere."
"What do you mean everywhere?" Jo prompted.
Lucia gave her a disdainful look and said, "Ya know what I mean, it's easy to get. Ya just move into a hotel at Lake Toba and ask for it. That's all. If the police are coming around, ya chuck it. Then ya just score more."
"So you spent the time stoned there," I said. "Did you learn any of the language?"
"Of course we were stoned," said Grant. "Isn't that the point, man? And why would you want to learn the language?"
This is a bit bloody tedious, I thought. Why on earth would anyone want to spend the whole time getting stoned when there was so much to learn?

"Yeah, *ganja*'s everywhere around Malaysia and Indonesia," Grant continued. "Some of it even gets to Australia. Have you seen those small cart traders here selling tobacco and cigarettes by the roadside?"

"Yes," I replied.

"If you ask them, they've got *ganja* under the fliptop of their carts. There's so much of it around. A lot of it comes from Aceh north of Lake Toba. They sell the stuff so they can get money to buy arms for their independence fight against Indonesia."

I'd heard a little of this back in Australia and my encounter in Singapore started to make a bit more sense now. I looked at Jo. She was making subtle signs it was time to move.

"I haven't been too well, so I need to rest this afternoon," Jo explained as she pushed her chair back and stood. "I must go…"

"Oh yes, tell me about it," Lucia interrupted. "We've spent a fortune at the Adventist Hospital."

"Really?" Jo asked. "Both of you have been unwell?"

"Yeah. We've been smoking opium and it stuffs up your gut. So as good as it is, we have to go to the hospital when we get too constipated."

Jo frowned in subdued annoyance. "Look, I must go," she said and slipped out of the dining room.

"Did we offend her?" Grant enquired.

"No. She's pregnant. She almost miscarried and she's exhausted."

"I know what ya mean," Lucia said. "Smoking the opium makes ya pretty exhausted as well. So do these dreadful people in Indonesia and here. They can't mind their own bloody business."

"Yeah," Grant said, "they're always asking 'Where are you going?', 'Where have you come from?' and 'Are you married?' Things like that. Bloody busy bodies. I tell you

From the Sublime to the Horrific

I don't like them."

Why don't you go home if you hate it so much? I thought to myself.

"I think you'll find this is a really chilled out place but I must go as well," I said. "I want to make sure Jo's comfortable. We'll see you before we go."

"Okay, see ya!" they said in unison.

For a moment I wondered if I had missed something. Are people here really rude and overly inquisitive? Our treatment had been courteous, even if at times out of accord with our values. Grant and Lucia's negativity and arrogance came as a complete shock.

Arriving at Ban Hat Yai late in the day, we were tired. It is a quiet railway town 30 kilometres inland from the port of Songklah in Thailand. We checked into the Railway Hotel. Few trains ran so it was a convenient place to stay.

Thailand was a completely new experience, a different script, less English, more reserve towards foreigners, police and military roadblocks, overt bribery of police and soldiers and significant signs of poverty. Confined to the narrow Kra Isthmus with its poor soils and limited irrigation infrastructure, Southern Thailand was at the end of an intense dry season. After an amble around the town, we detected a general disinterest in if not disdain for young backpackers, so eating in at the hotel restaurant seemed the best option.

We ordered fish soup and rice. It was delicious with a strong taste of coriander and lemon. As the level fell, slices of a familiar fish were revealed. It looked like puffer fish. Back home I'd often caught what we called toadfish or porcupine fish. When puffed up, their skin bristled with thorny spikes.

"Jo, I reckon this is toad fish."

"What! You're kidding."

"No, sorry, I'm not. I've caught enough of them to know what they are."

"They're poisonous!" Jo exclaimed.

"Yes, but I don't think every part is. We haven't eaten much so let's just put it aside now."

"For sure," she said. Silent for a moment she added thoughtfully, "From memory they're called *fugu* in Japan. Remember the Kurosawa film *Dodes'ka-den* at last year's Sydney Film Festival, the one about the street people who eat inexpertly prepared fugu?"

"I do."

"They died," said Jo, with more than a little concern in her voice.

"We've eaten very little, Jo, mainly soup and rice, and from what I know the poison isn't concentrated in the flesh but in the liver and intestines. We've only eaten clean flesh."

Almost all puffer fish contain the poison tetrodotoxin. It is deadly to humans and Jo had already eaten a little more than me. That night, dreaming or awake, Jo was disturbed by strong hallucinations while I was untouched by toxicity. I first thought Jo was being a little dramatic about the whole episode, finding it hard to believe anyone would serve puffer fish, much less want to poison us. Years later, I researched the issue. Indeed, puffer fish were legally sold as food in Thailand until 2002. Even today, they are caught on both sides of the Kra Isthmus. Their sale is banned yet substantial quantities are still being sold in Thai fish markets.

After this disconcerting experience, both of us were keen to move on so we headed north to Nakon Sri Thammerat, arriving late the following day. This was as far as we managed to venture before weariness and a serious bout of bacterial diarrhea struck Jo, forcing us to turn to back and head for Kota Bahru in Malaysia where we had the name of a doctor for Jo.

Kota Bahru is the capital of Kelantan, a Malaysian state noted for its strong and traditional Islamic values. Arriving there at night on the eve of a holiday left us with only a few Ringgits, nowhere to cash travelers' cheques and nowhere to stay. Making matters worse were growing complications with Jo's pregnancy. Our only option was to ask for hospitality at the Sikh Temple, which was readily granted. So we settled in to wait out the holiday period on string beds, our only food some powered milk and vegemite. To supplement this meager fare, we managed to find half a loaf of bread and a street vendor selling cheap sticky rice wrapped in leaves that we found was impregnated with kerosene and inedible.

Three days later, our wait was over. Cashed-up and settled into a cheap hotel room, we went straight to the hospital expecting a quick consultation. This was not to be. The doctor wasn't available but would attend the hospital soon. In the meantime, Jo was admitted, the only way they would allow her to consult him.

Entering the women's ward was a journey back to the Middle Ages. It was a nightmare of unsanitary conditions. A bloodstained sarong lay in a corner where it had been thrown. Bedpans full of faeces and urine littered the toilet floor while goats and chickens roamed about on the verandah outside where families prepared food for patients on small charcoal or kerosene cookers. This was an assault on all our previous notions of health care.

Mid-afternoon the doctor arrived. His reaction was curt: "You're bleeding, so I can't examine you."

"Then how can I know whether it is safe to travel or even leave here?" Jo asked, a sense of panic rising.

"It seems you are miscarrying."

"Then the medical procedure is straight forward enough," she pressed.

"There is nothing I can do. My suggestion is get out of here."

"Nothing?" She grew alarmed.

"You could well die if you stay here," he answered.

Arriving minutes after this encounter, I found Jo in distress. "Right, Jo," I said, "we're out of here. Pack up. I'll be right back for you."

At that, I made straight for the Malaysian Airways office bought two tickets to Kuala Lumpur and returned with a taxi to see Jo out of the hospital.

That night, we waited. Outwardly strong, she was happy to walk along the banks of the river to a small night market. She didn't eat much; I bought a plate of cockles, ate one and realized they were rotten, so topped up on nasi goreng. Early next morning, we were on the flight over the central highlands and before long meeting our contacts at the airport.

By this stage, I'd developed a significant case of projectile vomiting and diarrhea but managed to accompany Jo to the university hospital where yet another doctor explained there was nothing he could do under Malaysian law. He referred her to a clinic in Singapore and the next day we were on the train. In Singapore, Jo's miscarriage was confirmed and safely managed.

It was almost a year before we saw Singapore again, retracing our steps from Europe to Australia.

Walking down Bras Basah Road one evening on our way back from the Orchard Road hawkers' market, we were surprised to encounter Lucia and Grant. They looked well.

"So, how have you been?" I asked.

"We've been fine," said Grant. "Hanging out in Goa

for most of the last year. A cool place to chill out and get healthy."

"Yeah, really cool," chimed Lucia.

Jo asked where they went after Penang.

"After you left the Eden, we were just hanging out and smoking a bit of weed that we picked up from one of those street sellers. The staff were a bunch of arseholes. They hated us. We reckon they dobbed us into the police."

"Yeah," Lucia broke in. "Suddenly, there was this hammering on the door and a voice saying 'Police! Open the door'. Grant grabbed the ganja and hurled it out the window. Then I opened the door."

"They were only looking for trafficable quantities so they overlooked the few crumbs on the bed. They told us to get off the island. I can tell you, man, we were glad to be out of that hole."

I could sense Jo's impatience and exasperation. She said nothing.

All I could say was, "It was a lucky escape."

The Dream

With bilateral relations at a low point, our dream of creating an Indonesia based field study centre for Australian students was ambitious, yet an idea whose time had come. That year, 1984, saw Red Gum release 'I've Been to Bali too'. It was a measure of the overwhelming interest ordinary Australians were showing in this tropical paradise. They sang positively of Ubud, a place in the hills of Bali, a place no one wants to leave.

Our field study centre was also in Ubud. Inspired by time spent in its child friendly atmosphere, Adrienne Truelove and Matina Pentes had just launched the book *Travelling with Children to Indonesia and South East Asia*. It attracted a national award from the Indonesia's Director General of Tourism, Joop Ave, and, in this atmosphere, with cheap promotional airfares secured from Garuda Indonesia plus strong support from the people of Ubud, Asian Field Study Centres was born. Its mission was to provide a rich array of interdisciplinary field study programs to students visiting Indonesia.

Surrounded by *sawah* (rice fields), off the mass tourist track, and with a long history of openness to visitors drawn by art, music and broader expressions of Balinese culture, Ubud seemed ideal. However, we were yet to appreciate its cultural depths, those other dimensions that challenged our understanding. At this time, we were content with the simple explanations forming the foundations of our intercultural program, as we awaited the arrival of our first group.

Over coffee in Murni's Warung, Adrienne said to me: "It's gratifying to know all's in place for the first group.

The Dream

Drama, dance, painting and batik are timetabled, tutors arranged, notes are written and printed. We can relax."

"We've achieved a lot already," said Matina. "I'm happy we've stayed the course and kept a fine eye for detail along the way."

"Well," I said, "without the accolades you two drew in Jakarta along with the national press and television coverage, it would have been a lot harder." I was conscious of the huge impact Joop Ave's imprimatur had back in the village.

Delicate negotiations from ministerial to village level concluded, accommodation, buses and local teachers organised everything was ready to roll.

"One more thing," said Matina.

"What now?" Adrienne and I asked together. The exhaustion of doing business Western-style in a developing country where time was 'rubber' and humidity was enervating was taking its toll. We needed a few days' rest before the group arrived, not another job.

"We need staff transport, not just for us, either. Any accidents or lost students will be a problem without it. We need a safety net."

Up until then, we used day-hired mini-buses and local utility trucks with bench seats in the back, *bemo* as they were called.

Matina added: "We need something that's reliable and immediately available to move students in a medical emergency."

"But transport's so damn expensive," I said. "I don't fancy paying tourist prices for transport long term. We'll need a special rate."

"Cody came up with a good idea the other day," Adrienne said, "buying an old bemo, of our own. We can sell it later, or keep it if it works well."

"You mean the type with a canopy," I asked, "and wooden benches at the back, not the other type."

"Yes, a *bemo*, like that one there," she said pointing out through the restaurant's open windows towards a bemo that had just stopped by Campuan bridge.

"A great idea but it could be like buying a pig in a poke," I replied, aware just how hard the old buses were worked. "I don't think anyone would let one go unless it was completely clapped out."

"Maybe not," replied Adrienne, "but they're everywhere so they must be cheap to repair."

Matina said, "I don't think buying transport is a viable option because there's nowhere to store it when we aren't here. Long term leasing's the only way to go. Nyoman said there's a trader next to Rai's shop that might have a van to rent. I'll have a word with them, and see what's on offer."

Eventually, we negotiated a price to rent a van from Gus, the trader next to Rai's shop even though Gus didn't have one available just then. We were left uncertain as to whether a van was actually available. In those days, there were very few private cars in Bali. With nothing on paper, we were merely given an assurance that one would be available "soon" – which might mean tomorrow, or might mean never.

Over drinks one evening, our neighbour George, who imported artefacts from Bali for his large emporium on the outskirts of New York, asked how we were going with preparations for our first group.

"Transport's the last hurdle," I told him. "Everything else is in place. We've agreed on a price to rent a van but the owner can't tell us when we can have it. We also think the price is too high." Typically, the price asked was more than seemed reasonable, but the laws of supply and demand applied.

George had a hard-nosed approach to business. When told the price he snapped, "That's a joke! The price is outrageous! And you don't even have a date. You need an actual van and a better price."

He was right. We decided that as nothing was signed, it wouldn't hurt to keep looking.

The next day, Matina found a bargain down in Kuta, a new Suzuki Carry and at a rock bottom price, thanks to her negotiation skills. Even better, the owner, Ida Bagus, lived close to Ubud.

This time we wanted a written contract, so together we engaged a notary and both parties signed on the dotted line. Then all of us headed off to an insurance company so we could take out cover for any incidental damage. Money paid and policy signed, we made to leave.

"One moment," said Ida Bagus.

"Something else?" I asked.

"There is a new cassette deck in the van. It should be insured as well."

"We could have included it as a separate item on the policy," I replied "but it's too late now."

"I will make another policy."

So Ida Bagus paid a modest premium with our funds and we all went our separate ways.

Driving back to Ubud, we were in high spirits as we hit the long stretch between Batu Bulan and Batuan. The cassette deck was a big hit – we had stocked up on tapes and were listening to Bob Dylan as we rolled along.

"Now that our transport is sorted," Adrienne said, "I wonder when they'll roll out more telephones around Ubud. I think at last count there were only two in the whole village."

"I reckon they'll need to upgrade the whole network," I said. "It's a new build. The Ginyar exchange is still manual, cables and plugs. Looks as if it's built out of a Meccano set."

"My biggest worry's over," said Matina, her relief palpable. "At least we can move any sick or injured students now. The thought of chasing local transport in an emergency was a nightmare – but, of course, now nothing will happen."

Being the qualified nurse amongst us, Matina was under some pressure if accidents or sudden illnesses arose. Having the van meant that, whatever happened now, we had quick options.

Our collective mood was buoyant and when Adrienne met an interesting French anthropologist, Vincent, our mood was buoyed even more. Conversations in the evening were stimulating and focused on the very elements of Balinese culture and the setting of the field study. We chatted late, enjoying both the wine and the coffee and thought there was time for a lazy morning sleep-in.

But it was not to be; early morning brought news of an angry and intense visitor. Entering the lobby, I was confronted by a man wearing a motorbike helmet and clutching a set of keys, an air of menace about him. When he removed his helmet, I realised it was Gus, the man who'd been unable to deliver a rental van the week before.

"Why you not come to see me and collect the van?" he demanded.

"We didn't know you had a van ready."

"When you take the van?" he asked angrily.

"I am sorry but we found a much cheaper van."

"You take these." He slammed the keys down onto a marble topped table. "I pay Rp 125,000 and rent motorbike to replace van. No good. What I do with motorbike?"

Acutely embarrassed, all I could say was, "I don't ride a motorbike and I don't have a motorbike licence." In those early days we were all learning Bahasa Indonesia, so the conversation relied on his simple English. I didn't know how to explain our understanding of contracts to him and was a loss to make amends.

Wordlessly, he grabbed the keys and stormed out.

With the benefit of hindsight, I realise that I should have offered him at least half the funds and helped him return the bike but I didn't, more through ignorance and surprise than a desire to stand on a point.

Several days later, our batik tutor whose wife, Rai, operated a business next to Gus's shop asked, "What happened with Gus's van? I heard you didn't take it."

I struggled for an answer, settling on, "Well, we didn't have a written contract. We have a written contract for the van we rented."

I realised this was a Western way of reasoning and that I'd lost both face and trust. From then on, I was always careful not to make agreements of any kind unless I was definitely going to honour them. Nothing more was said by anyone about the incident, as if it hadn't happened.

The Northholm Grammar group arrived and we were fully focused. Orientation ran smoothly, all the batik, woodcarving, dance and painting tutors were brilliant. The tour buses were punctual. The accommodation was well appreciated the food delicious, no one had a medical disaster and as a bonus, the students even met the Australian Consul. Despite every obstacle, we delivered an excellent educational experience.

At the end, the group farewelled; a glow of tears, thanks, and ceremonial departure lingered as we entered a relaxed mode.

Once again, however, I was woken early in the morning. This time entering the lobby, I met the van's owner Ida Bagus. He looked intense. I hadn't encountered this energy before. It wasn't anger. Was it fear or was it guilt? It was indeterminate. Mysterious.

"I dreamt about the van," he said. "So I come to check. Please, come and see this."

We stepped outside. The van was in its usual place near the manager's Nissan Patrol. Then I realised the passenger side window was broken. Inside, wires protruded from the place where the cassette player should have been.

"What happened to cassette player?" he asked.

"Looks as though it's been stolen," I replied.

"It was in my dream."

"You say you dreamt this. When was that?"

"In the night."

It was hard to assimilate. Visions in dreams couldn't be dismissed yet I was disinclined to buy it. He had insisted that the cassette player be insured. Why had he left it until the morning if he was so concerned? But these were private thoughts. I'd no intention of voicing them.

"We will need a police report for the insurance claim," I said, half expecting him to back off at this point given the implausibility of it all. "I'll meet you at the police station as soon as possible."

Of course there was no calling the police to come and inspect, without telephones. Adrienne and I drove to the police station ready to devote the whole morning to paperwork. Ida Bagus followed on his motorbike.

There was little detail I could offer in reporting the incident just that the cassette player was in the van when I parked it the night before. The owner had roused me with his concern in the morning and we'd discover the window broken and the cassette player missing. Surprisingly the owner repeated his story about the dream.

Without question, the police typed up a report and gave me a copy for the insurance company.

There was Rp 60,000 excess on the cassette player, which cost Rp 125, 000 to replace with the balance paid by the insurance company. The replacement cassette player was identical, the latest model.

Left puzzling over the affair for years, I couldn't decide what really lay behind it. Was it some form of *kontak batin*, a mystical conduit allowing for some sort of precognition, or was it something more mundane? I didn't ask Ida Bagus if he knew the man with the motorbike.

Seen and Unseen

The Thief and the Angels

Julie and Grant, old friends from Sydney, had spent the past four years balancing the demands of professional life and children. Now it was time to use up some long service leave for a quiet break in Bali, with their four year-old Ian and a toddler Tim, during the dry season of 1988. For a modest outlay, they rented a beautiful bungalow on the outskirts of Ubud. It came with kitchen, sitting/dining room and children's bedroom plus a spacious attic style bedroom with woven bamboo walls that opened to reveal magnificient views over Campuan and Ubud. Accessible via a steep stairway, the attic could be closed off and locked using a light wooden door that dropped into place. It was the perfect parent's retreat. The bungalow afforded a wonderful sense of space and continuity flowing seamlessly into the surrounding gardens.

"Can I pay the rent in advance?" enquired Julie, as the last of their luggage was carried in from the car. "It's all in cash and travellers' cheques."

"No, rest, relax; enjoy your welcome drink," replied proprietor's wife, Made. "You can pay me tomorrow."

"Thanks, Made, the children are tired," Julie replied. "I'd like to show them around and then settle them down." Relieved at the opportunity to unwind, she was happy to attend to business later.

Early in the evening, all four lay in the attic bedroom, parents waiting for the children to drift off, luggage partially unpacked. Exhaustion rapidly overcame them. They slept the innocent sleep of a small family on their first night in an apparent paradise on earth. Locking the attic door was the last thing that came to mind.

Julie's first moments of morning wakefulness were infused with a nagging dread. Lifting her head and glancing across the room she exclaimed, "Oh no!"

Grant's upturned bag lay on the other side of the room.

"Where's my bag with all the money?" Julie wailed. "Damn it, I should have put it under the bed at least!"

Grant woke in a start and bounded out of bed.

"The leather suitcase! Where's that?" he yelled as he slid down the steep stairway stumbling over the sturdy leather case at the bottom, its tightly compressed load of disposable nappies sprung all over the floor.

"The compression must have surprised the thief," said Julie, for a moment glimpsing the humour in the situation and almost managing a chuckle.

"You said it, darling. The thief. We've been robbed," said Grant in exasperation.

Julie's bag with their passports and airline tickets turned up in nearby rice fields later that day. Meanwhile, the proprietor offered a list of local restaurants explaining that the family could have dinner at any one of these venues and his family would provide both breakfast and lunch. As an added bonus, although not then apparent, when it was time to settle up, they found all their meals were discounted.

Speculation on the thief's identity proved accurate and was confirmed many years later through painstaking investigations, but then any forensic efforts on my part were abruptly terminated when early one morning, two days after the theft, the phone rang. It was Julie's voice wavering and emotional.

"Tim has fallen off the bed and cracked his head on the paved floor. He's semi conscious and vomiting. We need your help and your vehicle now. Please come!"

Within 20 minutes, we were consulting the village doctor who advised rushing Tim to the new emergency department at Sanglah Hospital in Denpasar.

Seen and Unseen

Arriving, we found the emergency department quiet. We were promptly ushered into a small room with plain white walls and polished concrete floor. An examination table stood to the side and next to it a cabinet with basic medical instruments. Simple, clean and functional, a smell of antiseptic iodine hung in the air.

An Australian baby with head injuries was an uncommon event so we'd soon attracted a gathering of cleaners, ward staff and nurses who leaned in the doorway and spilled into the examination room. Moments later the doctor arrived, the crowd parting and dispersing somewhat as he stepped into the room, only to reform.

The doctor, a man with fine Indic features, common amongst some of Indonesia's old aristocratic families, spoke basic English. Having established the sequence of events with Grant and Julie, it seemed useful to tell him the story in Bahasa Indonesia.

I explained that the baby fell off the bed onto a hard floor and had been vomiting and semi-conscious since.

The doctor looked into Tim's eyes. I assumed he was doing a rudimentary check for concussion.

I explained further that we were worried he might be concussed or have a fractured skull.

"I'll examine him first," the young doctor advised.

Julie was still holding Tim, so motioning for her to lift him up onto an examination table, the doctor gently worked through a series of diagnostic tests.

"There's nothing conclusive from the physical examination. I'll need to x-ray his skull," he said.

Julie nodded.

We moved into the corridor. Julie and Tim were led into a very large room next door. Peering in, I could see the same well-kept polished concrete floor and neat white washed walls. There was an x-ray machine with some other equipment shrouded in sheets of plastic in an unlit back corner.

Julie was handed a heavy lead lined protective apron and a smaller one draped over Tim. The doctor showed how he wanted Tim's head positioned and left the room.

As we waited for the results, the crowd still milled around in the hall outside. Once the print was done, it was passed around the assembled group even before the doctor had seen it – such was the level of interest.

When the doctor returned, he gathered the x-ray from the hands of an orderly, stepped into the room and without a word slapped it onto a light box. He studied it intently then turning towards us said, "The x-ray doesn't show an obvious fracture though there could be one."

"So there could be a fracture after all," I said.

"Yes, I get it," said Julie, exasperated. "So there might be a fracture, a hairline fracture that can't be seen in an x-ray. So the next step is a CAT scan in that case."

"There's little chance of that," added Grant. "Look over there." He gestured to the equipment covered in plastic. "There's a CAT scan but it's still in its plastic wrapping."

Acutely aware of our predicament and not daring to speak aloud at this point, I began to think through the options. The nearest operational CAT scan was in Surabaya maybe even Jakarta, but what if it's Singapore or Darwin? I tried to stop my mind running in that direction consoling myself with the relief that there was no obvious fracture. The thought of something more serious conjured up images of slow bus trips through Java, a ferry trip to Singapore or even a low-altitude flight back to Darwin if that sort of thing was possible. All were daunting prospects. Eminently practical, Julie enquired, "What do we do about the vomiting?"

The doctor replied, "Don't let him fall off the bed again."

I puzzled over his reply wondering if I'd translated the question correctly.

"I'm a little puzzled by the answer," I said. "He says, 'Don't let him fall off the bed again'. I know that's not what you're asking but on the other hand it seems the doctor isn't all that worried about the vomiting. My suggestion is that we just get out of here now and keep fluids up to him. What do you think?"

"Yes," Julie replied. Turning to the doctor she said, "Terimakasih, Doctor. We go now?"

"Yes, my pleasure," he answered.

On our way to the car, I kept thinking about the doctor's strange reply. Then I realised it wasn't so strange. He was stating the obvious. Balinese children were not left alone and were almost always carried by mothers, fathers, grandparents and siblings. What's more, not until a child's first Oton at the age of 210 days, one Balinese year, were they permitted to make contact with the ground. On those occasions when they weren't held, they were suspended in a sling fashioned from a sarong well out of harm's way and close to family. They were never placed alone on beds.

"We need to replace those stolen travellers cheques," said Julie. "Russell, do you know a bank that has a client relationship with Westpac?"

"Yes, my Bank, EXIM. It's not far. It's got great air conditioning and a water dispenser as well."

With Tim either refusing fluids or vomiting up what little fluid he could be encouraged to take, I was mindful of the swiftness of dehydration in the mounting dusty heat of dry season Denpasar. Bank EXIM seemed like a good place to go.

Grant sat squirting minute quantities of fluid into a tiny, reluctant mouth as we sat in the comfortable air conditioned atmosphere of Bank EXIM, rendered all the more benign by its austere marble lined interior. With Julie engaged in the task of replacing the travellers' cheques, there was little to do except wait for completion of paper work.

After a 30-minute transaction, Julie joined us proudly holding a bundle of new travellers cheques.

"So, Julie," I said, "how would you like to approach things now?"

"What are our options?"

"We can either sit here in this fantastic air conditioning," I said, "cool Tim right down and wait and see, or we can go straight back to Ubud where it will be several degrees cooler, anyway."

"Well, we can settle him down on the road and I'll try to get him to drink something more."

While Julie and Grant continued offering Tim fluids, I drove north to Ubud. By the time we arrived, Tim was still far from well. As Grant lifted a limp and lethargic Tim from the van two women approached.

"What's the matter?" one asked.

The other added, "Is the baby sick?"

From their voices, they were just a couple of Australian travellers, well attired for the tropics in tee shirts and loose fitting cotton trousers. Yet there was something assuring and confident in their voices.

Julie told them that he'd banged his head and kept refusing fluids. "Anything that we can get him to accept comes right up again. We've been to the hospital and now we've come back here hoping that he might settle down."

"There's an easy solution to that problem," suggested one of the women. "Young coconut water will help. There are lots of young coconuts around here."

"I'm Gabbie, by the way, and this is Michaela," she explained, a loving tone of assurance in her voice. "We're both nurses."

"We've just arrived from Cambodia," added Michaela. "Up there we had to be careful small children didn't dehydrate when they were unwell so we used young coconut water."

"*Air kelapa muda*, young coconut water, the tropical miracle water," I said. I wondered why it hadn't occurred to me. "I'll organise some."

Soon Tim was accepting young coconut water and, by nightfall, he was back to his bouncing best.

Gabbie and Michaela had arrived that morning, en route to Sydney. They hadn't booked and just happened to find the bungalows. They stayed for a few days and then left.

For years, Grant and Julie sometimes encountered them, usually in Balmain, most often in the street or at the supermarket. They always asked after Tim, who completely recovered.

Magic, Polygamy and Triangles

When using a traditional method for map-making, triangles are the key. Setting the location of any one place by confirming its relationship with two others is the basic technique. An easy way to do this is with eyesight, compass and pace, though measuring the distance between places can be challenging, as the length of one's stride is apt to vary. The technique is called compass traverse and the final stage involves transforming figures and jottings into cartographic substance, demanding intense concentration.

Sitting on my verandah long immersed in the process, I was vaguely aware of the rising heat of the day and an electric chorus of *onceret-onceretan*, the cicadas, that built in waves as the day advanced.

"This is beginning to look like a cartographer's drawing room."

I snapped the lead in my propelling pencil.

"Oh! . . . *Bonjour*, Vincent. You startled me."

Vincent was a French anthropologist doing fieldwork in Bali. Medium height, wiry and always sporting half moon glasses, he was absorbed with Bali's many deities and endless rituals.

"Sorry! You were very focused."

"I'm making a map of Palakaja village. It'll be accurate enough with a few major landmarks. Students can annotate it and I'll be happy if all they do is capture a sense of *Tri Anggah*, high, middle and low, and show the village surrounded by rice fields, the *sawah*."

"So easy yet so difficult," he smiled. "But how do you work with their cultural filters?" I knew by this he meant the way meaning is influenced by the cultural values of an observer.

With Vincent, conversations moved like this from greeting to analysis in moments.

"Naming the problem right from the beginning, we ask them to delay judgement; to observe, collect data, discuss, ask questions, compare and then try to suspend that moment when they draw a conclusion. It's like sketching with a pencil and eraser." I gestured to the empty wicker armchair on the other side of the table I was using as a drawing board and he sat, and smiled.

"Sound advice, but what about things like *ilmu hitam* (black magic), *leyak* (witches as balls of light) or even something as mundane as polygamy?"

"I can always rely on an anthropologist to rake up the pond. Vincent, they're only high school kids but it doesn't take them long to catch a thread that might run deeper. Someone always sees a swastika, which sets off a discussion that leads to samsara."

"Do you talk to them about *ilmu hitam* and *leyak*, the realm of magic in general?"

"Balinese belief in earth bound entities like *bhuta* and *kala* (names for earth-bound spirits) are discussed as soon as they notice the offerings on the ground."

"And how do you deal with that?"

"We don't censor or dismiss this as a superstition. I tend to say that belief has the power of reality and that consciousness is both absolute and shaped by experience. I chunk it down into bite-sized concepts for high school students. We try not to leave them with a fear of dark forces either, or obsessing about magic, but it's a point of great difference and interest."

"Mmm, interesting. So what about easier things like polygamy?"

"Ah, you anthropologists can't leave kinship alone."

It was a sound question and cause for reflection. Polygamy is a common enough practice in certain Balinese circles. In the past, royal families practiced polygamy as a way of consolidating networks of alliances within the realm. Beyond Bali, the practice was found throughout the ancient world, from Egypt to China. Marriages often followed conquest of new territory consolidating geo-political affinities and loyalties. Delicate balances and arrangements between competing kingdoms and empires were easier to maintain when there was common blood at the top, at least this was the theory.

"What fascinates me is the way it endures," observed Vincent, as he leaned back in his chair and toyed with strings of *kepeng* coins that dangled from a small representation of Vishnu hung on the wall beside him.

"It's experiencing something of a renaissance with tourist dollars transforming family compounds into palaces for foreign tourists and new palaces rising in the rice fields."

"What's that got to do with polygamy?"

"The new wealth is the key," he said as he let go of the kepeng and leaned across the table towards me. "This will sound judgemental, but when in the course of history the functional aspects of cultural practices no longer apply, their pursuit by the newly rich can be tawdry in its most innocent form and tragic in its more ego driven and rapacious forms. Some of them have embraced polygamy with enthusiasm."

"I see what you mean. Like the situation at Cerdik Bungalows?"

Made Cerdik, a successful artist and gallery owner, was an upwardly mobile Sudra turned land developer. His lavishly decorated bungalows on the outskirts of Palakaja, conveyed an air of luxury and artistic refinement drawing on his interpretation of older forms of palace and temple architecture.

Vincent nodded, "Yes, exactly. You know the story?"

"Some of it. I won't say who told me; I'll just call him Ketut. Some of this I know firsthand as well. Would you like me to tell you my version?"

"*Certainment*! I can't resist a tale well told. Please go on."

"Well, this is in two parts: Ketut's and mine."

"May I make notes?" he said, as he stood and produced a small notepad from his back pocket.

So now I'm becoming Vincent's informant, I thought. I smiled waiting to see what he would do. Telling him the story included a risk of embellishing or of being induced to speculate, and so altering the tale. I wanted to keep this recounting as close to evidence-based as possible but even with someone as practised at listening, recording and recalling as Vincent, the mere telling of a story always offered opportunities for distortion.

"Well, where do I start? I guess you know that Cerdik is a better than average artist and quickly acquired sufficient wealth to take a second wife. It seems he thought all would go well with the second wife but she was quite assertive and more than a little wily. Some say she had an eye for beautiful younger men. Before long, they agreed to a divorce but not without a most satisfactory settlement for her."

"Ah! Perhaps this explains the souvenir shop on the main street," he suggested, as he sat back in his chair.

"I don't know but shortly after this, he married an attractive widow who happened to have a very beautiful 16-year-old daughter, Ayu. The widow became wife number three, though many insist he married her so he could have the daughter as well and Ayu was sufficiently mercenary to take advantage of his advances. Within a short time, Ayu became wife number four."

"I'm tempted to repeat the old cliché 'Truth is stranger

than fiction'," said Vincent.

I was amused, in turn, to be able to illuminate the complex nature of relationships for an anthropologist.

"Maybe and maybe not," I teased. "Many had their own thoughts on this but little was said publicly after all there was a long-standing tradition of polygamy."

Leaning forward on the table, Vincent peered intensely over his half frame reading glasses.

"Ayu soon grew bored with Cerdik. Then a rich seam of tales processed in village rumour mills chronicled her many affairs. I don't think any of these are accurate. The truth is far plainer."

"So in Bali, it can be both plainer and stranger," he grinned.

"She did have a lover, Komang Nemu, someone of her own generation. He was in another part of Indonesia when she married. I assume news of the marriage reached him. Then a year later he returned to the village with a new wife."

Raising his finger, Vincent asked, "So how did Ayu react when she learned that he was married?"

"She had a secret relationship with a rich builder from another village, Dewa Kereta. Several versions of the tale are told each one with subtle variations but, in all of them, the lover is eventually outed and the aggrieved Cerdik tracks him down to a nearby village as he lies with Ayu. Brandishing a *parang* (machete), he pursues Kereta, whose only escape route is the nearest roof."

Of course this was beginning to assume something of the drama of the Ramayana. The Balinese love a good story.

Raising his finger again, Vincent said with sudden insight, "This reminds me of a story I heard from an American woman, a long term Bali resident. She lived on the outskirts of Palakaja. She said one day, alarms sounded and she ran to the centre of the village with others discovering a man brandishing a parang and threatening to kill another man perched on a roof."

"Yes, that's what happened. It sounds like the same event. Kereta was terrified but terror turned to relief when he realised that the huge crowd was only trying to pacify Cerdik. All Kereta lost that day was his dignity but from then on Ayu was ever so closely monitored."

"So was that the end of the matter?" Vincent asked.

"No, it wasn't. Irrepressible in her legitimate desire for mates her own age, Ayu's eyes roamed far and wide in search of the ideal partner but her every move was known and her finances kept tight until Cerdik made Ayu manager of the bungalows because his land development interests were occupying a greater share of his time. Ayu then had opportunities to visit markets and to travel to the regional centre with staff in search of stores and provisions."

Traditionally Balinese women don't own houses but they do enjoy considerable scope to manage financial affairs in households and run small businesses. When they are involved in the marketing of produce, it is easy enough for them to get access to money but if, like Ayu, they are dependent on husbands who live by selling art, land development, building and renting hotel rooms, the books must be kept and hard cash pursued in tips from tourists and any other chances that might arise.

"Vincent, some of this next part of the story I know firsthand or I've managed to piece together over the years. It began when the beading industry was developing in Palakaja. Ayu's old lover, Komang, had a thriving beading business with production outsourced to various families in the village. As an astute and creative entrepreneur, he had prospered and looked for other opportunities. Soon he had sufficient capital for land development and Cerdik was an obvious business partner. Besides, his passion for Ayu had never dwindled and perhaps he intended this as a way of reconnecting with Ayu."

"How do you know about it? Were you living in the midst of it?"

"I rented a place in the bungalows for a time, and this is when I began to notice subtle indications of a special relationship between Komang and Ayu."

"So it was that obvious? Maybe they wanted you to see it."

Vincent raised an important point. Secret relationships can be involuted. While they run counter to the needs of humans as social beings there is often a dangerous pressure to seek discreet forms of social approval thus outing the secret themselves.

"It's hard to believe Cerdik didn't see it," he said with a puzzled frown.

"Yes, it is, and I still don't think I have the complete picture. Anyway I moved to a large house in another village. It was more appropriate for conducting field study groups. It had a big front verandah and was surrounded by bungalows. Student groups stayed in the bungalows and the verandah provided the perfect classroom."

"I remember that place," Vincent remarked. "It was demolished for a new hotel if I'm not mistaken."

"That's right. It was all natural materials then. At its centre was a bale patok just a thatched roof supported by poles and open at the sides. This was the formal meeting place for the whole compound."

Vincent settled back now engaged with the story, his legs crossed and balancing the note pad on his left knee. It was difficult to know why he was so interested. I reasoned it might be that he had already heard a version and was cross-referencing, perhaps testing the veracity of his other informant or both of us for that matter or perhaps the anthropologist had relaxed and human interest had taken over. Jealousy, after all, is a universal human trait.

"As background, I must tell you I sometimes booked visitors into Cerdik's bungalows."

Thinking back over what followed, I wondered whether to present it as a comic event, given the transparency of the deception that was attempted. I wasn't certain. But to be authentic it must be told without interpretation I thought.

"Vincent, my housekeeper is in the kitchen and she features in this next part of the story. It might help if you go and introduce yourself so you can form your own impression of her. Perhaps while you're at it, you could arrange for her to bring us some coffees as well."

"Good idea. Bali coffee?" Vincent always pronounced Bali as Bally – an endearing eccentricity.

"Yes, please, but bring the sugar separately. Don't let her add it to the brew."

Gathering my thoughts, I recalled one day around midmorning, Rai the manager called me as I walked up from the spring below the bungalows."You have three visitors waiting in the bale patok."

"Who are they? I wasn't expecting anyone."

He seemed irritated and didn't answer.

Approaching the bale, I saw Made Cerdik, Ayu and Komang Nemu. Made appeared in a state of shock, his body rigid his eyes down caste and a depressed expression on his face.

I greeted them, "Selamat pagi."

Only Komang responded. "Selamat pagi, Russell. We've come to ask you for help."

"How can I help?"

"There is a problem with your friends."

"Who? Bill and Paula? How could they be a problem?"

Magic

"It is their *pembantu* (housekeeper)."

"Ketut?" I had recruited her, so this came as a complete surprise.

"Yes, she must go," said Ayu in a grave tone.

"Why? What has she done? The children like her." The thought of pressing Bill and Paula to dismiss her was out of the question.

"Russell, you know that in Bali there are special dangers," said Komang. She is creating a dangerous situation for Made. He is unsafe while she stays there.".

Inwardly irritated by the indirectness and reluctance to name the problem, I asked, "Do you mean *ilmu* (magic)?"

Made flinched at the very mention of the word and then resumed his ridged posture. I'd never seen him in such a state before.

"It's dangerous for Made," Komang assured me with an intense look as if to say you have no choice.

Sensing that the unseen forces at work had little to do with black magic, I waited for an answer. "Why would she be doing this?" I asked, finally, hoping one of them would identify something tangible. Still there was no response, just a palpable intensification of Made's fear. Irrational as it was, and knowing there was much more to this, I had to think quickly. There was a field study group arriving within days but in the interim the family could stay with me.

"We can't dismiss the child minder. It will disturb the children. The family is very happy with her. The only solution is for them to move."

Immediately, some of the darkness seemed to dissipate; I sensed that this was an acceptable suggestion.

"It will take time to find them alternate accommodation. You will refund the room charges," I suggested as if a foregone conclusion.

"Yes," was Made's response.

Seen and Unseen

Vincent returned with the coffee.

"We had an interesting conversation," he said as he placed the coffees on the table. "I didn't realise Ketut spoke English so fluently."

"Oh, yes. She's worked with me ever since the events I'm about to recount."

As I told him the story as objectively as I could, Vincent made meticulous notes, stopping me from time to time to ask about my feelings in respect of this or that part of the drama.

"So in the end, my friends moved in with me that day and, while I was tempted to see the whole matter as a ruse and accept that all's well that ends well, the question of ilmu *hitam* (black magic) left me with a nagging doubt."

"So you believe this is what was happening?" asked Vincent.

"I thought it was a remote possibility because it's a common practice in Palakaja, but my real concern was Ketut being distracted by such things and not getting on with the task at hand. I needed to discuss it with her and clarify matters. That's all."

"So you aren't a believer in *ilmu hitam*?"

"No, but I see people believing and being harmed. From my perspective, *ilmu* is mere spiritual tinkering, a ripple on the cosmic spirituality centring my own life."

I thought about Ketut and what a fine woman she was, the contribution she has made in helping me raise my own children, her life as a devoted mother to her children, and the many conversations we've had about all manner of things. I also thought of her selflessness and her innocence.

"So, Vincent, I took Ketut aside and confronted her with the story. She broke down sobbing in sheer anguish with an emotion I'd never encountered amongst Balinese people before. In that moment, there was no doubting her innocence. She was the real victim. I thought of witch burnings and the scapegoating of innocent women through the ages. As we chatted, more emerged."

"Oh! So there is more to the story?" he asked.

"Not a great deal more. The truth was plain enough. I'm sure you see it, Vincent. It was all a ruse, not *sekala* (the unseen), merely undisclosed politics. She often accompanied Ayu on business when the point of the journey was a secret meeting with Komang. She knew too much about the affair. She had to be silenced and her credibility damaged so the triangle wasn't broken and business continued as usual."

Black magic is a potent force amongst some Balinese and in Palaklaja it was often used when attempts at resolution failed. Yet for all the belief in *ilmu hitam* the more universally recurring reality of the love triangle dominated this situation. I thought again about triangles, how important they were in planning Bali's complex irrigation system and dividing myriad plots of rice land but now I had a different sense. I pictured an unseen web of human triangles layering back through the generations – Cerdik, Ayu and Komang's just one among many.

Beyond Bhoma's Powers

Penyor, like vibrant green flags, cascading over Ubud's streets and lanes were a striking reminder *Galungan* and *Kuningan* had passed for yet another Balinese year. Bridges between an unseen world of spirit and our corporal realm, the displaying of the *Penyor* symbolise that time when Balinese ancestor spirits visit their corporal families. Christmas in my own tradition came to mind. There is much connecting these seasons. Both are times of goodwill, conviviality and happiness one grounded in an endless cycling of souls the other in a singular incarnation of the supreme.

Turning north at *Puri Saren*, I approached Agung Niang's Warung Ayam Tutu, smoked chicken restaurant. It was a simple structure beside Puri Kantor, one of the many puri, or palaces, occupying this central part of Ubud. I often stopped there for breakfast.

I took a seat by the open window and watched someone wash a car across the road as my thoughts turned to an old friend, I Gusti Made Sumung whose passing I still mourned. We often sat here. Now in this place, there was sadness and comfort, sadness at my loss and comfort in the remembering of our many conversations as they flooded back.

I first met I Gusti at a showing of John Darling's film *Lempad of Bali*. As I Gusti Nyoman Lempad's eldest son, he also appeared in the film. He spoke plainly without awe as an observer of the great man. Over time we became friends. Though without the global notoriety of his father, he was an experienced cultural interpreter, fond of recounting some of his earlier encounters with Margaret Mead and Gregory Bateson.

"Bateson worked hard photographing and filming what he saw," I Gusti observed. "Mead directed him a lot as well."

"I read that he was a pioneer in using still and cine photography for fieldwork."

"Yes, he was yet sometimes he had difficulty seeing things that were not so obvious, much less *Niskala*, the unseen."

"*Sekala* (Seen) and *Niskala* (Unseen) must be a challenge for any anthropologist here in Bali."

I Gusti reached over and picked up a mangosteen from a basket on an adjacent table. "I held a mangosteen just like this," he said. "Then I said to Bateson, 'There is much that's unseen in Bali but some can see it. How many segments do you think there are in this mangosteen?' Bateson answered, 'I don't know, do you?'

"'There are seven pieces,' I said, and when he opened the mangosteen, there were seven. Then I took another mangosteen. Again I asked how many pieces were inside. He didn't know and again I told him exactly how many."

"So, what did Bateson say?"

Smiling, I Gusti answered, "He asked, 'How do you know this?' and I replied, 'Do you think it depends on me having a special power?'"

"I Gusti, I'm assuming there's no special power here. It must be something to do with the size of the fruit. Didn't Bateson suggest this?"

"No, not the size, but that's a good answer."

"So you convinced the eminent anthropologist that you had special powers?"

"Not really," he said as he turned the stalk side towards himself revealing the base of the fruit. "See, the pattern at the bottom shows how many segments are inside."

"So we must not assume the supernatural is in play just because something is unseen."

"Correct. Perhaps it's unseen because it hasn't been turned over."

I Gusti always enjoyed rhetorical exercise and games. He was a thoughtful man with a great sense of humour much of it quite mischievous.

"I Gusti, I've a question about the unseen."

"What question?"

"The Bhoma faces your father created here in Ubud –where did he find his inspiration?"

"Ah, a good question. Our family came from Pejeng. They lived in Bedulu. Do you know this area? It was the site of the old Balinese kingdom before Majapahit."

"I'd like to know more about it. It has lots of ancient sites, doesn't it? Did this influence him?"

"He grew up surrounded by rich traditions and a landscape full of opportunities for rediscovering ancient ways, images and architecture."

"I know he had many talents."

I Gusti went on: "When he was about 13, our family left Bedulu because of persecution by the local lord. Cokorda Raka granted us refuge in Ubud."

This part of the story I knew. Lempad was indeed fortunate to enjoy the patronage of Ubud's royal family but he also enjoyed a remarkable opportunity. There was a major earthquake in 1917; Bali sustained extensive damage and Ubud was no exception. Rebuilding and repair was essential. As a brilliant architect, engineer, sculptor, carpenter, draughtsman and painter, he was able to make a significant contribution to Ubud's reconstruction. While some contributions like Pura Saraswati are grand, it's frequently in the detail and sometimes in the absence of detail that this work is most interesting. Amongst the most striking are the powerful Bhoma faces he created.

"So his inspiration for Bhoma came from the ancient sites around Pejeng?"

"Yes, the ancient sites and also the stone face at Goa Gaja. Have you been there?"

"Of course, it reminds me of the kala figures found in Java, but Bhoma here in Bali is far more elaborate."

"True. Why do you think he's different here?"

"I guess because Lempad drew Bhoma's visage from the ancient forms and then reinterpreted them in his own distinctive way."

"Do you know the story of Bhoma?"

"Ah, yes a little. He's called the son of the earth and he's depicted with bursts and tendrils of leaves and flowers around his face and head sometimes even trailing from his nostrils and the corners of his mouth."

"*Ngeh*," he said, "Yes, son of the earth. His name derives from two Sanskrit words: *bhumi* meaning earth; and *bhauma* meaning that which comes from the earth."

"Is he a god?"

"He is the son of Vishnu and Ibu Pertiwi or Mother Earth. He is of the gods and of the earth. Anyway we can talk further." Standing and reaching for his money he added, "I must go now."

"I'll walk with you to the crossroads," I replied.

We paid the bill and stepped out into Jalan Suweta walking in silence. I Gusti had given me a partial answer. Now it was time for me to reflect. This was his usual approach.

Since Vishnu is the god of the waters, Bhoma is an entity whose place is intrinsically connected with the conjunction of earth and water. In terrestrial environments, earth, water, atmosphere and biosphere all meet. All four domains are present in a space where energy is exchanged and fundamental transformations in states of matter occur. So, I had a sense that Bhoma was also associated with transformation.

He is common enough in Bali. His face appears on the Kori Agung the gateway between the middle and inner precinct of Balinese temples. The gateway symbolises the lower slopes of the holy mountain Mahameru that is covered with large trees. In simple terms, Bhoma is a symbol of Bali's trees and plants, but the entrance to the inner courtyard of a temple is also a place of transformation. In this material space people pray and have their most direct contact with the gods, the unseen realm.

I Gusti turned to the west towards his rice fields by the cremation ground and I headed east towards Nirwana.

Turning off Ubud's main street, I walked down Jalan Gotama utill I reached the entrance to Nirwana, the name Nyoman Suradnya had chosen for his pension gallery and batik workshop. Approaching it down the long pathway was always a passage of pleasant anticipation. We had worked together for years conducting student study groups. I enjoyed our conversations, his coffee and his more concrete exposition of Balinese culture and religion.

Stepping into the compound, I found Nyoman sitting by a small table on a verandah near the kitchen.

"*Apa kabar bapak?*" He asked how I was with a smile.

"Fine, Nyoman. May I join you?"

After the usual pleasantries, I said, "I've been thinking about Bhoma."

"Ah, now that is a good subject for thinking."

"An important character. Is he God or demon, or do we locate him somewhere between demonic earth bound presence and deity?"

Nyoman thought for a moment. His explanations were never off the cuff. He was careful in choosing his words. "So Bhoma actually is the . . . the son of Mother Earth, Ibu Pertiwi, and son of Visnu. When Visnu came down to visit Ibu Pertiwi she still is beautiful and Visnu looks like a pig and they make love and *anaknya* (their child) became Bhoma."

"So when Visnu comes to earth, he is in the form of a pig? I didn't know this, Nyoman."

"Yes, Visnu travelled down to end of the earth as Varaha the pig."

"So if Bhoma is between Visnu and Ibu Pertiwi, between heaven and the earth, what is his role?"

"Well, you see him above every door as a protector."

"Yes, I often see this but I also see him on funeral towers.

"Ya, the tower, ya," Nyoman affirmed.

"So I wonder, when we go through the door or pass from this embodied form into spirit, there is a transformation. Is Bhoma responsible for transformation?"

"He is known as a foundation of the earth as a protector. He is actually located in bottom part. You never see the Bhoma on the top of the temple or the top of the tower." Nyoman hesitated. I felt he hadn't quite understood my question but in his hesitation I sensed he grasped my meaning. He continued, "Actually if we think more deeply he is involved in transformation. Bhoma is supposed to be like a gate. People have to pass through that gate."

"Does Bhoma have a role in transforming dead plants, leaves and forest litter into things of beauty?" I asked.

"He is responsible for transformation; he is like a recycling machine. Not God, not demon; between the two and he take care of recycling. That's why we must be kind to Mother Earth otherwise we will have punishment from Bhoma."

Traditionally, almost everything used in Balinese villages was biodegradable. Food scraps were fed to pigs and the pig manure used to fertilise fruit trees and vegetables. Coconut palm leaf plates were thrown away after a meal so they could rot and return their nutrients to the soil. Cooking pots were made of soft pottery. People drank from coconut shells, stirred their food with coconut shell spoons and cooked with coconut oil. Grated coconut flesh was added to food for flavouring. Every morning, yards were swept. Leaves collected from this sweeping were thrown beneath fruit trees or into drains and irrigation channels recycling the organic waste.

Provided humans played their part, acting in harmony with nature, then natural processes remained intact and unimpeded so all remained in equilibrium and Bhoma was free to carry out his work skimming across the earth and transforming rubbish into the food of life.

Nyoman's housekeeper placed two steaming glasses of thick Balinese coffee and a small plastic sugar jar on the table. Picking up the plastic jar I turned it over between my fingers watching the sugar tumble.

"It seems Bhoma isn't very good at eating plastic," I said.

"Oh no," Nyoman chuckled ironically.

"So, Bhoma's role was best suited to a traditional setting before modern times when Bali depended almost exclusively on its rice economy."

"Yes, when farmers planted two rice crops each year, the cattle pulled ploughs and the ducks grazed on the sawah eating snails, grubs and worms. Before *kimia* (chemicals), Bhoma enjoyed this world," Nyoman said with a smile.

"I'm sure he did. I can see some of the problems Bhoma might confront these days."

"Indigestion, in a word."

"The heartburn of *Tri Hita Karana*." I refered to the dynamic equilibrium between humans, biophysical environment and gods.

"So, if *Tri Hita Karana* is harmony between humans and God, humans and humans and humans with nature, we are unwell," said Nyoman.

Nyoman has a gift for brevity and humour. It couldn't

be put more succinctly. For Bhoma, plastics, aluminium and cocktails of chemicals are impossible to recycle. For many traditional Balinese people as well, these products are outside their usual way of dealing with waste. Plastic bags and bottles are a highly visible problem. Some people think they can be recycled if they are thrown into rivers and irrigation channels, others simply burn the plastic bags and bottles in the way they burned off rice stubble.

"Nyoman, I know Bhoma's powers are limited. He might be the spirit of recycling and transformation but he doesn't know much about 21st century products, much less climate change and global warming."

"He knows about them. It's up to *manusia* (humans). We must become aware, accept that there is a problem and try to bring the world back to balance."

Seen and Unseen

Balikpapan: Looking Backwards and Forwards

Balikpapan was rainy and grey. Before this journey, I had only a general awareness of its location and significance in my own country's history. Watching numerous ANZAC Day marches, I knew that Australia's 7th Division AIF was in Balikpapan in the closing stages of World War II. There was a view that this involvement contributed little to the final defeat of Japan and was more a matter of General Douglas McArthur sidelining the 7th Division so that United States forces might control the final assault on Japan.

Cruising in an air-conditioned Land Cruiser from the airport, I mused on the Australians arriving here 44 years earlier under different circumstances. What had it been like in 1945? Macarthur's forces went on island hopping while they, many of whom were veterans of Tobruk, Alamein and Kokoda, were left to flush out pockets of Japanese resistance between Balikpapan and Samarinda.

Images of young soldiers emerged in my mind. Hazy black and white images gathered from grainy post war documentaries, they stirred me; history arched toward the present in that Land Cruiser, just as it does in the sacred, storytelling ritual of the *wayang*. The *wayang* is the mythic realm created with shadow puppets by a master puppeteer, the *dalang*. The shadows, cast upon a fine cotton screen for the audience, enact archetypal and epic events – the deeds of gods and of men. In this space of the sacred story, the *dalang*, his puppets and the supporting musicians draw substance from this shadowy realm.

I pondered the name of this city: Balikpapan. *Balik*: to turn; *papan*: a board, reminiscent of the screen that holds the puppeteer's shadows. In *wayang* performances I saw, the men could walk behind the screen to see the *dalang* at work and to ground the myth in present reality. If only I could turn the board around and look back. The shadows of those soliders danced in my mind; the old projector within me flickered like the *wayang* flame.

As the Land Cruiser slowed before my hotel, I remembered the purpose of my journey and the soldiers slipped from me, soft as shadows. The car door opened, and I remembered that I was there to plan a rainforest tour of Borneo, to help people connect with this beautiful place and its rich history.

Checking into the hotel, I caught site of my travelling companions sitting in armchairs off to the side in an annex. My own musings meant little in this context. We were here to develop a cultural tourism product, Walks on the Wildside.

"Hi Paul, how are you?" I said as I approached them. "Have you been here long?"

"*Selamat datang di Balikpapan*, Russell." Paul welcomed me to Balikpapan. "We've been here an hour or so. Did you have a pleasant flight from Denpasar?" He extended his hand.

Paul was a fine looking man of dark complexion, seemingly from the south of India but from Ambon in Indonesia's east. Rather portly, given his comfortable Jakartan lifestyle, he was fluent in English, Indonesian, Javanese and Dutch and understood the travel industry inside out. I was looking forward to travelling and working with him. He grasped my hand warmly.

"Russell, may I introduce our photographer, Henky?"

I extended my hand and greeted him: "I'm pleased to meet you, Henky,"

"*Senang*," Henky replied, meaning pleased, and shook my hand without smiling.

A serious man of few words, I reasoned.

Paul continued, "Henky has been working with PT Puri Astrinata for a number of years. He is well travelled in Indonesia, working also with UNICEF and the Catholic Church. We are very lucky to have him."

"That's good news. If this goes ahead we need produce a new line of brochures, itineraries and advertising materials for *Walks on the Wildside*. We'll be competing with the mass market into Bali so this product must be clearly positioned as soft adventure with elements of cultural and eco-tourism."

That afternoon, we took a short tour of the city but its status as oil industry boomtown limited its tourism potential. There were some comfortable Dutch style cottages, a small but busy downtown and an interesting *kampung* or village perched on stilts out over a small section of the bay.

Little remained of the Balikpapan of 1945. That evening as I waited for Paul and Henky in the bar of the hotel, I found the most tangible historic references to the 7th Division decorating the walls as a series of photographs. I reflected on how different my life had been compared with these men, but the thoughts quickly faded and I came to think, more pertinently, how different my life had been compared with my two middle class Indonesian colleagues. How could they know of April mornings watching the old diggers marching, of the little symbolic tin hats we wore securing a sprig of rosemary?

For dinner, Paul selected the best Indonesian seafood restaurant in town. We dined on a spread of barbecued fish, prawns and chilli crab served with rice and *sambal*. Spoons and forks were provided but fingers were the preferred eating utensils.

Balikpapan: Looking Backwards and Forwards

Over dinner, I spoke of the images I hoped to create in the tour materials.

"I would like to convey a sense of the great rivers like the Mahakam, Kayan, Rejang and Kapuas as the highways," I told Paul and Henky, "the vital corridors of access to the interior. People like the idea of romantic journeys into the heart of Borneo."

"Yes," Paul said. "Well, we will certainly be making a journey."

"I want people to appreciate the magnificence of the rainforests of the thousands of species of plants and the rich ecosystems," I enthused.

"They will see forests and animals," Paul replied, a little tersely.

I was gaining a sense that perhaps I was too effusive. Paul was very measured in his responses and, so far, Henky had barely said anything to me.

When Henky left the table briefly I spoke directly with Paul.

"Why is Henky so quiet, Paul?"

"Some Chinese Indonesians are a little reserved at first when they meet new people."

"That's a relief. I thought maybe I had committed some cultural faux pas."

"Not at all, Russell," he replied. "It's just . . ." he stopped as Henky returned.

I was so excited about our imminent journey into the rainforests, my thoughts drifted on into scenes of a myriad plants and animals, of complex ecosystems optimising the life force and climaxing in total profusion.

"I guess logging will be an issue for some," I said.

"It's an important industry but our focus will be on some of the unique animals and the different Dayak cultures," Paul said with an air of unexpected formality. "You will enjoy all of that I'm sure, Russell."

Henky nodded. "*Betul*," he said, meaning 'correct'.

I wondered about the impact of logging. I knew it wasn't well managed but my romantic notions persisted.

"We have an early start so let's go back to the hotel," said Paul.

"Yes," I replied, "I'm sure we'll have plenty of time to talk on the river."

Heading north out of Balikpapan on one of Borneo's few major sealed roads, my sense of romantic anticipation was tempered by a sudden blunt and rational awareness. Close to Balikpapan, settlers had established *ladang* (cultivated farm land) entirely replacing primary rainforest. Further along the road, the full impact of logging without any reassignment of the land to agricultural uses was soon evident. Where once there had been rainforest providing abundant cover for the Japanese, a wasteland appeared. Massive stretches of forest had been clear-felled with the litter of branches and chaotic secondary regrowth surrounding the road. This devastated land was depressing but I reassured myself with romantic visions of the interior.

Paul's reserve the night before began to make sense. He knew this would be one of my first impressions and was embarrassed by the devastation. In typically Indonesian fashion, he didn't want to offend me by dampening my fervour with reality.

In the distance, a high wooden platform appeared; it looked like an observation platform surrounded by a picnic area. Beyond it were neat rows of plants set out on a grid system and extending over many hectares as far as one could see.

"What's that platform over there?" I asked. "It looks like an observation deck."

"That is *Bukit Suharto*," Paul answered, "a gift from our President so that visitors can enjoy the natural beauty."

Accustomed to the official television documentaries of the Suharto era colloquially termed *Cinta Negara*, which meant Loving the Nation, I sensed that while Paul's words were in this genre they were also subtly and deeply sarcastic.

"The natural beauty, Paul?" I queried.

"Well, Russell, you can see for yourself."

"Can we stop for a moment, Paul?" I asked, eager to have a closer look at the plantings.

"Yes, sure but we can't stop for long. We must meet the river boat by 1pm and there is a museum to visit in Tenggarong." Then Paul turned to the driver and asked him to stop: "*Tolong berhenti di sini.*"

We pulled in where the verge was wide and the plantings came close to the road.

"So what have we got here?" I said aloud not expecting an answer.

"This is for our enjoyment and future production," Paul answered.

A species of mimosa had been planted in straight rows, alternating with rows of acacia running back from the road and over the hills. Between the rows were small plants. They looked like recently planted tube stock and were all rather similar in appearance. After a few moments, I thought I could detect about five different species.

What was happening here was plain. Mimosa and acacia are fast growing and hardy. They were the shade plants. The smaller plants appeared to be *Dipterocarpaceae*, that in ideal conditions would grow to become towering rainforest trees.

"Paul, this looks like an attempt to simulate some of the conditions found in a rainforest," I observed.

"Yes, it's called a managed tropical forest," he replied

tersely. Again he used that elusive tone. I couldn't determine whether it was commentary or criticism.

"I reckon there are only five species of large rainforest trees at most here, Paul. In a forest there would be around 300 or more along with ferns, palms, vines and countless other small plants. This is a very limited selection."

"We are very grateful to our President," he answered.

Now his sarcasm was undeniable.

"I guess we had better get on the road again," I replied, ignoring his sarcasm. "I hope the real thing is a little more complex than this. Yes, we must be grateful to President Suharto for small mercies."

I wondered if I saw a flicker of a smile on Paul's face. At best, this is a managed tourist experience. At least it involved a cleanup of debris left behind from logging. In most of the clear-felled areas I saw along the road, a tinderbox waited for a firestorm. Fire in logged areas was a regular occurrence in East Kalimantan and ten years after this visit, the inevitable happened. The El Nino of 1997-98 exacerbated yet another outbreak that went on to burn 25 percent of the forests in the province. The event was so severe that even Australia's New South Wales Rural Fire Service was involved and people in cities as far away as Singapore and Kuala Lumpur developed respiratory disorders.

Bukit Suharto was soon a bad memory as the road wound on past neat lines of Javanese transmigrant huts surrounded by ladang, cultivated areas. No one spoke further of the devastation, a silent consensus prevailed that this was just another dramatic New Order ecological catastrophe in the making.

Mounting a small rise above the village of Loajanan, the immensity of the Mahakam River confronted us. Nothing of the scale of an Amazon but its status as a highway for the coal and timber trade was obvious. Sweeping down

Balikpapan: Looking Backwards and Forwards

towards the river's edge, elegant and simple timber houses on wooden piles came into view, then as the road twisted again, a vista of vast floating carpets of tethered hardwood logs appeared. Each bend in the road was either an encounter with beauty or another confrontation with a voracious, unsustainable harvest.

"How long can this logging continue before Borneo is depleted of rainforests?" I asked.

Paul was silent.

Henky answered with "The forest trees will grow back in 80 years."

"I hope," I replied. "But I don't think the forest will grow back with the same biodiversity." I then added, "Besides, there's the problem of erosion and soil loss."

"I'm sure these thoughts are occupying the President's mind," said Paul, his sarcasm now fully revealed.

Aboard our riverboat in Tenggarong, we saw that the muddy colour of the great river was an indicator of the unseen exploitation now extending deep into the headwaters. On these lower reaches of the river, no primary rainforest was visible though secondary regrowth was common, a few species of trees predominating.

My sense of ecological despair, however, was constantly challenged by the extraordinary adaptations I saw people making to life on the river. Senoni, for example, was an impressive floating village doing a brisk trade in the darkening evening, its several rows of floating shops and *warung* supported by massive rainforest logs. Further on in the short equatorial twilight, proboscis and black-faced monkeys gathered in trees above the riverbanks. A brightly lit floating shop travelled swiftly upstream. Ferries and barges slipped past us as night darkened, sometimes raking us with spotlights. Indeed the Mahakam was a major highway. I remembered Mark

Twain's words, "The laws of Nature take precedence of all human laws. The purpose of all human laws is one – to defeat the laws of Nature."[9] So it was that facing rampant exploitation, in quiet places Nature was still triumphant.

"Look at the fireflies along the riverbank," said Paul in one of the dark intervals between passing riverboats.

"Yes," I said, "so reassuring to see the beauty that remains."

---

[9] *Autobiography of Mark Twain*, Vol. 2 (2013), p. 127. Dictated 18 June 1906.

The River Guide

Anchored in a Mahakam River dawn, our boat was blanketed in a thick fog. Roosters crowed and the Fajar prayer cut through the brume: a town was close. As the sun rose and the mist lifted, we saw that we were moored near a floating riverside bathing platform and toilet. People from the town of Muara Muntai ambled sleepily down for their morning ablutions as we emerged to greet the day.

Paul sat on the gunnel, struggling with sleep inertia, his body wrapped in a sarong for protection against the morning chill.

I wished him good morning: "*Selamat pagi*, Paul. Did you sleep well?"

"No, not so well, I kept waking up with the sound of that diesel running all night."

"Me too. I heard you snoring though, even above the sound of the diesel."

He looked embarrassed. I felt like biting my tongue. It was a very insensitive thing to say.

"I mean it wasn't your snoring that woke me; it was the engine." I attempted to save the situation then thought I should just shut up. "May I get you a coffee?"

"Thank you, yes." He reached for his cigarettes and sat on the bench forward of the engine pit that served as our dining table.

"So this is Muara Muntai," I said as I prepared the coffee.

Henky stirred in his bunk, waking from a deep slumber. I envied his abilty to sleep so well in these conditions.

"*Mau kopi,* Henky?" I asked him if he wanted a coffee as his eyes appeared from beneath his sarong sheet.

"*Маauu,*" he affirmed that he would through a large yawn and stretch.

Slowly we assembled around the table and sipped our coffee.

Flicking open the guidebook I'd brought, I said, "*Muara Muntai* appears to be something of a Wild West town. It's a market town on wooden piles in the Mahakam's flood plain, connected with Lake Jempang, the largest lake in Kalimantan. It says here that there are distinctive, wooden two storey Kutai houses along here, adorned with fret-worked facades and lining a network of iron wood boardwalks and thoroughfares. Paul, can I ask you a couple of questions?"

"Ah, Russell," he said. "Maybe. I'll try.".

"How much primary rainforest will we see on this trip?"

There was no immediate reply so I prompted him.

"I mean forest that hasn't been commercially logged at all."

Paul sipped on his coffee and slipped a cigarette from the packet he'd brought to the table. Lighting up he took a deep morning draft of nicotine. "Russell, that's a difficult question. There are some areas of swamp forest around Gemuruh near Melak and some well-established secondary forest near Longiram. Then there's the Kersik Luwai National Park and orchid forest."

"I've read about Kersik Luwai. It's on peat deposits. So what you're saying is there's none, right?"

"There is, but it's beyond Longiram, up stream from Rukun Damai. There are rapids and waterfalls, so we can't go there. We would need to fly there from Balikpapan or Samarinda."

Deciding not to press him any further on the environmental issue, I continued on another tack, "This is a simple question. Who are the Kutai people? Where are they from and why aren't there Dayaks here? Dayaks don't live in two storied timber houses, do they?"

"I thought you said simple," he exhaled cigarette smoke.

"Well, each question's simple enough," I said, hoping my grin might appease his morning mood.

"The Kutai were probably refugees from Java, possibly from the Hindu Singosari Dynasty. They've lived along the lower Mahakam since the 13th century and eventually converted to Islam. They also live around the shores of some nearby lakes and compared with other groups they are rich making a comfortable living from fishing. It'll be obvious when we're in Kutai territory because you'll see mosques, coconut palms, areas of sawah and almost no dogs."

"Got it. So why so few, if any, Dayaks in these parts?"

"It's a similar story to other parts of Indonesia. Later settlers pressed the earliest settlers into the interior just as the Batak were pressed in around Lake Toba in Sumatra. The lakes near here are a natural division between the lower and middle Mahakam. Beyond here is a lot more forest, and more and more Dayaks."

Not wanting to push Paul's goodwill this early in the morning, I turned again to my guidebook for more detail on the Dayaks. It informed me that more than 50 Dayak ethnic groups settled in Borneo over 4500 years ago, each with their own cultures and languages. Many converted to Christianity during the Dutch colonial period, but many assimilated both Christian and primal religious practices.

"*Aduh! Sudah bikin kpoi?*" Our guide, Alex, who also doubled as head chef and providore, observed that we were already making coffee. In all, our boat carried eight people on this stretch of the river, Paul, Henky, the captain, an engineer, two deckhands who doubled as kitchen hands, Alex and myself.

"*Selamat pagi,*" he said good morning to Paul and nuzzled up against him in an affectionate way. "Paul, I need a special favour from you."

"And what would that be, Alex?" Paul wore a look of resignation on his face.

"I must go shopping with the boys. Adi has already prepared some *nasi goreng* (fried rice) for your breakfast but I want him to come with me to buy some fish, prawns and vegetables for our meals. So will you take Henky and Russell to Muara Muntai without me?"

"Fine then," Paul answered in a weary tone.

"Don't be like that, Paul. Do this for me and I will take good care of you." He smiled broadly and slapped Paul on the shoulder.

After breakfast, the three of us set off for Muara Muntai.

By midmorning, we were all back on the boat ready to cast off for our next destination.

Alex was already supervising the cooking but when we returned, he came up to the bow where we were seated around the table. He carried a large plastic bucket, saying: "Just so you know, I haven't been lazy. Look at this." He reached into the bucket and retrieved a huge river prawn, which was more like a small lobster with mean-looking claws. It twitched and wriggled as he held it aloft. "This is what we will be having for dinner, Paul. I know how much you like them," he said as he thrust the huge prawn close to Paul's face.

Paul feigned dismay but he knew Alex all too well to be perturbed.

"Delicious!" Henky exclaimed. "I like these prawns. How many did you buy, Alex?" "Four. Fish as well. We'll have a feast later on."

Alex was an extraordinary character. Animated and charismatic, he combined the features of a grand dame from traditional European pantomime with the rotund, humorous and astute clown figure *Semar* from the *wayang*. *Semar* is associated with *Arjuna*, one of the *Pandawa* brothers in the Mahabrata and is renown for authenticity and truthfulness. *Semar* is represented with a squat body and big eyes; this was Alex to a tee. Although inclined to joke a lot, Alex reflected great wisdom and insight. Even a short conversation with Alex revealed his remarkable acumen. Although playing the fool like *Semar*, he did not suffer fools lightly.

As the days passed and we travelled upstream, Alex's knowledge of the river revealed a mind that was a map of values and relativities, of flows, surges and eddies in the price and availability of things. His astute powers of observation weren't simply confined to the dynamics of riparian commerce along the main channel; he was equally at home when we made side trips into anabranches, tributaries and backwater swamps or when walking through tracts of secondary rainforest.

On one forest amble, Alex demonstrated his prowess with a Dayak sumpit or hunting blowpipe and was a crack shot. He also had a wonderful, opportunistic eye for the myriad culinary delicacies one encountered in the forest. "Look there," he said, scraping away leaf litter to reveal brightly coloured inflorescences sprouting from the buttressed roots of a tree. "These are sweet and delicious. Here try some," he said as he ran a blade beneath them, presenting them to the group.

Initially we all passed except Henky who exclaimed, "Really delicious. Sweet!"

"Oh," I said, "I'd better try the fungi," and pinched several segments between my fingertips and I bit into them. "Amazing! An explosion of sweetness. Tastes a bit like *Monstera deliciosa*."

Further along I spied a fine example of *cauliflory*, with fig-like fruit sprouting out of a tree trunk. They looked ready to eat. "What about these figs, Alex?" I called. "Can we try them?"

"You can, but they won't taste very good and you won't live long. They're poisonous," he added with a knowing smile.

He moved ahead down the shady track in a twilight world of muffled sounds where seldom a ray of sunlight was seen. The humidity was oppressive; my head pounded as profuse sweating unbalanced my electrolytes. Alex was moving swiftly and it was hard keeping up with him. A few hundred meters on, he stopped under a large tree with a huge spreading canopy and trunk. He looked down; there was something beneath the tree. Approaching, I realised that it was a very old woman gathering fallen pods.

For our benefit, Alex asked, "What are you looking for grandmother?"

"I'm looking for *kemiri* nuts," she told him

Henky shot off half a dozen candid photos of her and when she realised, she looked disapprovingly at him and said, "*Lima ribu,*" Or five thousand, her price for the photos.

Undaunted, Alex began the charm offensive, saying, "Grandmother, may I help?" He then added, "Wow! You're so beautiful, grandmother."

She smiled, distracted.

"Grandmothers here are so beautiful," he effused.

Unaccustomed to such flattery, she soon forgot the issue of payment. Alex again addressed her politely, "With your permission, grandmother. We must go to our boat. Please excuse us."

"Please do," she smiled.

So off we went down the track.

Nearing the river, my pounding head worsened. Alex kept ahead of us, spotting out new attractions then stopped and beamed, pointing with his large knife. He said, "Look at this!"

It was a massive clump of brown wood fungus growing on the rotting branch of a fallen tree. Cutting it off the rotting branch, he pressed it towards me. "Smell it!"

I hoped it was good for my headache and sniffed in a deep draught. "Mmm, it smells like fresh mushrooms. I bet it's delicious."

"Would you like me to cook it for you?" he asked.

"Yes, thanks. I've had it before in Chinese food but I've never seen as much fresh fungus as this."

He gathered it up.

"We'll be in Longiram tonight. We cross the equator three times on the way so I think we should have a feast tonight. I will cook this with soya sauce and garlic. It will be delicious."

Longiram was the limit of easy navigation for larger riverboats, pushing further upstream required a local Dayak river pilot. A natural stop over, we also found ourselves close to the renowned black orchids of Kersik Luwai.

A hot steamy place and an important trading centre, Longiram comes to life after dark so Henky and I wandered along the main street in the *petang*, that fleeting almost imperceptible equatorial twilight.

By this time and after a period of uncertainty, Henky and I had become quite close. At first I was puzzled by his standoffishness but came to understand that this often marked the early stages of getting to know many Indonesians of Chinese descent and was a common condition under the New Order regime where personal opinions were cautiously guarded. Now we realised that we shared much in common, particularly our liking for leisurely ambles spotting out visual attractions.

"Look at that, Russell," Henky gestured, lifting his head and pointing his chin towards a man carrying a large rattan basket of what looked like porcelain.

"I think that's porcelain," I said, without expecting an answer.

"Definitely from a Dayak longhouse," he said.

"If that's so maybe it's trading porcelain from the Ming or Ching dynasties. I'm interested in that type of porcelain."

In a couple of steps, we were right alongside the man, his basket brimming with porcelain. Although now dark, there was sufficient streetlight for us to see it was trading porcelain.

Henky greeted him, "*Selamat malam pak.*"

"*Selamat malam bapak-bapak,*" he replied.

"I see you're carrying a lot of porcelain, Sir," I remarked, looking down at the basket.

He told me it was just a small amount and I asked if there was any more.

"There is. Come over to my house; it's just there," he said, beckoning us to follow him toward a plain timber hut.

Taking a few steps up onto the boardwalk, he unlocked the door and flicked a light switch as we followed him. As my eyes adjusted to the weak lighting, I was amazed. The floors were covered with hundreds of Ching and Ming trading items: bowls of many sizes, plates, cups and even porcelain rice spoons. Recognising that this was a mere glimpse of what must have originally been traded, I was astounded. In the larger cities of Indonesia, I'd have been circumspect about the authenticity of such items but these were unmistakably genuine.

Before hard currency made an appearance, porcelain was the medium of exchange. Ming trading porcelain was carried up stream and exchanged for forest products, tying the Dayak cultures into an emerging international trade. Trading continued well into the 19th century, spanning the Ching Dynasty and overlapping the period of Dutch colonialism.

Though dwarfed by the new extractive industries of mining and logging, ancient patterns of trade continued in a manner. Gone were the Ming and Ching Emperors but in their place, a global middle class emerged with a passion for the rare and unusual. Trading porcelain grew as a fashionable curiosity not only throughout Indonesia but also internationally during the second half of the 20th century.

Bugis and Banjar traders began to scour the upper reaches of the river systems, exchanging currency for trading porcelain. Packed on river boats and inter-island ferries, their finds were shipped across the Makassar Straits to Ujung Pandang then south and west into the antique emporia of tourist and commercial centres in Bali and Java.

"Looks interesting, Henky," I said softly.

"There's lots of it," he replied.

"I bought a few bowls in Ujung Pandang last year, so I understand a little of the prices."

"Be careful," he cautioned.

While I had a sense of value, my means were limited and my capacity to carry much was restricted. Remembering the struggle I'd had carrying eight Ching porcelain bowls out of Ujung Pandang the year before, I curbed my impulses and approached the matter conservatively.

I picked up a bowl similar to the sort I'd bought Ujung Pandang and said, "How much for a bowl like this, Sir?" I tried to appear only academically interested and not seriously in the market.

"*Bowls like this,* Rp 55.000," the trader answered, with just the slightest hint of uncertainty.

Based on my knowledge of the market in Ujung Pandang, I reasoned he was asking for three times the original price. So if he was paying no more than Rp 14,000 for a bowl, this meant I should pay no more than Rp 28,000 for the same. At least this was my rough and ready reckoning. Applying this logic after browsing through the collection I ended up buying three fine Ching plates for Rp 48,000.

After this encounter in the house of porcelain, I began to wonder what other treasures might be found. Strolling back towards the mooring with Henky, I scanned the footpaths and shop fronts for treasures.

As we reached the riverbank, Henky decided to hurry ahead, wanting to wash before dinner so I took in the scene. Apart from the usual riverside clutter of timber, boxes and small up turned boats, there was an evening bird market prompting recollection of a conversations I'd had before leaving Bali.

A Balinese friend, Made Rebing, joked about me bringing souvenirs back from the jungles of Kalimantan. Like other Balinese, I knew he was caught up in the endless cycle of temple festivals. Cockfights were often associated with these events as a means of appeasing malign earth bound energies with a blood sacrifice. Made and others I spoke with were keen to crossbreed forest fowl from Kalimantan with the domesticated birds used to supply their stock of fighting cocks. While not asking outright, several of them were apt to comment on how valuable these birds might be in Bali. So I entertained a half crazy idea of picking one up and somehow traveling back to Bali with it.

A couple of men enjoying an evening *kretek*, aromatic clove and tobacco cigarettes, leaned on a railing across the street from the bird market near the steps that led down to our boat. Cooler air was already flowing down the valley and they were happy to chat.

We began exchanging the usual introductory lines spoken in so many conversations along the archipelago, establishing that Iwan and Joko were transmigrants from Java who worked land not far from the town and I was an Australian living in Bali.

"Where do you stay in Bali?" Iwan asked me.

"In a village called Ubud," I replied.

Glancing back at the bird market where twenty or so cane cages hung from simple wooden frames set up for the evening, Joko inquired, "Are birds kept as pets in Ubud?"

I explained that they were, and my friend Nyoman liked keeping birds as well as turtles and fish.

Iwan suggested that there was a lot of cockfighting in Bali and I replied that they were held before temple ceremonies and that another friend was after a forest fowl to breed stronger fighting cocks.

Iwan looked enthusiastic. He said, "I have a friend with a forest fowl. It's been raised with ordinary chickens."

Buying and transporting a forest fowl was awash with difficulties and it all seemed a little too coincidental to be true. Assuming this was just a story and the last time we were likely to meet, I said, "I must apologise. I almost forgot dinner is ready on the boat. If you want to bring the bird to the boat tomorrow morning, please do.".

The following morning, as the mist lifted, three men arrived at our boat carrying the most beautiful forest fowl, looking to me like a member of the family of *Phasianidae*, which includes jungle fowl, partridges, pheasants, ptarmigans and grouse.

Greeting our visitors, Alex conversed with them in Javanese. I had no idea what was said, though I was left with then impression that Alex had a more than casual interest. After the brief exchange, Alex turned to me and said, "This bird is ready to mate with domestic birds. It will be valuable in Bali."

I said nothing but in the cold light of day I'd wondered about the challenge I might face negotiating with airport authorities in Bali, assuming I managed to get the bird back down the river and onto my return flight to Denpasar.

Thinking that I could always back out of any negotiations by claiming that the bird was far too expensive, I tentatively asked, how much the bird cost

The third man, obviously the owner of the bird replied, "Only Rp 100.000."

Perhaps my caution was obvious because the price translated as a mere 25 Australian dollars. If price wasn't something I could argue about, then what? All I could think of was the special care the bird might need and the difficulties of getting it onboard a flight at short notice. This would have to do.

It worked; the potential sellers understood.

"You don't want to buy this bird?" asked Alex.

"Certainly the bird would be very valuable in Bali, but it will be too difficult to carry it there."

Alex then turned to the owner saying he would pay Rp 80,000.

The owner replied, "Brother, its food is very expensive. Rp 90,000."

Alex agreed to the price, paid him and and our three visitors left looking very pleased.

"What will you do with the bird, Alex?" I asked.

"I will take care of it and breed it with a village hen."

The poor bird had its legs tied and spent the remainder of trip downstream on the deck. Worried about it dying from exposure, I sprinkled it with water from time to time and made sure it was in a warm place at night.

The River Guide

I saw first-hand how the rivers in Kalimantan offer countless opportunities for the movement of things, but they are also corridors for the unexpected, for the less tangible and the unseen. Amongst the less obvious flows were ideas, language, cultural nuance or simple things like trends and fashions. Then there were also the biological flows. All have a demonstrated capacity to flow upstream with great rapidity stimulated by growing global connectivity.

Henky and I became firm friends and several years later, when visiting him in East Jakarta, I reminisced about our Mahakam trip.

"Russell, I have some news." He spoke slowly.

"What's that?"

"Paul rang me yesterday. He said Alex died last week."

Stunned, I asked, "How? Do you know?

"Yes, it was AIDS."

Siberut and the Simple Life

Accustomed as I was to the wide Mahakam River, journeying up the Rereiket River from Muara Siberut to Rokdok village was more like travelling up a mining sluice. It was a raging turbid torrent of sediments and tree trunks fuelled by a constant downpour. Sitting in the centre of the motorised canoe, I was amazed at the debris that came tumbling past me. Beneath my broad brimmed hat and plastic cape, I roughed out notes on the surroundings whenever the downpour eased enough for me to peek out.

Paul and Alwi, our link to the local area, sat behind with Henky. Andre, our guide and translator with his brother Daniel, sat near the bow. At the stern was our boatman, Pak Eddie, gunning the outboard motor across pools while deftly avoiding rocks and snags at every riffle with practiced use of rudder and throttle.

"Russell, are you still taking notes?" Paul called above the noise.

Henky turned around and told me: "Paul thought you were a journalist when we first met in Balikpapan."

"Yes, I guess freedom of expression is a precious commodity in the . . ." I hesitated not wanting to start a political conversation in this situation where basic survival was a more pertinent concern.

"Apa, Russell?" (What, Russell?) Paul asked.

"That's funny, thinking I was a journalist. I'm just trained to take notes. I forget things too easily otherwise . . . bloody hell . . . look at the size of that tree trunk floating past!"

"Big log," shouted Henky.

Siberut and the Simple Life

"Did you hear that, Russell?" asked Daniel.

"Hear what, Daniel?"

"Pak Eddie said there's no forestry in the headwaters of this tributary we're passing. So there's a clear waterfall and natural swimming pool two kilometres upstream."

It was hard to imagine struggling upstream through this riparian gateway. Forestry was the problem, although that was the wrong word for it. Forestry itself conjures up a sense of husbandry of orderly enterprise while nothing remotely orderly was responsible for this turbidity. In recent years, cash cropping had followed the timber cutters and there was nothing orderly about that process either. It was a systematic rape of a fragile environment and culture unrestrained by the rapacious demands of the market place and the corruption of Suharto's New Order regime.

After an hour, we made it to Rokdok.

Andre called, "Let's go, get off!" over his shoulder as he and Daniel leapt into the shallows and pulled our boat up a sloping bank. Here the water eddied back into a quieter pool protected by a long slope and sand bar further up stream.

"We'll spend the night here," Andre told us.

"Where will we stay?" Paul asked.

"We must ask the people in the village," Alwi suggested. "Maybe we will stay with a family."

Since the rain had eased, we waited on a grassy bank while Alwi and Andre walked off into the village in search of accommodation.

It was only a hamlet. In the centre, a single storey building stood with rendered brick walls capped by a rusting corrugated iron roof. It was ringed by several traditional structures with high peaked thatched roofs, timber walls and small covered verandas. The entire hamlet area had been cleared, the forest cut back beyond the huts.

Wanting to relieve myself, I wandered up to the central building, quickly realising it was a small school building. Henky followed some distance behind, looking for a photo opportunity. At one end, I found the toilet block only to discover that it lacked running water and that all the rudimentary porcelain toilets were smashed.

"These toilets are smashed. Where do we…?" I said.

"In the river for sure," Henky answered.

Just then, Alwi and Andre appeared with a young man.

"May I introduce Mas Trihono," said Alwi. "He is the teacher. He has invited us to stay with him tonight. His is the house nearest the boat."

We moved our bedding and food supplies into the teacher's house just as the rain started and looked to rain all night.

"It's amazing how efficient this house is," I said, "how watertight the roof is. It looks like it's just sago palm thatch and yet, it's as dry as a bone in here."

"'Dry as a bone' – I've never heard that before," said Andre. "Mentawai houses are very well built," he added.

"They also have a very stable inside temperature," Alwi said, "usually around 25°C but they can't stop mosquitos so you should all hang your nets now. Make sure you put the edges under your sleeping mats."

The simple split bamboo floor was firm but far more yielding than floorboards so once our nets were strung up over our mats, it felt luxurious after the hair-raising boat trip.

At dawn, the rain eased and we looked out at a dripping landscape. After a breakfast of instant noodles, we loaded our bags and bedding into the boat and set off on foot. The boat went upstream without us, to round several sinuous meanders more easily.

As we walked, I remembered what Alwi said about Siberut's forests when we first met back in Padang.

"Siberut's forests aren't just a random collection of species but an established equatorial garden created through hundreds of years of careful modification. They are part of a slow transformation unfolding along the archipelago of Nusantara and beginning as far back 40,000 years ago. Such sustainable change is all but invisible, yet the very language and culture of the archipelago's forest people is enmeshed and entwined in this process."

He was right. While the illusion of the virgin forest remained wherever we looked, the hand of human intervention was evident in the regular occurrence of fruit trees, sago palms and trees supplying specific resins or timbers.

Siberut's shales and marls weather into sticky water-retaining soils so walking on the forest floor was like stepping into deep, wet cement. Progress was only possible using a series of slippery logs set end-to-end, a path that tested our balance at every step and there was great satisfaction in not falling into the slush.

"Oh!" said Paul, falling again, "I have such bad balance!"

"Try moving faster and looking ahead," I suggested.

"Paul's shoes are too slippery," said Henky, "that's the problem."

Progress was slow at first then, as confidence built, we all moved a little faster. After a time, I broke into a fast stride before the ground disappeared and I found myself suddenly confronted by an open, raging watercourse. Abruptly, the forest ended and we stopped on the verge of another cleared area, Ugai village. Several large timber houses with big verandahs faced a central square.

The click of Henky's heavy brass bodied Nikon caused me to follow the direction of his lens, glimpsing a young woman sitting peacefully on a verandah, oblivious to our arrival. Click and click again went the Nikon's shutter.

She had striking features, pale skin and long dark slightly wavy hair. Strung about her neck falling onto her chest were dense strings of tightly packed blue, red and yellow beads. An infant suckled at her right breast; iconic I thought, but any sense of this was immediately shattered when she raised a thick conical cigarette to her lips and drew deeply.

I lifted my camera and snapped one shot just as she caught sight of us. A sullen disapproving expression fell over her face. She said something that I didn't understand but Andre, who spoke the regional language, translated and told me that she didn't want her photo taken.

"I'm sorry," I said, letting go of my camera so that it hung out of sight behind my arm.

"Have any white cigarettes?' she asked me, making the price of a photo abundantly clear.

Paul handed her a packet. She placed the cone behind her ear and light up one of Paul's.

The experience saddened me. Tobacco smoking is endemic in Siberut and life expectancy short, but my thought was quickly distracted at the sounds of our boat and Pak Eddie calling. We piled in and headed upstream against a more subdued flow now the rain had stopped.

A few hundred metres upstream, a solitary figure stood on a long, curving sandbar. He waved and our boatman nudged towards the shore.

A wiry man, his muscular body was taught like steel cable. Dark tattooed arcs were visible beneath each collarbone with a prominent arc across his chest. The remainder of his body was tattooed with straight lines mapping out something reminiscent of the meridians in Chinese acupuncture.

"*Kai pa uee?*" he asked where we were going in his own language while motioning for us to land.

Siberut and the Simple Life

"Upstream, to Matatonan," Andre told him in Indonesian as our boat hit the sandy shore. Once again, Andre and Daniel were quick to secure the craft as the rest of us jumped out.

After the formal greetings, Andre explained, "This is an old friend of mine. He is a Sarareiket elder; the head of his Uma. His place is further upstream, about half an hour's walk. He is making sago just upstream. Would you like to see?"

"Yes!" several of us answered. So we set off on what proved to be a much easier track with some rocky surfaces that allowed traction and greater security.

Isolated from Sumatra since the end of the Pleistocene era, Siberut's traditional economy is sago based, supplemented by taro and bananas. While not the most nutritious food, sago affords the largest yield of edible starch for the least effort of any known plant, one day's work yielding 17 days supply at 241 calories per 100g.

After a ten-minute walk, we reached a clearing. There a simple sago processing plant had been built on a wooden platform, set on thin piles in the marshy surface. On the platform, two rectangular tanks had been fashioned from sago palm bark.

The process was simple. The elder stood on dry land above the platform and chipped out the pith from a split palm trunk. He used a simple wood and stone adze. Gathering handfuls of the shredded pith, he threw them into the first tank already close to brim full. As the water became cloudy, he added more scooped up marsh water, forcing the first tank to overflow along a conduit of sago palm log and leading into the settlement tank, where the sago starch accumulated. From there, a thick white sludge was dropped into a cylindrical basket, also fashioned from sago palm bark.

Seen and Unseen

Andre translated as the elder told us: "Much of our traditional life must remain hidden and unseen if we are to protect it."

He went on, "However, if there was some way of showing the value of our culture perhaps even selling examples of our tools, this would help us with money. At the moment, we have no money."

He told us he was proud of his work but he also spoke of threatening forces beyond this simple life, of frequent police raids, the destruction of traditional tools and clothing and the pressure to move to a settlement camps where children and families could be educated in the ways of the government.

He spoke at length, explaining his world. It was a familiar story. "For us, the land and our forest is our life. Before, we didn't use money because everything we needed was here. Men hunted pigs, deer and monkeys. We use poisoned arrows. Our women gathered leaves, fruit and taro roots. They also netted small fish."

On our way back to the boat Andre explained a little more of the traditional lifestyle. "People live in separate isolated houses or *uma* set on the higher grounds upstream."

"Something like a Dayak *lamin*?" I asked if these were like the Dayak longhouses.

"No, smaller, and the difference is they have just one big family. Sons stay and daughters move to their husband's *uma* when they marry."

"A patrilineal system?"

"Yes, it is," answered Andre. "Before, only a few people lived in an area maybe as few as four people per square kilometre. There was plenty of forest. Sometimes there was warring between clans but mainly people were at peace amongst themselves, at harmony with forest spirits and living with a sustainable traditional economy. There was no tobacco, alcohol or betel nut."

Siberut and the Simple Life

"Forest spirits, mmm," I said. "So the people aren't Muslim or Christian; they're still animist."

"The group we're meeting are also Sarareiket. Some say they are Christian but that just means they've had contact with missionaries. Actually I think the Baha'is have also had contact with them recently."

Once back onboard the boat, we continued upstream in relative silence. Sometimes there were women fishing along the shore, sometimes we passed a dugout canoe, and occasionally one swept past on a downstream run.

Arriving in Matatonan was a complete contrast with all Andre had recounted. Here some 80 dwellings occupied a flat area at the mouth of a small tributary. It was a resettlement missionary village. Houses were set in a tight grid pattern with a vast silver domed mosque on higher ground at one end. It was difficult to imagine a more dramatic departure from the Mentawai tradition of solitary dwellings in subtle relationship with river, rainforest, gardens and forest spirits.

Landing, we climbed a trail leading away from the village to a small hill, our destination a large *uma* commanding the high ground above the village. Dress on our arrival was t-shirts and skirts or shorts. Even in this attire, the extensive tattooing on the adult bodies around us was apparent: the density and complexity of the designs roughly accorded with age.

Smiling and welcoming, they had gathered outside the *uma*. Two brothers headed the family, the older formally the head of the *uma*, his younger brother, the shaman. In all there were eight adults and seventeen children.

Children were everywhere; not just from the *uma* but our arrival attracted scores from the village below. After formal greetings, we followed family members up steep steps into the *uma*.

A wide, sweeping palm thatch roof protected a solid rectangular timber structure set head high above the ground. At the top of the stairs, we entered a large room where the smell of smoke was strong. Light from beneath the eaves filtered in through long narrow windows on either side, creating a subdued twilight and revealing hardwood and split bamboo floors. To the rear, a corridor emitted a shaft of light through a wood panelled back wall. Eyes slowly adjusting, I noticed scores of animal skulls hanging above the rear wall: monkeys, pigs, goats, perhaps the skull of a fresh water crocodile and others.

Relaxing after a short time, the family quickly shed their western clothes. Sitting on a rough bench by one of the side windows, Andre was chatting with the headman. I sat beside them and Andre began to translate. He said they were wary when our boat first arrived. His words were, "We thought you were government officials."

"It must have been Paul's hat," Andre surmised.

Paul's navy blue hat with gold insignia, like one worn by a minor officials in the tourism department, rested in his lap as he sat crossed legged chatting with a cluster of children by the other window.

"We are worried that the government is trying to destroy our way of life," the headman continued. "We hope the tourism you could bring will help us."

"Yes, you'll be able to sell examples of your tools," said Alwi, as he sat to join the conversation. He waited silently while Andre translated his suggestion.

The headman nodded.

"Tourism can also destroy culture," I said, hoping Andre would translate for me.

It was Alwi who replied. "Yes, so it must be on the right scale and not disrupt traditional life but give people a small cash income so they can survive now that their world is being destabilised by logging and cash cropping."

"I agree, Alwi," I said, "but their resources are limited and basics like water and sanitation will be challenging."

"Water and food must be brought in and garbage carted out," Alwi agreed. "That is essential."

I was happy we were in accord because he would be responsible for local operations if our proposed *Walks on the Wildside* tour ever got off the ground.

By now, everyone was in traditional clothing. Men wore loincloths fashioned from bark and women, a type of *lap-lap* or skirt. Both men and women wore multiple strands of bright coloured African beads, originally traded into the area by pepper traders, supplemented by amber coloured ceramic electrical insulators introduced by the Dutch. The men wore cheap silver watchbands as a final touch.

Women were both ministering to the needs of older children and breast-feeding babies. Their minimal attire made the signs of frequent pregnancy and childbirth obvious. All had noticeable stretch marks and many were lactating. As a father, I found their fertile femininity beautiful.

In remote communities such as these, people who attended secondary school spoke Indonesian well, even if they only completed the middle years. Others preferred to converse in their *bahasa daerah*, the regional language, opening up many opportunities for misunderstanding when discussing relationships or responding politely to traditional status. Pronouns were very important; the simple word *you* found in English might not even have been used. By contrast, there was intimate *you* and respectful or plural *you*. *We* could be inclusive of the person being addressed or exclusive of them. With such rules operating, it was easy to give offence without even being aware it happened. Sensitivity, politeness and patience plus a good guide was a great help to me.

Despite my developing linguistic and cultural fluency, I was the only non-Indonesian in our small group so I was often the butt of elaborate intercultural jokes. Frequently, these had a patriarchal twist when we visited isolated indigenous communities.

Just before arriving in the Mentawai islands, we'd been eating a lot of durian. Many Westerners baulk at its unusual smell, their reservations reinforced by Eurocentric guidebooks likening it to eating crème caramel in a public toilet or some other equally disgusting image. In truth, it was delicious and could be mildly intoxicating with a disinhibiting effect not unlike a couple of glasses of red wine. In such disinhibited spaces, my companions' conversation was apt to stray into more risqué realms.

"I trust you will be safe when we visit Siberut," Paul chided. I could tell from his tone this was about to be a joke at my expense. "Well, as in Kalimantan," he prompted, "you remember that isolated village I told you about?"

"You mean the one where the headman wanted the tourist to sleep with a woman from his *lamin*?" I said. "I thought that was a joke."

"Oh, no that happened in an isolated area south of the Mahakam," he assured me with a most serious expression.

"Really?"

"We can't be certain about the situation in the Mentawai Islands. If the same custom applies, to refuse such a request from a patriarch would cause profound offence."

I listened, laughing inwardly. My inclination was to dismiss it all as fantasy but the story stuck in my mind.

That evening, as we sat chatting with our hosts what emerged above all else was the peacefulness of their lives. Conversation also confirmed that some of this family had converted to Christianity while in more recent years, several had also been exposed to the Ba'hai faith.

Our local guide, Andre, was exceptional in his rapid translation skills, allowing me to converse at length with the shaman and as evening progressed, I came to rely less and less on Andre's translation. Somehow we managed to conduct a conversation in very simple Bahasa Indonesia and sign language. As the evening drew to a close, he eventually smiled and said, *Mau tidur sama kita?* asking if I wanted to sleep with them. As he asked the question, he gestured to part of the *uma* where a woman with most arresting features was sitting.

He'd used the inclusive *we*. Combined with the gesture, it sent amber lights flashing in my head. Is the story I'd dismissed as fantasy true? What was the level of individuation in this culture? I didn't know.

With whom was I being asked to sleep? Did he mean us in a broad sense, meaning the whole extended family or was he indicating this woman in particular and meaning one of us. Was it her? Were the stories true? He must mean her, *wow*! What do I say next? I was terrified. She was most beautiful, sitting barebreasted, looking towards us. How old was this woman? It was impossible to be certain. I was drawn to her beauty but then pulled sharply in the opposite direction registering an equally negative impulse.

Privileged Westerners preying on innocence distressed me. There was a feeling of anger that my guide and Indonesian companions had allowed this situation to arise. There was no way I was going to sleep with her but how to extract myself from this situation. It didn't make sense that the people claimed to be Christian and yet could maintain such practices. On the other hand, I was aware of how nominal conversion could be. Perhaps the whole Christian story was for Andre's benefit, after all he is a Catholic.

The moment pressed in on me, what to say. Finally I blurted out in Indonesian, "Sorry, I can't. I'm already married."

The silence seemed endless but the laughter, when it came, was a blessed relief.

The shaman smiled at me and said in precise Indonesian, "Not that. If we want to sleep with our wives, there is a room at the back. Do you want to sleep with the men, over there?" He pointed again to the same spot on the floor.

Now it was clear. I was mortified. He gestured again to the place where the woman still sat. Now I got it, this was the spot where the men slept.

I quickly agreed to save any further embarrassment.

Soon it was time to bed down. Dressed in a long sleeved shirt, track suit bottoms and thick socks as extra protection against dangerous *falciparum* bearing malarial mosquitoes, I was hot, to say the least.

Swiftly, the men hung up their mosquito net, not the light nylon type that I had but a heavy shroud of unbleached calico. It covered a double bed sized space for four men, so they could only sleep draped over one another. I didn't fancy this: one more made five and the body heat would be intense.

There was only one way out. I strung up my net right next to the men and invited them to share it. Much to my relief they all preferred to sleep draped together under their calico shroud. We slept soundly.

The Pig and the Cockfight

"*Okaylah*. Let's have a look around here," said Nyoman, in that distinctive blending of English and Indonesian he so often used. Far from obscuring communication, it marked his accomplishment as a linguist and his capacity to move into an independent space when in dialogue with those from outside his culture.

Just as well I'd met this guy. There's no way I could have started this without him. He had come along just at the right time.

Nyoman was an erudite communicator, not a tour guide but an artist, an intercultural translator and interpreter with an immense generosity of spirit. Establishing a business in Indonesia, Bali in particular, was only possible with such help from Nyoman and many other such knowledgeable and generous people. Nyoman was the first, introducing our team to his village and its lands.

Arriving early in the morning, he'd say "Take a short walk with me; there is something I want to show you," and immediately he had my attention.

Approaching what I reasoned was the south west corner of Ubud; we leapt down off a bund onto a flat dry area, apparent wasteland.

"Here's the graveyard."

I must have looked puzzled.

"Yes, the graveyard. We bury the dead here. Do you notice anything?"

There were some twenty headstones marking the graves of people who'd all left us within the last two years.

I thought Balinese Hindus cremated their dead and wondered if there had been some epidemic, or a catastrophe.

He added, "Cremations are expensive, so people might need to save up, or wait for relatives to return. Sometimes the whole community comes together and we have a mass cremation. In the meantime, bodies remain here in shallow graves."

Now he had my complete attention.

"This is the domain of *Dewi Durga*.[10] See that small temple over there? That's the *Pura Dalem Marajapatih*, her temple. It has her form on the front. She looks scary, ya?"

"She certainly does." I snapped a picture of her demonic form.

"Balinese people avoid this place after dark because of unseen powers. It's not a safe place for the living after sunset."

Over the years, the graveyard became an essential stop on the study tours our team conducted through the village. Thanks to help from another remarkable informant, our housekeeper, Ketut, so too did her village. It became familiar territory.

In Ubud, our company office and residence was towards the west of the village, about halfway between Jalan Bisma and the graveyard. Balinese people often asked, "Where do you live?"

It was an element of polite conversation, *basa basi*, as it is known, but also a subtle way of determining where we sat in the village context, whether we were rich or poor, close to the Balinese, or amongst that aloof clique of foreigners who lived in relative luxury.

I would invariably answer, "I live just east of the graveyard."

A common response often accompanied by a concerned expression was, "Near the graveyard. You're not scared?"

---

[10] A feminine aspect of Shiva who governs the domain of the unpurified dead, those who await cremation and an opportunity to be one with the purified spirits of their ancestors.

The Pig and the Cockfight

Mostly, at the end of each working day, I drove Ketut home. In the rapidly darkening early evening, she would never get into the car outside the office.

"I'll wait here; you turn the car around first," she said, displaying a non-negotiable reluctance to climb up into the kijang, knowing that I would use the graveyard's verge as my turning circle. She was adamant that this was the domain of Dewi Durga and not safe after dark.

Ketut lived in her father's household. Balinese households, organised around kitchens, are generally within family compounds and compounds might contain several families. People in Balinese compounds are related through the male line, as inheritance is patrilineal. Sons bring wives in and daughters marry out.

One day, Ketut told me she was getting married.

"You haven't met him," she said. "He grows orchids in the Bupati's garden. He's from Singaraja."

"So you're moving to Singaraja?" I asked, trying to stifle my disappointment about losing her and also aware of how difficult the move would be for them. They both had jobs in Ubud.

"No, he'll move into my place."

A little confused at this point, given the inheritance system, I decided this was a question for Nyoman.

"Yes, a woman moves into her husband's compound, but there is flexibility. Basic rules can be adjusted. We call it *desa-kala-patra* or place-time-situation. Rules can vary, provided that we make special arrangements. Maybe in Ketut's compound, it was decided that it is better for everyone if her husband moved in because he comes from a place where paid work is hard to find."

This made sense, I thought. If they'd moved north according to the custom, they'd have little work. I wonder what special arrangements were made and later I discovered that her husband had to pay a small fee to

161

the local *banjar*, or village ward, to secure his place in this arrangement.

When we visited Ketut's compound, many hours were spent sipping glasses of sweet tea, chatting, laughing and enjoying informal instruction in basic *Bahasa Bali*.

"How many people live in your compound, Ketut?" I enquired, mainly to see if the census data plate on her front fence was correct.

"There are about 66 people sharing six kitchens. They share the pigpens at the back as well. It's crowded and our only clean water is at the front of the block all our other water has to be carted from a spring. It's women's work."

"That's a lot of people in a small space, Ketut."

"It is not always so healthy. I worry for my children sometimes."

I was aware of the conditions. People worked hard to keep things in good order. Women did their clothes washing in the river or at a *pancuran* (spring), people also used the river for bathing and toileting. Despite their efforts, gastro-intestinal upsets were common, there was active tuberculosis in the compound, and scant informed appreciation of the unseen world of microorganisms.

"Aside from these difficulties," Ketut said, "there is much *ilmu hitam* (black magic). A lot of people are victims of *ilmu*. We face many challenges."

Black magic was a problem in her village and in her compound, which was always full of people, coming and going. On the surface in this social place, interactions were amicable but beneath the surface, there was a complex world of disputation, jealousy and rivalry. Such complexity was extended by the practice of first cousin marriage and polygamy. With such complexity, many disputes were settled, within the unseen world of *ilmu hitam*.

As my friend, I Gusti Made Sumung observed in one of our many philosophical discussions: "The Balinese world comprises a hierarchy of spiritual entities and practices. In time, you will come to learn more about this."

For me, it was apparent that this unseen world wasn't merely the spiritual domain. It also included elements that I understood as having a rational, scientific explanation. In this category was the microscopic realm of bacteria and parasites and I learned to deal with microecology and had strict, non-negotiable rules: there could be no *desa-kala-patra* in this realm. In the Balinese understanding, things weren't this clear-cut.

We continued working in this environment, grateful for Ketut's help, our main concern being just how to compensate Ketut for all of her service. It wasn't possible to start paying her substantially more than the going rate for cook, housekeeper and office assistant. Paying too much was just as likely to cause jealousy and trouble for her and her family, if the extended family began to pressure her for additional funds. So we resolved to turn a blind eye to the slight skimming of the domestic budget and Ketut was often given small items of gold like earrings and eventually, a pig.

The idea of buying Ketut a pig came out of a conversation on domestic economy. "Women often raise pigs," Ketut advised as we examined a basket of cute piglets in the market one day. "It's a way of making a little extra money."

She continued, "Traditionally, men might own the land but women manage the household budget and if the family grows rice they're responsible for selling the rice crop or any other produce over and above family needs."

Ketut went on, "Women run the markets and understand the value of goods and money. They are good money managers. We have skills in bargaining and can establish the correct prices for most things. Men often don't have these skills."

Outside the marketplace, values weren't always easy to determine. Fortunately, Nyoman was very helpful with this explaining, "Gifts are assessed on an invisible scale that ranges from refined to vulgar. If something is refined it is *halus*; and if vulgar it is *kasar*. Everything can be located on this scale. Everyday objects are assessed according to their capacity for transformation. So, it is quite *halus* to give someone money or gold as these can be used in a many of ways, giving someone cooked food is *kasar* as it has a single purpose."

On first explanation, this was most disconcerting, mainly because I realised just how vulgar some of my efforts at showing appreciation, like passing on second hand clothing, must have had been.

I remember thinking then that giving Ketut the pig must have been the right move. Even though it was an experiment it seems to have worked, the pig was thriving and soon she would sell if for a little profit.

Giving her the gold earrings was also a good move. It was common knowledge that giving a woman gold protected her asset in the patrilineal system. She could keep it and cash it in if she needed to. Cashing it was easy as every substantial market place had a gold merchant.

We often asked after the pig until one day Ketut said, "The pig's sick. Taking it to the vet is too expensive."

I was disappointed but consoled myself with the thought that if it died, we could simply buy another. Since it was the anniversary of the Pura Dalem, Ketut's father invited me to the festival at the Shiva temple and with everyone involved, nothing more was said on the matter of the pig.

Walking over to the village, in response to her father's invitation, I was excited by the festive atmosphere.

The Pig and the Cockfight

"*Selamat pagi Bapak,*" I said good morning to her father as I entered the compound. *Bapak Ketut,* as I called him, had little English and not a great fluency in Indonesian either. Our conversations were usually a mix of Indonesian and Balinese

"*Bagaimana Bapak?*" I asked how he was.

Pulling me by the hand to a seat in the *bale sikepat*, the main pavilion, he beamed and said, "Fine! It's busy at the temple today! This is the climax!"

The last time I'd encountered Bapak Ketut in such a mood was at Galungan, when ancestor spirits return to celebrate with their families. Important events like these invariably lifted his mood. It was contagious.

"Let's go to the temple – there's a cockfight." He motioned for me to follow.

I told him I'd come along but all the while I was thinking if this was in Australia, I'd have profound reservations about such a request. There it was common practice. So, this was a halus gesture; there was a spiritual purpose and he wanted my companionship.

Understanding the setting for these events is the only way to begin making sense of them. The key is in the spiritual geography. One of the first explanations Nyoman had offered about his village concerned the doctrine of *Tri Angga*. He said, "Towards the mountain and the east is high or *utama*; the village itself is middle or *madya* then seaward and west are low or *nista*. We can relate this to a person's body, their head, trunk and legs. Everything in the village aligns with this spiritual geography. Family compounds have three main parts and there are three main temples within a village comprising three parts, the *Jeroan* or inner courtyard, the *Jaba Tengah*, middle courtyard, and the *Jaba* or outer courtyard. Once you understand this you can easily find your way in Bali. Everything can be traced back to this underlying principle."

Bapak and I walked into the Jaba of the Pura Dalem.

"This is a really big celebration. Very busy," he enthused.

There were ice cream and fairy floss stands, helium filled balloons, plastic toys and trinkets and stalls selling traditional Balinese food assembled around the vast courtyard. He told me that these traders visit every temple anniversary.

Looking around at all the buzz, I imagined a similar scene every 210 days when each of the 1400 major temples in Bali, held its anniversary. Lots of work for hawkers, I thought.

Cockfights were held outside, in the *Jaba* the profane outer courtyard of the temple, in this case it was a large open space outside the temple walls. To one side was a big permanent pavilion or *bale*. Stalls lined the remaning two sides and the cockfight took place in the middle where a ring of men shouted out the odds and called for bets. In the centre of the ring, the owners of the two cocks stroked and preened their birds, pulling their neck feathers, stirring them up before the contest began.

"You want to place a bet, Bapak?" I asked.

He told me that he didn't gamble anymore.

Clutching a 1,000 rupiah note, I edged into the tightening circle, instantly meeting another man's eyes, "I want to bet on the brown cock," I said.

He nodded and within 30 seconds, the brown cock's cruel shiny steel blade delivered a mortal thrust to his opponent. Reluctantly, I collected my 2,000 rupiah in winnings.

I don't like cockfights even though I find the human spectacle fascinating. These events are charged with subdued macho intensity that is seldom encountered elsewhere. Big money changes hands and when the cash runs out, the title deeds to land are often used to borrow more.

The Pig and the Cockfight

Ketut's uncle made a lot of money this way. I suspected that even Ketut's father had fallen victim since he was no longer able to gamble.

I wondered what my friends back in Australia would think about this. They'd find such violent blood sport entirely inappropriate for a religious event and I didn't think I could explain that in the Balinese world, blood must spill to appease earth bound demonic presences prior to devotions.

Events such as these reminded me how far I'd travelled outside my culture. Yet for me, blood was blood; a complex organic fluid with a myriad of physical properties. If only it were that simple here. In this unseen domain, blood retained the spiritual essence of the creature that spilled it and there, it's the essence of things that is important.

On that day many cocks shed their blood.

"Let's go and eat," Bapak motioned.

I followed him to a stall at the far end of the open space where a succulent and crisp pig carcass was being portioned out to customers. Bapak placed an order and we were handed plates of food piled high with rice, roast pig, crackling, *sambal* and *lawar*[11]. It looked delicious.

In a slight panic, not wishing to offend Bapak, I confronted a major problem, the *lawar*. White *lawar* is a fine nutritious food, but this was red and I knew what it meant: it was prepared with raw pig's blood.

My mind raced. I remembered the time I ate some at I Gusti Made Sumung's son's wedding thinking it was a brightly coloured vegetable dish tinted with tomatoes, but it had a metallic, salty taste. Even though they said it was raw duck's blood, I wasn't about to go down that path again. This was pig's blood and definitely beyond the pale. There are good reasons why Jews and Muslims don't eat pork: parasites like trichinosis are debilitating.

[11] A mixture of vegetables, coconut and meat mixed with herbs, spices and raw blood.

Pig physiology is also remarkably similar to ours and clean pork is sometimes difficult to find. On purely pragmatic grounds, I knew I had to be extremely cautious with this. I thought for a little longer.

"Don't you like pork, Russell?" Bapak asked.

I told him I did, but that the *lawar* was made with uncooked blood, which didn't concern Bapak so I strategised. I flicked the *lawar* away from my rice, and set up a quarantine line on my plate – some rapid border protection.

As I shifted the food on my plate, I pondered the unseen armies of parasites and bacteria marching from the raw blood across the surface of the rice into pristine territory and hated to think of them setting up camp and colonising my gut.

If I don't eat this, I thought to myself, it'll be profoundly offensive. This is major festival and Bapak's paying for it out of his meagre means. I have to eat what I can.

So I ate heartily, pushing away my concerns. The pork was delicious, the crackling was excellent, the sambal intensely hot. Placing the plate back on the counter I said, "Thanks, Bapak. Very delicious."

He asked me if I wanted more.

"No, thanks, Bapak," I replied.

As we left the stall, he confided, "The pork was delicious, wasn't it? That was the sick pig. We sold it."

Kanda Empat: The Four Siblings

Before the era of mobile phones, being woken early in Bali invariably meant something urgent had arisen. Early morning was the time to catch someone at home, a time to connect with people on all manner of important matters.

Somewhere outside, my name was called and I was propelled from sleep into alertness. First struggling with the mosquito net, I stumbled across the cool tiles, composing myself as I lifted the wooden latch and pushed open the door. Standing below in the garden were Bapak Ketut and his son-in-law, Nyoman.

Taking several steps onto the verandah, I offered a customary greeting, "Good morning, Bapak and Nyoman. How are you? Please come up."

"Fine," they answered and stepped onto the verandah.

"Please have a seat," I said, gesturing towards the comfortable chairs. "Coffee?"

"Already," Bapak said with his characteristic brevity.

They were sombre, conveying an impression that something important was on the agenda.

"Sorry, I've just woken up and would like some coffee," I explained. "Are you sure you don't want coffee?"

"If you are making coffee, we will have some," Nyoman said, without reference to Bapak.

Returning with a tray and three steaming glasses, I served my grave guests then settled into a chair knowing that if they had a problem I was likely part of the solution.

Finally, with Nyoman translating, Bapak spoke. "There is a problem with my new grand daughter."

"You mean now that Ketut's back from hospital?" I asked, remembering that a friend from the same village lost a newborn only a year before. Here, infant mortality was quite high.

"Yes. If I don't take action, it will cause many problems in the household," he said with certainty.

I was relieved. It's not a health problem but I knew with 66 people living in the household, small problems easily escalated. "How does this concern me?" I enquired.

Nyoman said something to Bapak in Balinese and then explained, "We must take my daughter's placenta to my family in Singaraja. You have transport so we need your help."

"Fine," I answered. "We could leave early tomorrow."

"We must go today," Nyoman urged.

I'd long since stopped asking lots of questions. With Balinese friends it was better to go with the flow. Adopting this approach meant that whatever had to be accomplished was done in a spirit of good cheer.

"Fine, then let's go," I said, with a smile.

Entering Ketut's compound, few people other than Ketut's immediate family and a *pemangku* (village priest) were visible. The *pemangku* sat passive on the verandah of one family room. Below him, a small hole had been dug into the earth and a woven pandanus leaf mat placed beside it. Ketut stood nearby holding her newborn, a grave look on her face. Catching sight of me, she said. "*Selamt pagi,* Russell. We must take my child's placenta to Nyoman's compound."

"Yes. I'm ready, Ketut," I said in an assuring a tone.

Her tense expression softened.

Back in Sydney, this request would be considered eccentric. Here in Bali, it made sense. In that moment, many conversations with Bali experts came to mind.

"Balinese Hinduism is a syncretic blend of ancestor worship and the more recent Hindu notion of Samsara," I recalled Vincent saying.

"I was told that reincarnation is understood as occurring within families," I replied.

"Yes," he affirmed. "Purified ancestor spirits wait their turn for rebirth in each new generation. So Balinese Hindu families are a complex of the corporal and the incorporeal."

"So would you say that keeping harmonious relations within a family involves maintaining healthy and respectful relations with ancestor spirits as well?"

"Yes! It is an obligation for each individual and every family and of course every 210 days, at Galungan, ancestor spirits and deities come to earth and take up residence in family temples."

"An exciting time, Galungan. It's amazing how villages are transformed not just in the most obvious ways with *penyor* (woven palm leaf decorations mounted on tall bamboo poles) lining streets and towering over family compounds, but with a huge infusion of cordiality. Everyone's mood is elevated."

"Yes," said Vincent, "and all that ephemeral art; the *janur*, the fine woven and plaited coconut leaves hanging from the *penyor* bridges between the seen and unseen worlds intrigues me."

More relaxed now, Ketut gently ushered me to sit beside the *pemangku*, saying, "Please sit here, Russell."

Here we're dealing with another aspect of the unseen I mused, recalling a conversation with I Gusti that arose after a visit to Puri Saren Agung. I asked him: "I noticed some stones beside a *bale* (pavilion) in Puri Saren Agung. Each stone had the name of a family member engraved on a small metal plate. What do these mean, I Gusti?"

"Each individual is connected with unseen elements of themselves," he explained in his generous manner.

"Not only do they have a soul or *atma*, but each person has a relationship with four brothers, the *Kanda Empat*. Understanding this is easy if you have seen a human birth."

"I have, I Gusti, both my sons. You say brothers but I think in English we might say siblings."

"Yes, then you know about the four elements that accompany the child?"

"Well, the placenta is obvious. So what are the other three? Let me think, there's blood and amniotic fluid and I guess the fourth must be the vernix.

"Correct, here in Bali the placenta is buried in a special place at the child's house. The other three don't need as much attention."

"Does a person have any special obligations to their four siblings?"

"They do. It is most important that they ask permission if they leave the village to live somewhere else."

Leaving the verandah, the *pemangku* assumed a lotus position on the woven pandanus mat and began chanting, casually waving a bunch of freshly cut aloe vera fronds over the hole. Leaning forward, he lifted a white calico bundle out of the hole and handed it to Ketut who placed it inside a woven cane basket. Then he placed the aloe inside the hole, carefully scraping earth back into place to conclude the ceremony.

Catching the *pemangku*'s eye as he stood, I asked him respectfully why he placed the leaves in the hole.

In basic Indonesian he replied, "Because take must give."

I understood: something was taken from the earth, something must be returned.

Ketut was already making for the compound entrance so without further conversation, Bapak Ketut, his wife, Ketut, Nyoman and I piled into my mini-van. It was early, well before the daily onslaught of tourist coaches made their way up into the mountains, so I chose a route via Goa Gaja and Tampaksiring, along the edge of the Batur Caldera past Kintimani and Puncak Penulisan to the north coast.

The next ceremony was over in a few moments and after coffee and snacks, we headed back via a more westerly route through the coffee and clove gardens of Pujung to avoid the tourist traffic that had followed us up into the mountains. The drive back was more arduous but a scented delight as we passed through coffee trees in full blossom and the bouquet of cloves drying on mats beside the road.

Several months elapsed before I asked Ketut whether her daughter now living in a village far from her placenta was at a spiritual disadvantage. "Was the problem with the placenta because you are living in your father's compound and not your husband's?"

"Usually wives go to live in their husband's village but we have permission from the village for Nyoman to live here," she replied, not directly answering my question.

"I understand that but what about living in your father's compound? Did someone in the compound object?"

"You remember I told you my uncle tricked my father?"

"Yes, I do remember. You said he wanted to borrow your father's land title to raise money."

She nodded.

"Why doesn't your father just ask for it back?" I pressed, again in a direct manner.

"Father would like to have peace, so he will not ask," she explained with a look of dismay. Ketut's capacity to demand justice and fair play reminded me of an instance when she was travelling with Matina during the period of Suharto's New Order regime, a time when police corruption peaked. She had fearlessly argued with police who had stopped their car for no reason other than to demand cigarette money.

"Is your uncle frightened of you?" I asked.

"He is always frightened."

"So he sees you as a threat and thinks that you might find a way to claim the land when your father eventually dies. Is that it?"

"Maybe, but I also know much about him and his tricky ways."

This was beginning to make sense. Not only had she boldly brought her husband into the compound where power and inheritance were patrilineally apportioned, but she probably had the goods on uncle. Knowing so much about him and being such a resolute, and fair-minded woman must have been deeply threatening for him and the prospect of a consolidating a spiritual presence on his patch alarming.

"Ketut, I have just one remaining question. Doesn't separating your daughter from her *Kanda Empat* weaken her spiritual safety?"

"No problem," she answered. "I've dealt with that."

She never did tell me how.

A Day of Departures

Australian Foreign Minister Gareth Evans marked his term of office with a sincere attempt to transform Australia's relationship with its largest neighbour, Indonesia. Commenting on that relationship he said, "No two neighbours anywhere in the world are as comprehensively unalike as Australia and Indonesia. We differ in language, culture, religion, history, ethnicity, population size, and in political, legal and social systems."[12]

Aligned with his attempts, the Australia Indonesia Institute (AII) invited expressions of interest for the production of a social geography and history of Australia, one that could be used by Indonesia secondary students. To be written in Indonesian, it was to emphasise bilateral links and the advantages of cooperation.

Asian Field Study Centres[13] (AFSC) won the tender for the project. Competition was tough with Oxford University Press and two Australian universities. AFSC was set to hold initial first meetings with the Australian Cultural Counsellor and the Indonesian Department of Education and Culture (DEPDIKBUD), in Jakarta on 2 October 1994.

Matina and I decided to travel down from Ubud, stay over night in Kuta and take an early flight to Jakarta. All that remained was to call our driver, Agung Raka, and tell him we were ready to leave..

---

[12] Evans, G. and Grant, B. *Australia's foreign relations in the world of the 1990s*. Melbourne University Press. 1991. pp.184-185.

[13] Asian Field Study Centres Pty Ltd was established in 1984. Initially its mission was to provide interdisciplinary field study programs for Australian students visiting Indonesia. Its role gradually broadened to include consultancy services. The Directors at that time were Russell Darnley and Matina Pentes.

Before I could ring Raka, our phone rang. Answering and half expecting to hear his voice, I was surprised to hear my sister Meg. "Hi, Russell. I've some news and it's not that good. Mum has refused any more dialysis and she has fallen into a coma."

I had known this was coming, and knew the impossibility of returning at such short notice. The meeting in Jakarta had taken months to arrange but Mum was dying.

"My goodness, in a coma and off dialysis. What can I say? I can't get back right now." I felt a lump forming in my throat.

"I know you can't," she replied lovingly. "You need to know that she won't be with us for much longer. If there was any way…" she choked on her words.

A feeling powerlessness enveloped me. How could this be, right now?

"Ask her if she's with your mother," Matina prompted.

"Meg, are you with Mum in the hospital?"

"No, I'm at home now."

"Please let me know if anything happens. We're staying overnight in Kuta and flying to Jakarta early tomorrow. I'll ring you again as soon as I can."

Replacing the handset, I stood in silence. The medical registrar I first spoke with was right about Mum's prognosis. He had said about three months and it was almost to the day. "What do you want to do?" Matina asked.

"I feel powerless. If I go back, chances are she'll have gone by the time I get there."

"You can always ring her," she suggested.

"Ring?"

"Yes, she's lapsed into a coma, not a drug-induced one by the sound of it. She'll be able to hear you. Why don't you ring Margaret and have her go back to the hospital so you can speak to your mother?"

After ringing Meg I went and sat on the front veranda. A farmer was hoeing a recently harvested rice crop. Ducks were grazing over a flooded area. A Javan kingfisher with iridescent blue wings sat in a tree by the compound.

Not much for you today, I thought. Time passed. I pictured Mum lying alone in her hospital bed. The image was clear. I'd visited only two weeks before. Of course, Dad would be there. At least she's not entirely alone. More time passed.

"Russell," Matina called, "I'm on the phone. Margaret is back with your mother."

I felt a rush of adrenalin as I took the phone from Matina.

Meg's voice spoke first: "I'm back with Mum and I'm going to put the receiver to her ear."

"Thanks."

I could hear Mum's deep, irregular breathing.

"Mum, this is Russell," I said, struggling to keep my voice clear.

She responded almost instantly, "Yes… son." Her voice was remote. I could feel her struggling back from another realm, stopping momentarily on a journey that had already begun.

"Mum. I can't be with you in person. My body can't be there with you to hold you." I was surprised how clearly my words flowed. I knew I had to make every moment count. "But I'm here in the room… with you… in spirit. I'm holding your hand."

"Yes… I… feel you."

Every word was a strain for her. Tears flowed, yet I felt entirely lucid not even needing to think about what I was saying. "I'm going to stay with you in spirit. I won't leave."

"I… know… thank you."

"I love you, Mum."

"Love… you… Son."

Mum was struggling to answer but completely aware of my presence. The strength she needed to summon the words must be exhausting her, I thought, best I let her rest now.

"I must hang up now, Mum, but I'm staying there with you."

"Yes."

My sister gathered the phone. "She heard you, Russell."

"This is the last time I'll ever hear her voice. Please kiss her for me." With that, I burst into tears, not just tears of sadness but tears of joy that I could be with my mother even from this great distance.

When I'd gathered myself a little, I said, "Thanks, Matina. I'll be forever grateful to you."

My thoughts stayed with my mother. I felt the strength of her love for me, a love so strong that she would interrupt a journey already begun to be with me.

I recall little of the drive to Kuta, a night in the hotel and the early morning transfer to Ngurah Rai Airport.

Sitting in the terminal, I drifted through the layers of sound that inhabit such places, largely shapeless noise punctuated by flight announcements. Unexpectedly, out of the soundscape a voice called: "Russell!" It was Mum's voice. Not the one burdened by slowly ebbing physical strength but a clear energised voice freed of earthly worries. I knew what this meant. While I cried for my loss, I was grateful that she'd given me this last great gift, a reassurance that beyond physical existence there was consciousness and a capacity to reach out and communicate with the embodied tangible world.

Kampanye – The Campaign Procession

Returning to Indonesia in October 1999 after the nationwide violence accompanying Suharto's fall was a daunting prospect. Reason suggested that a new era of stability was emerging but certainty was elusive. In Australia, both mainstream media and government were emphasising the instability inherent post New Order. Despite years of travel throughout Indonesia, long periods staying in Bali and the countless conversations at all levels of society, I wasn't immune to the fear and polarisation that was already a mark of the Howard era. I was seduced by the constant criticism and worried by megaphone diplomacy, unsure just how we'd be received.

Paul Arbon and I were about to conduct a series of teacher workshops that were the culmination of four years' work. Weeks prior to departure had been spent preparing the content for plenaries and small groups then working on translations with Rochayah Machali at the University of New South Wales. Now completed, it was time to work them through with Paul. Though functionally fluent, my Indonesian was not strong enough to carry an entire staff development conference alone and Paul was an excellent linguist with a comprehensive knowledge of Indonesia.

Boarding the plane in Sydney presented an immediate reminder that this was the low season. "This flight's full of Bali bargain hunters, Paul."

"Off for the cheap five star experience at Nusa Dua, eh?"

"Yeah, there and Kuta. Time, tide and political upheaval hasn't dampened the quest for a holiday bargain. Looks like business as usual."

Touching down at Bali's Ngurah Rai Airport confirmed first impressions. Budget tourists many already sporting Kuta chic holiday clothes flowed through the airport precinct.

Things were not quite as my direst of imaginings foreshadowed and in those I wasn't alone, even friends with sound political antennae had reservations. I recalled a conversation with Steve Storey, an old friend who dropped in a few days before I left: "You're taking a chance going to Indonesia in this climate. Things are by no means stable, particularly with the election campaign in full swing. You don't know when the slightest disruption might develop into a flair-up. You could easily become a target." He was worried and understandably so.

"I appreciate this," I replied, "but I've learned a few things about survival in Indonesia. A lot of the fear and apprehension in Australia is a direct result of the Howard government reorienting foreign policy settings away from what they see as the pro-Asian leanings of the Hawke and Keating era."

Despite the emergence of Bali as a budget tourist destination, many Australians across the political spectrum, from the xenophobic right to the internationalist left, held reservations about Indonesia. Howard played on this and his politics fell on fertile ground. The Howard doctrine amplified such uncertainties refracting regional affairs through a neo-colonial lens and attempting to tip the balance of perceptions. Reality also became more difficult to discern when filtered through Australia's concentrated and biased mainstream media.

"Why d'you have to go anyway? You've done all the work," Steve said.

"It doesn't work that way."

"Can't you just send the book and stay here? They can take care of it over there, surely."

"I can't hand over a pioneering book like this to strangers who don't know it and expect them to run meaningful workshops. It's taken four years to bring it to this stage. There…"

"And the security situation's changed," he interrupted.

"Yeah, it has but there've been all sorts of delicate bilateral negotiations. We've seen it through the fall of the New Order regime plus three Indonesian Ministers for Education and a change of government in Australia. No, I must be there."

"Well, just take care, Russ."

I couldn't blame Steve for his reaction. He was concerned, not obstructive. It didn't help that travel warnings still applied but suggesting these were about the government limiting its liability seemed to carry little credibility even amongst friends with a normally healthy scepticism about government claims. Still I wasn't going to miss the opportunity to launch the book *Geografi Australia* with workshops in Surabaya, Semarang and Palembang, particularly with the New Order regime at an end. It was an exciting prospect an opportunity for a political pulse check. Paul was of a similar mind.

Clearing arrivals in Surabaya's Juanda Airport, Paul and I were met by a driver from Grasindo, the Indonesian publishers of *Geografi Australia*. He welcomed us to Surabaya with "*Selamat datang di Surabaya,* Mr Russell and Mr Paul. How was your flight?"

"*Baik!*" we answered that it was fine.

"We will take you straight to our hotel," the driver explained. "We don't have time to look at the venue for the *lokakarya*, I mean, workshop."

"Oh," I said, "then we will need to get there early tomorrow so we can set up before all the teachers arrive."

"Of course."

Aboard our mini-bus, our driver was the consummate tour guide as we drove on into the city. Paul and I were in a state of alertness, scanning the city for any hint of the political drama that was unfolding and maintaining our own quiet dialogue, attuned to the growing signs of *Reformasi* while politely responding to the driver's commentary.

"Amazing. These streets are just avenues of flags," Paul said beaming with an excited smile.

"Mainly red, red and more red. Wow! Megawati's party has been active."

"Ah! There's a splash of green. So the old *PPP* still has numbers on the ground."

"Haven't seen any Golkar yellow yet. This is such a contrast with the 1997 elections Paul. Yellow was everywhere back then. Golkar said beforehand they'd get at least 70% of the vote."

"You mean Suharto's Festival of Democracy?"

"What an extravaganza that was," I said. "I was here for the lead-up but not on the day."

"Look at that!" said Paul, excited to see a huge billboard displaying the symbols of the 48 contending parties slide by. "That's great. I wonder if there's a poster available?"

Teachers are compulsive collectors of resources. We were yet to realise it was actually a facsimile of the ballot paper.

Settled in my hotel room, I began to wonder whether without the flags, bunting and billboards, anyone would know there was an election campaign in progress. The answer to this question came as soon as I turned on the television. All channels were in full election coverage. Most carried panel discussions comprising no more than three keynote speakers delivering statements on their party's platform and responding to questions from the audience. There was no great clash of philosophies and little presentation of firm policy. Audiences were balanced between supporters of each of the three speakers. The parties participating were also chosen so that they didn't represent opposite ends of the political spectrum so there were no major polemical clashes.

Night passed without incident.

Opening my curtains in a city etched against the sunrise, I was struck by a huge banner for PAN, the National Mandate Party. Draped from 18th to the 6th floors of a partly completed city office block, the banner was coupled with a strident statement and supported by the most fundamental expression of the monetary crisis: a stalled building site.

In the foreground, an orderly *kampung* extended right up to the forecourt of the hotel, eight floors below. People stirred, women hung out washing, *Pedagang kaki lima* prepared their wares and corn merchants stripped leaves from fresh cobs that would soon be served steaming hot from street stalls. Pigeon coops stood prominently above the *kampung*, reflecting the architectural creativity of their owners. Above all, large red PDI-P flags fluttered in the steady monsoon wind with no sign of Golkar, and precious little of *PPP*, the former Muslim umbrella party.

Arriving early at the workshop venue, Paul and I found Gregson Edwards, Australian Cultural Counsellor already there. "Good morning, gentleman," he said effusively.

"Good morning, Gregson." I extended my hand. "Glad to finally meet you."

Gregson greeted the others in an equally enthusiastic manner as I gazed around the vast dimly lit auditorium. Tables were set out on a grid system each designed to sit eight to ten people and so dispersed that casual contact between participants would be difficult beyond these small clusters. A lectern stood on a platform at the front. To the side at room level was an overhead projector so positioned it was impossible to operate from the lectern. Some seating was so far away from the overhead projector that reading text or decoding diagrams was not an option. This room was this structured to project and reinforce the authority of officials, one-way transmission of information.

"Just as well the text on the overhead transparencies is embedded in the spoken material Paul," I said despondently.

"Just as well," he replied obviously aware of the same challenges I saw.

"Any idea who set up the room, Gregson?" I asked.

"That would be the DEPDIKBUD, not Grasindo. We just asked them to provide a space."

In those days, the Department of Education and Culture, known by the acronym DEPDIKBUD, controlled all levels of Indonesian education, particularly the curriculum. While there is an ancient tradition of participation and discourse at the village level in Indonesia, it hadn't been reflected in the configuration of this vast space.

"Mmm, I thought this was going to be a workshop but the way the room's set up, it's talking heads only. How's the sound system?"

"We can try it now," answered Gregson.

"Paul, since you're doing most of the talking, you want to have a go?"

"Sure thing." He made his way down the long centre aisle to the lectern.

As he walked down the aisle, I struggled with the task reminding myself that our objective wasn't simply to promote the book but also engage teachers in a pedagogical discourse around possible uses. This room was working against us.

Paul reached the microphone, lifting it out of its cradle and switching it on.

"Test… test… test… We could do this Oprah Winfrey style and move around the room."

"I think that's the way to go," I shouted down the aisle. "Each of these tables will have to become a syndicate group for the workshops."

Turning to Gregson, I asked, "Would you be prepared to help with the workshop activities later in the day?"

"Sure!" he answered without hesitation.

"It's easy; everything is on printed sheets and we can explain it using the microphone."

Just then an attendant joined our group. Without introduction he announced that there were two more radio microphones: "*Ada dua mikropon radio lagi.*"

"That makes life easy if the batteries are charged," I said. "Paul you're closest, would you switch it on the overhead projector please."

Paul walked over to the overhead projector. A dusty patch of light soon shone onto the screen behind.

"There's not enough time to clean the lens so we'll just have to go with it," I said wondering why I'd even bothered to make 30 or so coloured overhead transparencies.

"*Saya akan bersihkan proyektornya.*" The attendant volunteered to clean the projector with a smile and I thanked him.

Despite all the up front speeches from officials dragging on through a hierarchy of set piece performances, the rest of the day ran well thanks to the proactive efforts of our small team. Paul and I had to wing our way through the now severely compressed timeframe, pencilling out passages and hastily summarising others. Our teacher hosts were delighted to have an opportunity to meet, confer and engage with Australian educationalists. My only real difficulty was the East Javanese accent.

After our short stay in Surabaya, we embarked on a train trip along the north coast to Semarang. Rocked by the train, my last rail trip through Java in the El Nino year of 1997 drifted into mind. Harshness was over the land the earth cracking, rice crops failing and farmers digging cassava roots, their emergency food supplies. Amidst the intensifying drought, President Suharto announced the floating of the rupiah, which plummeted into a rapid free fall. Inflation hit levels not experienced since 1965, another El Nino year and a time when President Soekarno vainly encouraged Indonesian farmers to seek self-sufficiency in rice production. Within months, economic and political turmoil saw his downfall and Suharto's rise amidst mass violence. Now the cycle was repeated and by May 1998, Suharto had fallen.

In Semarang, we stepped out of our hotel into the midst of the rally staged by Megawati's Democratic Party of Struggle (PDI-P).

"This is overwhelming!" I shouted above the din uncertain whether Paul could hear me. "I've never heard so many motor bikes being revved in unison before!"

"They're all so young – mostly under 25," Paul replied.

Motorbike engines revving rhythmically, with the heat, fumes and pulsing surges of energy, had an emotional impact like listening to very loud music. Many of the motorbikes had pillion passengers, young men daubed with red and black face paint, swaying trance like in the energy charged atmosphere.

Trucks packed with teams of painted youthful supporters and the occasional car had also joined the parade. In the distance, brightly dressed pedestrians also followed this noisy motorised vanguard.

Numbers of our hotel's staff were already out on the street holding placards aloft then suddenly a phalanx of PDI-P rally marshals, dressed in black paramilitary garb with red insignia, emerged from our hotel's basement car park.

Paul shouted: "I had no idea we were about to step right into the middle of this campaign rally!"

"Me neither! So whether we like it or not, we were in it. It's emotional but there's not the slightest sense of threat!"

How could one possibly explain this to friends back home, worried by the threats they imagined we might face in this transformation, much less the Howard minions who bought it all and ran on fear.

People wanted their photos taken and gestured OK to us with PDI-P salutes. Being *bule* (white people), we stood out as there were no other foreigners there.

Overwhelming, energetic, optimistic and partisan, this was a massive release of emotion: a gestalt, an historical adjustment manifesting around us. Energies suppressed throughout the New Order era now burst to the surface in a convulsive correction.

Here was the process of *Reformasi* in action, perhaps even the birth of democracy; there was such hope. It was friendly and engaging. There was openness, a preparedness to step forward, to take a chance. While there was something strong and potent there was something incredibly innocent as well.

I remembered the words of my friend Henky whom I rang every night through the terror of 1998.

"Henky, how are things today?" I'd ask.

"Fine," he would answer. "There's no problem here. It's peaceful."

I started to get embarrassed; worried that he might think I was unduly neurotic about his safety. Then finally one evening I rang and everything had changed.

"Henky, how are things today?"

"Destruction," he replied. "Total destruction."

I wished Henky could see this unfolding. The next best thing was to ring him but surrounded by this wall of sound, it wasn't an option.

Tears welled, tears of empathy with Henky, with these young people with their struggle, tears of grief for those who had suffered and tears of optimism. They were the product of months of feeling restrained and impotent, of late night telephone calls to friends like Henky who stood by as provocateurs terrorised their neighbourhoods, burning their shops and businesses, of horrifying reports of the systematic rape and brutalising of Chinese women.

My Indonesian friends had much to contend with as they confronted the cynical and increasingly desperate struggle of the failing New Order regime. I felt released; I had an urge to jump up onto one of the tabletop trucks amongst the youth and shout my support for the struggle but I was constrained. It was enough to bear witness.

Somehow through this I lost sight of Paul though we'd barely moved since emerging from our hotel. I then caught sight of him chatting with bystanders several metres away as the campaign procession entered Semarang's central square, the Lapangan Pancasila.

"Russell!" Paul called.

We edged towards one another.

"Let's see if we can find a place where we can get a view of the whole event," he suggested. "Over there," he pointed. "I think there might be a hotel with a terrace overlooking the Lapangan."

"Good idea. With any luck it'll serve good coffee as well."

Skirting around the edge of the crowd, we made our way towards the hotel, set between the square and a shopping mall. Once inside, everything seemed detached

Kampanye – The Campaign Procession

from the rally. There were even a few other foreigners and behind the hotel in the retail area it was business as usual. There was a bustling trade in mobile telephones, CDs, clothing, foodstuffs and household effects. No sign of a monetary crisis here.

While waiting for our coffee, I wandered over to the edge of the terrace. With overwhelming street level sounds muted, I rang Henky. He answered promptly. "Russell, where are you?" he asked, without any formality.

"In Semarang. I'm watching a PDI-P campaign rally."

"Big?" he asked.

"Big, and lots of young people."

"Good, Russell. When are you coming to Jakarta?"

"Next week. Just before the election."

"There is a PDI-P campaign rally next week. I'm going." Then he added, "Until next week then. Maybe you can join in."

"Maybe. Okay, bye, Henky. It's very noisy here."

"Bye."

Paul was reading a copy of *Jawa Pos* when I rejoined him. He looked up.

"Russ, I'd like to find an Internet connection to check my emails. The waiter tells me the *Telkom* office has connections."

Neat plantings of street trees and imposing New Order government offices marked the administrative area. Away from the rally, all was quiet.

Turning a corner, we happened on a large contingent of riot police. Quite relaxed characters, they weren't taking an interest in the rally and were only too happy to welcome us as a convenient distraction and confirmed the location of the Telkom office. They seemed interested in us out of sheer curiosity. It was then we realised there was a distinct likelihood they thought we were international election monitors after all what else would *bule* be doing here on such a day?

Pemilihan Umum – The General Election

Several Kampanye, grand processions of the faithful, were planned for the first week of June 1999, the final week of general election campaign. Optimism and exuberance were pervasive, even eclipsing tangible political agendas. Exercising the right of political expression en mass on the streets in huge manifestations was an end in itself, yet touches of the old remained with separate days reserved for the different party rallies. Speeding along Jakarta's airport toll road, Paul and I knew what to expect after our earlier encounter with a PDI-P Kampanye in Semarang. Anticipating major traffic disruptions for the Muslim parties rally involving PKB[14], PAN and PPB[15] and PPP[16], we reasoned that our early arrival from Palembang might just allow us to sneak into Central Jakarta before the action began.

Chatting with the driver, one thing was clear: his rejection of the New Order Regime. Whizzing past the national parliament buildings, he taught us a little ditty popularised by the students the previous year:

> Bang-bang tut
> Acar gulang-galing
> Bambang, Tommy, Tutut
> Bapaknya raja maling

---

[14] Partai Kebangkitan Bangsa (The National Awakening Party) Leader – Abdurrahman Wahid.
[15] Partai Bintang Bulan (The Crescent Moon and Star Party) Leader – Yusril Ihza Mahendra.
[16] Partai Persatuan Pembanganan (The United Development Party) Leader – Hamzah Haz

It can't all be translated, but the last two lines address Suharto's children, Bambang, Tommy and Tutut, reminding them that their 'father is the king of thieves'.

After the tollway at Semanggi, we dropped down onto Jalan Sudirman and, swamped by a tide of young campaigners, our smooth passage came to an abrupt halt.

"This is too good to miss," Paul enthused.

"Everyone seems happy," I said. "It doesn't feel threatening."

"There's a mass of election material out there," Paul exclaimed as he wound down the taxi windows.

Our driver flinched. Undeterred, I did the same thing waving at the young people who flooded around us. Within minutes, we sat amongst a virtual avalanche of election pamphlets and posters. As fast as Paul could load them into his bag, more popped through the window sliding off our laps and littering the floor.

"Your classes will love this Paul," I chuckled.

"Sure will. It doesn't get any more current than this."

Kampanye in Jakarta converged at the roundabout on Jalan Thamrin, in front of Hotel Indonesia. Here floats and mobile stages narrowed the way and motorbikes drew into every available space, wedging the slow moving traffic to a standstill.

"Do you hear that?" asked Paul. "Someone's calling out the names of lost children over a PA system."

"A bit of a contrast with the story being pushed back home, eh?"

After a short pause, the familiar Al-Zuhr burst out over the loud speakers focusing attention, the noise and bustle abated. At the closing of prayers, someone called for God's help in bringing about a safe, orderly and honest election then asked people to clean up the area. This was not the chaos projected in the Australian media.

A pity it is unseen back home, I thought.

Amidst the mounting noise of motorbikes, cars and thousands of conversations, crowds began moving forward. Finally the bottleneck broke and we resumed our journey.

"Paul, after we've checked in, do you want to visit Glodok and West Jakarta?" I asked as our taxi was pulling into the Sabang Metropolitan.

"You reckon it's been patched up after the terror squads hit it last year?"

"I don't know. I've only seen television coverage but I'd like to get a sense of the scale of the carnage."

"Let's check in and meet in the lobby."

During the racially inspired violence of May 1998, it was Glodok, Kota and West Jakarta with their large Chinese populations that sustained most damage.

Later as we drove down Jalan Gajah Mada, I looked for one of my favourite shopping places, the old Pasar Glodok. Passing Jalan Pancoran, it was nowhere to be seen. "That's so weird. I used to shop in the old market here. I can't see it. It was a great place for T-shirts, sarongs and that sort of stuff."

"Are you sure you've got the right place?" Paul asked.

"I remember this area distinctly. Jalan Pancoran runs down to a canal. I've often walked around here. Down the end of the road in the 80s, there were people living in packing case houses cantilevered over the water. It was a very poor area. It's stuck in my mind."

"Maybe you should come back on foot and poke around."

"I will, for sure."

We moved on towards Kota and the railway station. All seemed much as before here but further on, we entered an area where buildings had either been razed or burnt out with those still standing revealing facades scorched by fire and peppered with marks from fusillades of stones. An eerie experience, it suggested a type of Jakartan Kristallnacht. A part of Jakarta I once knew so well had disappeared.

The next day, Paul left for Central Java while I settled into a sumptuous borrowed apartment at Puri Casablanca off Jalan Rasuna Said, not far from the Australian Embassy. For the first time ever, I had my own space in Jakarta. On one side, I looked out over the *TPU Menteng Pulo* cemetery on the other was a small *kampung* (village) and a school.

The phone rang. It was Henky. He asked "Do you want to go to Glodok with Dachlan?" He wasn't long and, within the hour, we were browsing around the street markets in the Glodok.

"Dachlan, do you remember the old multi-storey Glodok market? I couldn't find it when I took a taxi through here two days ago."

"It's gone," Dachlan answered. "It was badly damaged by fire in the riots and the remains were demolished."

"Okay. That explains it."

"They'll probably build a new market. There are more in the area. There's one on Hayam Wuruk. I must go there now to buy some lights for the Bogor project."

The three of us crossed over the road into the Glodok Plaza area. Teaming with people, despite the looting and the damage, it was a testament to the remarkable optimism, courage and resilience of Jakarta's Chinese community.

Making our way up to the second floor, we sat perched high on stools as Dachlan selected fluorescent lights. Suddenly there was shouting and the sound of roller doors slamming shut.

"What's going on?" I asked, surprised by a swift change in energy.

Seen and Unseen

"There's a disturbance," Henky said

That much was obvious: the noise of the shutters alone was disturbing but I took his meaning. He meant there was some sort of political disturbance.

Moments later, Dachlan handed over the cash and, with shouts reverberating from the street, the trader locked the till and shut the shop.

Nearby a woman was crying, trembling with fear. Like the effect of touching a vibrant sea anemone, one moment radiating brilliant colours the next an almost invisible bump on the side of the rock pool so this disturbance transformed a vibrant market place. Now, only walls of metal doors remained.

Walking back to our car through this shuttered space, no one spoke. Evening television news showed the extent of the disturbance. There was some rowdiness in a square about eight kilometres from Glodok. A motorbike was in flames. The next day, the mainstream print media had an appropriately low angle shot with flames from the motorbike's fuel tank licking higher than the nearby shops and government buildings.

Thursday, 3 June was the final PDI-P campaign rally. Henky and Dachlan called at the apartment. They wanted to drive out to Megawati's house in south Jakarta and follow the *kampanye* into the city.

"You're coming with us aren't you, Russell?" asked Dachlan, as if my answer was a forgone conclusion.

"I'd like to come but I have a problem."

"What problem?"

"Well, I'm here on official Australian Government business so I shouldn't be involved in Indonesian politics."

I felt really bad saying this. They had come to collect me but it was true. I wanted to go but I realised that it was inappropriate. Then on the other hand, if it was anything

Pemilihan Umum – The General Election

like the kampanye earlier in the week it was more like a big carnival on the streets.

"Just stay in the car," Henky suggested.

"Okay. But I want to see the spectacle. I know this is going to be the biggest political demonstration I've ever seen."

"Fine, then!" said Henky.

At that, we piled into Henky's car and set out.

An extremely orderly and enthusiastic crowd had gathered outside Mega's house. Shortly before we arrived, she left by helicopter for a rally at the old Kemayoran airport site in Central Jakarta but hundreds of her supporters remained on the large green in front of her home.

Discretion was impossible; climbing out and walking around amongst the crowd was the only option. None were expecting a *bule* outsider such as myself so there were countless questions and lots of *basa basi* (polite conversation). Conviviality reigned. No one talked politics, there was no need as such was the confidence of this partisan crowd it was as if Mega had already been declared President.

Soon we piled back into the car and the *kampanye* began. As it moved towards Jalan Sudirman, masses of people entered from side streets merging with the growing procession of red flag bedecked buses, bajai, becak, bemo, table top trucks, golf buggies, cars and thousands upon thousands of motor bikes conveying a river of red shirted supporters. Into a canyon of towering late New Order office towers, the *kampanye* rolled on through a blue haze of exhaust fumes searing noses and throats, burning eyes and blurring views of postmodern summits.

Many participants carried handphones and for those without the capital to participate in electronic reportage, there was always the illusion. Numerous teams of young people created their own video cameras and microphones from cardboard, aluminium cans and almost any available material in a unifying affirmation that the whole world was really watching.

This was a fusion reminiscent of a Vietnam Moratorium, Melbourne's Moomba Festival and with sufficient drag to contain elements of Sydney's Gay Mardi Gras. It was street theatre at its best but then Indonesia has a long and theatrical history and on this day there was willingness, perhaps a compulsion, to participate in the drama. Many hundreds of thousands now massed along the main artery of Sudirman.

"Wow! This is extraordinary," I exclaimed. "I've never seen a manifestation as big as this!"

"Too slow to drive any further," Henky observed. "We'll have to go on foot."

"I wanted to avoid that," I replied.

"It can't be avoided," Henky said. "We can park under the UNICEF building."

He was right. Driving became a futile exercise so we left our car and walked the last three kilometres to Hotel Indonesia. I was the only *bule*, yet no one cared as the streets were now a vast performance space.

Election Day dawned. From my borrowed apartment, I watched the first signs of voting in the *kampung* below. All was orderly. I grabbed my camera hailed a taxi and made for Kebon Serih, a *kampung* in the city centre, wedged between Jalan Thamrin, the National Monument and Menteng where Suharto and his family resided. Here all was well underway by the time I arrived. People were proud of their first democratic election since the 1950s and I mingled with voters and chatted with poll officials. There was a mood of subdued euphoria and pride in what they'd achieved.

Pemilihan Umum – The General Election

I thought I'd check out the rest of the area so I headed for an Internet café on Jalan Wahid Hasyim. Cutting through Jalan Jaksa, I was surprised to see its restaurants and bars bursting with foreign clients, an unusual event for 10.30 in the morning.

Catching site of a paperboy, I bought a copy of *Kompas*. Knowing that small boys selling papers on street corners are always full of the latest informal street chatter, I asked, "Why are there so many foreigners here?"

"They're foreign journalists," he answered.

This was a most unexpected reply. I'd always imagined that facing such an important event the fourth estate would be hard at work, in a country so long deprived of democracy and press freedom.

"Strange! Although there's a General Election they're just sitting around here."

He didn't reply.

I asked how long they had been there.

"A lot of them arrived two days ago," he replied.

When I asked what they'd been doing, he said, "They've just been eating and drinking beer."

Mildly shocked to think that foreign journalists could be just sitting, eating and drinking while this remarkable event transpired, I was interested to see how the foreign press described the progress of the election.

In the end, I pieced together the story of the day. Polling booths opened on time. People went about exercising their democratic choice. All passed with little apparent trouble. Voting was impossible in three districts in Aceh; some polling booths were found to be short of ballot forms; some were unable to mark voters with indelible ink when ink supplies failed to arrive; and, in some parts of Eastern Indonesia, there were no seals for ballot boxes. In two instances, angry voters burned ballot boxes and

Seen and Unseen

problems of voter intimidation characterised the vote in Timor.

The count was painfully slow. Political commentators offered various post election scenarios ranging from a clear majority to Megawati's Partai Demokrasi Indonesia – Perjuangan (PDI-P) to military intervention. Unseen and unanticipated by many was the political skill of Abdurrahman Wahid, Gus Dur, who crafted together sufficient support to assume the presidency.[17]

---

[17] Gus Dur was elected President by the Majelis Perwikilan Rakyat (MPR), becoming Indonesia's fourth President with 373 votes to Megawati's 313 votes.

Unspoken Realities

Jacob sat back, gazing out over that upper reach of Sydney Harbour known as the Paramatta River. A massive golden fleece of clouds adorned the western sky. We both enjoyed the spectacle at this time of the year when crinkly golden winter clouds reddened against a westering sun. We often came to the rowing club late in the day, since Jacob's son joined it. The club had good bus and ferry connections, so we didn't need to drive and the bistro served excellent food.

"It's such a beautiful view to the west from here," Jacob reflected. "To think it was once a grimy industrial precinct. We do live in a land of abundance. You know..."

"Our land abounds in nature's gifts, eh?" I interrupted. "It's easy to fall into the fantasy of living in the best country in the world."

"Oh! I thought we did," he said smiling. "You mean to say there are problems with this country, Russ?"

"Just a few," I said. "Coming back, I've a far greater sense of how we appear from the outside looking in, how others see our global citizenship. I've always thought diplomacy was about reducing conflict between nations and I don't think we're doing well."

"One thing's for sure, the Howard government's approach displays a marked lack of respect for other's sovereignty."

"That's putting it mildly," I exclaimed. "He's been banging on about pre-emptive strikes to protect us from terrorism for months now. It hasn't gone down well in Indonesia. Add to this a lack of emphasis on cultural exchange and aid along with a domestic narrative designed to keep people ignorant and then dog whistle up fears of the unknown."

"Russ, he's been working on this since the late nineties."

Both well-travelled Australians we were probably more sensitive than many to recalibrations in Australian Foreign Policy. Working globally, Jacob in a scientific field and me in education and tourism, had equipped us with an acute awareness uncommon amongst casual travellers.

I went on: "I couldn't believe it when they shutdown Radio Australia's transmitters on the Cox Peninsula in June of '97. Suddenly our capacity to broadcast the daily narrative of our lives or those of our regional neighbours in the languages of our region either disappeared or was barely audible over large areas. I relied on those broadcasts when I worked in Indonesia."

"What, in Bahasa, Russ?"

"No, I mean the Australian language broadcasts. Yeah sure, I heard broadcasts in Indonesian. Many people listened in. Once I was climbing Mount Batur very early one morning and the kookaburra call sign broke through the darkness. Reducing that footprint couldn't have been more poorly timed."

Back in 1997, I realised Indonesia was on the verge of a tumultuous period. When the change came, it saw economic crisis; the fall of Suharto's New Order Regime; widespread civil unrest often directed at Chinese citizens; a new democratically elected government; as well as the resurgence of the fanatical Islamic fringe group Jemaah Islamia with the return of its leadership from Malaysia in 1999.

I asked, "Did you come across people listening to Radio Australia on any of your visits, Jacob?"

"No, not really."

"Maybe this was because you were working with the scientific community. It seems that from the 1970s, the more educated were already tuning to the new local FM stations. Ordinary people still depended on AM and shortwave but these broadcasts were highly regulated and censored so Radio Australia had a receptive audience."

"Yes, I guess it attracted a big following amongst ordinary folk."

"It did," I replied. I was reading the book *Radio Wars* by Errol Hodge and found that in 1979-80, it received 198,000 fan letters in Indonesian, and these are just the people who chose to write."

"With all that appalling violence after the vote for independence in East Timor, a strong signal might have helped," Jacob reflected. "What is it with these conservative governments? Why do they want to kill off the ABC's capacity as an independent news service under the guise of budgetary restraint and economic necessity?"

"It's ideological," I said. "It has been since the time Hasluck was Foreign Minister."

"Hasluck! Now there's a name I haven't heard for a while. The man who pleaded for us to be allowed to join the Vietnam War?"

"They don't believe in a free press unless their privileged mates control it," I continued. "It would've been much easier to explain the INTERFET action to ordinary everyday Indonesians if we'd had a full-throated Radio Australia. Suharto's New Order regime didn't only abuse the human rights in East Timor but militarised governance and narrowed opportunities for democratic process throughout Indonesia. Potentially there was a most sympathetic audience."

In response to the violence in East Timor, the UN Security Council carried Resolution 1264, enabling the formation of the International Force For East Timor (INTERFET). Under Australia's leadership, INTERFET was to restore security in the territory. Logistically the response was well managed, efficiently led and temperate, but there was one problem. Just after Indonesia agreed to admit INTERFET the Australian magazine, *The Bulletin* published comments on foreign policy in which Prime Minister Howard is alleged to have said that Australia was becoming the USA's 'Deputy Sheriff'. This vulgar affirmation of the Howard Doctrine was most unpopular throughout the Asia Pacific region, particularly in Indonesia.

"Many people recognised that Howard had unhealthy Eurocentric, even racist leanings," said Jacob. "One Indian Australian friend of mine who lived in Howard's electorate said Howard had made lots of subtle racist comments in the local newspaper."

"Yes, I've heard that as well, and then there was his relative silence on Pauline Hanson's anti-Asian pronouncements."

"Don't forget his reluctance to support Vietnamese 'boat people' when he was a member of the Fraser Cabinet," said Jacob.

This disturbed me. I sat back thinking of the war, all the Vietnamese students I'd taught, some from thread bare associations of siblings and cousins, parents lost in the conflict.

"Regional foreign policy isn't simple. Timor is a good example. Much as I supported the notion of independence for the East Timorese, I felt that as a nation we needed to move cautiously. Sure, there were very strong feelings in Australia."

"Dating right back to Sparrow Force," Jacob reminded me.

"The Timorese helped a lot in the guerrilla struggle against the Japanese. On the other hand, in 1999 we had one of the world's most populous nations on our doorstep going through a political crisis at the end of 35 years of military dictatorship."

"You aren't arguing against East Timorese independence, are you Russ?"

"No, far from it, but when we became involved in INTERFET, it was done in such a triumphalist way. I was reading this commentary by M.C. Ricklefs recently and he made the point . . . I thought it was so important I saved the text . . . it's on my phone . . . just a minute . . . yeah, here it is: 'It was as if Australia, rather than partnering others in a regional police action, was again sending off troops to Gallipoli as the band played "Waltzing Matilda". Military triumphalism was the prime ministerial style of the day. Indonesians, who were humiliated by the collapse of their economy, by the secession of East Timor, and by the need to have foreigners to keep order there, were now subject to further humiliation by the Australian Prime Minister.' That's how it felt to me as well."

Sipping on his beer, Jacob gazed out into the darkening sky. We sat in silence allowing this discussion and its implications to settle for a moment.

Finally Jacob spoke, "I suppose many Indonesians worried that the whole operation was just a covert Australian attempt to break up the country. You know, to surgically remove East Timor and then maybe West Papua. Like an oil and resources grab."

"No doubt. And in Australia, there is a small lunatic fringe that envisages a greater Australia including Timor and West Papua. In my opinion, Howard's triumphalism and culturally superior tone fed into this delusional thinking."

Again the conversation lapsed as we struggled to make sense of just how far the Howard doctrine had shifted Australian foreign policy. Once Australia was so trusted by Indonesia that it was called upon to represent the fledgling republic in the United Nations as it struggled to deal with Dutch military pressure. The Howard government's grave political mismanagement and incompetence was plain. Restricting Radio Australia's Indonesian broadcasts created a news vacuum of sorts. Indonesians were forced to find alternate sources of news not all of them particularly favourable to Australia.

"Another problem for me, Jacob, was Australia's Foreign Minister, Alexander Downer. You know I was involved in educational and cultural initiatives with Indonesia. Well, I couldn't believe how inept he was. I don't know whether you recall this but at the 2000, Asian Leaders' Forum in Beijing, he announced that Australia could not so much view regionalism as cultural but practical, not something built on common ties but only mutually agreed goals. Now just think about that."

Jacob didn't answer. As if following my suggestion, he leaned forward sinking his chin into his hand raising his eyebrows. He sat for a few moments then leaned back in his chair. "It seems he was ignoring our significant Chinese, Korean, Vietnamese and Khmer Diasporas and that's just a few. Then there are the large numbers of Melanesians and Polynesians playing prominent roles in sporting codes like rugby. What on earth did he really mean?" Jacob answered his own rhetorical question with an ironic chuckle.

"I can only conclude that it's Anglo or Eurocentric ideology. This diminution of culture speech coincided almost exactly with the Pentecost in 2000. This is a significant date because it marked the beginning of a new role for Radio Australia's transmitters on the Cox Peninsula. Now the crusading zeal of Bob Edmiston's Christian Voice replaced the kookaburra's call, beaming an evangelical message across the old footprint. Anyway, you having another one, Jacob? It's my shout."

"I'll sit on this one, thanks. I have to drive tonight."

Unspoken Realities

Jacob toyed with his almost empty glass, head to one side and silent for a moment before continuing. "I'm still thinking through this idea of triumphalism," he said. "Howard is skilful in connecting it all with the ANZAC narrative; well, a version of it. It's a dangerous mix. What do you think?"

"He uses it but he also works with the fear of the unknown. Asylum seekers have been ruthlessly exploited. The 'Children Overboard' scam was an appalling and shameful business."

Jacob nodded then went on, "His support peaks every time he manages to inoculate the minds of electors with fear and insecurity. Then once he's infected people, he proffers his own particular brand of political snake oil to remedy the problem."

"Yeah, that's for sure," I affirmed.

"Mind you, the material he's had to work with has given him a lay down *misere*. Being in New York during the World Trade Centre attack put wind in his sails. We were in with the Coalition of the Willing right from the start. It was as if the wick was lit and to hell with the UN, we were all the way with the USA again."

"Yeah, once fear and xenophobia were activated, extremism began to rise."

"I agree with that, Russ, it's been very obvious. Didn't you tell me about someone you knew who wanted to respond by bombing the *Ka'aba*?

"I did. Having lived and worked with Muslims, I was shocked at his extremism, but it cut both ways."

"How do you mean?"

"I spoke with a Javanese Muslim friend in the weeks following the attack. Her concern was the sharpening of attitudes amongst otherwise moderate friends. She felt their responses were partly a reaction to careless statements like George Bush's. He said 'this crusade, this war on terrorism, is going to take a while.' That was a week after the World Trade Centre attack and the use of the word 'crusade' was a major problem."

"Osama Bin Laden was quick to pick up on it. He said something like 'We will fight the Crusaders and continue our Jihad.' It was an appeal to medievalist Wahabism a turning away from the 21st century and moderation. He even tied Australia in to some of his rhetoric."

"Yes," I said, "and during all of these utterances the voice of Radio Australia was was muffled in Indonesia."

For both of us, the world had changed greatly since we first met at university. Once the world was simple and as the Vietnam War finally drew to an end, we looked forward to a future of peace. The fall of the Berlin Wall and the end of the Arms Race inspired further confidence in a peaceful future but again, things were changing. A post Cold War future was simply a struggle between new fundamentalisms.

"I'm not optimistic about the future, Jacob. Apart from this new polarisation of the world, there is still an obsession with armaments, an increasing disparity between rich and poor, total denial in many quarters about climate change and an intractable resistance to the notion of environmental sustainability."

"All big issues."

"I can't let go of this Radio Australia issue and Downer's handling of Foreign Policy. How could he believe that our interests remain strategic and not cultural? What century is he living in? There has been more than 20 years of growing contact with Indonesia through tourism plus extensive educational and cultural contact. Places like Bali are shared spaces, in a sense both Australian and Indonesian, like a type of a third space. These aren't spaces that Alexander Downer is likely to visit, much less John Howard. Clearly they don't have a road map."

An Unusual Kind of Thunder

October nights in Bali can be most pleasant. Cool winds from the southeast begin to lose their strength and chilly edge as evening temperatures in Ubud can sit at 24°C with comfortably low humidity.

The night of 12 October 2002 was just such a night it was also a time of relaxation on the eve of my departure for Australia. That evening was full of happy and enthusiastic conversation with old friends comfortably settled on my spacious verandah: Nita Noor, who was involved in NGO work with poor communities in West Bali, and Melanie Templer, a long-term resident of Indonesia exporting essential oils.

Thunderous rumbles broke the conversation. Such events are common enough on this small island with its dramatic relief, but there was something unusual in this. Conversation paused and then naturally resumed. Idealistic and animated discussion absorbed us. We chatted of Nita's work in environmental management issues amongst people living within the margins of Bali's large national park and my plans for widening the field study programs for UK schools. Amongst old friends, optimism was dominant; I had no idea what lay ahead of us.

Tired and a little sunburned, I welcomed sleep. I dreamed of military trucks rumbling through a bombed out landscape, strewn with the shells of buildings. They were sweeping up people, taking them away.

I wondered what I was doing there as I wandered in this depleted space. Spotting two familiar people picking their way through the devastation, I called: "Nita! How did you and Giani get here? We're in a war zone."

"Yes, but where? In what time?" Nita was holding her nine-year-old son's hand.

"Truckloads of people are being removed. Look there's another load. Who are those men guarding them? They look like Nazi storm troopers."

"How did we get here?" asked Nita, pulling her son, Giani closer.

"I don't know but if we stay in the open, we'll be taken as well. We must hide . . . take shelter. The roads are too dangerous."

Shepherding my friends into a bombed out building, we crouched behind piles of rubble. Behind stood the remains of a wall several metres high.

"We're safe for the moment, Russ, but we can't stay here for long. It's too exposed."

"So what are our options? The roads mean certain capture." I looked for a way out. There were lightly timbered hills behind the building.

"If we can make it to those trees," I said, "we stand a chance of escaping. But we'll need to scale that wall. I'll get you and Giani up first then somehow you can help me."

"Yes," Nita replied, "though you realise we'll be visible from the road."

"We will, but it's our only option. Let's go!"

Just as we approached the wall, there was a screech of brakes outside and men shouting. We'd been spotted. Moments later, we were taken…

That morning, I woke to my mobile phone. It was Matina. She had news, the worst news I could imagine. "There was an explosion in Kuta last night. Maybe a bomb blast."

An Unusual Kind of Thunder

"What?" It has to be a gas cylinder or some mishap, I thought.

"We don't have much detail at the moment. At least 12 are reported dead and unknown numbers of injured."

"Bound to be lots of Australians involved if it's Kuta. So that's all you can tell me?"

"Yes. I think you'd better get down there as soon as possible. With your Indonesian, you can help."

"Sure. It's still early here. I'll get organised. There might be others want to come as well."

"Take care we don't know the circumstances yet. This could be terrorism."

Terrorism. The word struck a dreadful chord. Where will I go? To the hospital, I guessed. There was bound to be a need for translators.

Rolling off my bed, adrenalin already surging I stepped out of my room and across the small corridor to where Nita and Giani slept.

"Nita, Nita please get up; there's a problem," I called

Moving out onto the verandah to greet morning in the *sawah*, I caught sight of a duck man leading his obedient flock. Everything seemed at peace yet in some unseen place, I realised that people were suffering, perhaps dying, at this moment.

Footsteps and Nita's phone ringing drew my attention as she joined me on the veranda.

"*Aduh!*" she exclaimed in response to the caller. "*Di Kuta. Sari Club. Banyak tewas! Okay, ya, kita bertemu di muka Rumah Sakit Sanglah. Ya, ada mobil. Saya langsung ke sana.*" She said: In Kuta. Sari Club. Many dead! Okay, yes, we'll meet at the front of Sanglah Hospital. Yes, there's a car. I'll come there directly.

Turning to me, Nita said, "Well, Russ, there have been three bomb explosions: two in Kuta near the Sari Club, and one in Renon, outside the US Consulate."

"The US Consulate, eh? This elevates the significance of the event. So who would be responsible for this I wonder?"

"Just look at the political spectrum – pick anyone," she said with that intense resolve I knew so well.

"Islamic extremists, dissident elements in the Indonesian Army, one of Prabowo's gangs, the CIA, Mossad, some other security agency, it could be anyone."

Nita's phone rang again. She fielded several calls over the next period, sipping coffee and dragging on a *kretek* cigarette in between. Friends from various environmental groups and NGOs were organising a voluntary relief effort. All confirmed three explosions; two of them huge and the one outside the US Consulate apparently more symbolic. The toll in deaths and casualties was substantial. Our focus was now on providing what relief we could to the victims.

Collecting Melanie and leaving Giani in the care of her older children, our small group of volunteers was soon bound for Sanglah Hospital. The reality that lay ahead was far graver than any of us could imagine. Throughout the next four days, many were asking 'Why?' but this was overshadowed by the imperative of dealing with the consequences of this act of terror.

Approaching the Sanglah Hospital precinct in the rising, mid-morning temperature it was obvious this was big. Cars, mini-buses, motorbikes, and people were converging on the area.

"Have you ever seen anything like this?" I asked more by way of exclamation.

"No, Russ," Melanie answered.

"*Banyak orang*." Lots of people, replied Nita.

"Where am I going to find parking?"

"Look for a park elsewhere," Nita suggested.

We found parking a few streets away from the hospital and went on foot.

The atmosphere around the hospital was overwhelming. The crowd was huge; there were anxious and distraught tourists everywhere. The emotion was powerful and tears welled in my eyes. I felt the urge to pray: *Lord Jesus Christ, Son of God, have mercy on me a sinner. Lord Jesus Christ, Son of God, have mercy on me a sinner. Lord Jesus Christ, Son of God, have mercy on me a sinner.*

Composure returned. I had the strength to continue.

"This is major," I said, not knowing what else to say and not expecting a reply. "So where are we meeting the others?"

"Ah! There's Nyoman over there," Nita gestured towards a group of people, expatriate and Indonesian, setting up an information counter. Some were posting sheets of paper on the wall behind. Others chatted with tourists.

Many people were missing. Glancing down a list of missing Australians I saw no familiar names. Lists of the missing grew, filling the wall behind. Sometimes there was good news as a person was found, but usually it was bad news.

A note arrived at the information desk. Someone read it out aloud: "The Australian Consulate requests Indonesian speaking Australians to assemble outside the Melati Ward later in the day. People are needed to assist in the evacuation of the seriously injured."

"I can help there. At least it's tangible, Nita."

"Yes, Russ, you do that. I'm going to talk with the police. There will be many legal issues," she said as she headed off into the complex. This was the last I saw of her until late in the evening.

Expecting to fly out that night and resume work at Sydney Boys High School the next day, by three in the afternoon I knew that the scale of the tragedy rendered my plan impossible. Someone had installed an ISD line on our small information desk so I rang the school.

A recorded message played: "This is Sydney Boys High School. Absent teachers please leave your details after the tone giving an indication of the likely duration of your absence."

The tone sounded. Almost lost for words I wondered how much to say. The words came as if from another person: "This is Russell Darnley. I'm involved in the relief effort following a bombing incident in Bali. The situation is very grave. I must stay in Bali until emergency assistance is no longer needed."

Time passed in giving directions, reassuring people, photocopying lists of the missing, attempting to coordinate with other volunteers, struggling to gain some sort of an overview of what was going on and waiting for the evacuations that must eventually begin.

Periodically a loud speaker broadcast appeals for blood, for O type blood suggesting that there were lots of non-Indonesian victims. Although O is a universal donor, it's preferable to give people their own blood type if available. In Indonesia there is a higher incidence of my own group B. Finally, there was a call for B.

Comfortingly, the blood donation room was cool, quiet, calm and orderly. Some twenty or so people waiting. It was getting late and I wanted to make sure I was available for the evacuation.

A nurse sat at a desk just inside the door. I approached her. "Excuse me, sister. I must conduct some work for the Australian Consulate shortly so may I donate now?"

"Yes, of course, if you have an important responsibility. You will be next."

I sat and looked about me in a more studied manner. Most of the prospective donors were Indonesian, Semitic or Central Asian in appearance. Back in Australia, a friend from the research institute Walter and Eliza House had explained that B was more common amongst Asians and certain Judaic groups.

An emotional Balinese donor cried out, "The Muslims did this! Soon we'll go and kill them!"

He began repeating the general message, "We must go and kill the Muslims! Wipe them out!"

"Why must we go and kill the Muslims?" I asked.

"They did this; we must go and kill them," was his response.

There was a familiarity in his reactions an unreachable quality, a surety, and a single-mindedness that could take him to the point of exacting his form of justice. He seemed consumed by this notion. His passion felt transformational and dangerous.

"We are ready for you now, sir," the sister advised and gestured towards a newly vacant couch.

The man disturbed and puzzled me. Eventually, I spoke at length with Matina about him. She had many years experience in mental health. I told her: "Extreme events like these seem to give some people a licence to act out their aggressions. I thought he was definitely in an unapproachable altered state."

"It's hard to assess without being there," she said. "People can enter states similar to psychosis, under that sort of stress.

Someone raging like that can be difficult to deal with. The best approach is to be the still point and not react. You did the right thing disengaging. Eventually there would probably be a mental health intervention, but in the moment, safety would be the uttermost priority: both his and our own," she explained.

"I reckon this guy was definitely on the verge of running amok and if it had developed, I'm sure it would have been understood as a form of demonic possession." I realised that I didn't know what happened to the man. Hopefully the energy dissipated. "There were teams of Balinese priests working around the clock to disperse demonic forces."

"No doubt a culturally appropriate response," she replied. "My understanding is that if a person running amok gets really out of hand they could end up dead, particularly if they're wielding a weapon. From time to time that's happened to people experiencing psychotic episodes in Australia," she noted.

"In Balinese terms, the bombing represented a huge upwelling of negative forces, a concentration of sinister spiritual energies. I felt there was definitely evil afoot. In the end it was balanced out by the compassionate response of the volunteers and the love and the dedication of the doctors and nursing staff. Such a fine example of the positive spiritual energy. For me it was the Holy Spirit at work; others would have said it was an upwelling of Dharma, or something like that."

"I think it's largely a matter of cultural perspective," said Matina. "An interesting area for investigation. There's been some work done by anthropologists but there's a lot more could be done."

In the heat at Sanglah, I was losing a lot of fluid and donating 600mls of blood exacerbated the problem. My head pounded so I made my way to the *apotek* (pharmacy) and bought some paracetamol and then found some food and water on offer in the front courtyard. It was very gratifying that so many Balinese restaurants had responded with free food for volunteers.

Just after 5pm, news came that some of the seriously injured were to be flown out by the RAAF later that night and volunteers would be required to accompany them to the airport. This must be what the consulate was on about, I thought. I was keen to help.

Shortly after dark a young woman wearing a *hijab* approached the help desk. She had a sweet, almost angelic face as she asked, in fluent English, "Are any of you volunteering to help take injured people to the airport?"

Several people indicated they were.

"Please follow me," she said. "We are going to the Melati Ward."

I wished my unfortunate acquaintance that wanted to bomb the Ka'ba could see her. He bought the whole package of demonising Muslims. This sort of demonisation played into the hands of the extremists that might be responsible for this. Islamic extremists wanted to claw back what they saw as western deviations within the Islamic world. As part of this process they conveniently cast 'Westerners' as dangerous crusaders a tag that gained even more potency with George Bush's reference to the new crusade against terrorism.

Sanglah's walkways teemed with people. There was a constant murmur of conversation sometimes punctuated by louder voices calling to others or giving instructions. A group was clustered around the Melati Ward's entrance.

"Thank you for volunteering," said a well-dressed young man projecting a polite air of authority. "I'm David Chaplin, the Australian Vice Consul. We will need some of you to assist by accompanying injured people to the airport soon. Are there any Australians here who can speak Indonesian?"

I raised my hand. A woman also spoke out above the chatter, "I speak Indonesian as well." I recognised the voice and turned to see an old friend, Asri Kerthyasa.

We both accompanied David a short distance to an area where two small buses were parked. There, he said: "We need each you to take responsibility for a bus. Here is a list of small hospitals and clinics. Visit each one and liaise with hospital staff to determine whether there are any injured Australians that can be classed as walking wounded. We have Qantas flights bound for Sydney and scheduled to depart later this evening. No medical assistance can be guaranteed at Denpasar Airport, in flight, or when they arrived in Sydney. It's essential that no serious cases are taken."

"So we're engaged in triage; that means consultation with medical professionals is essential," Asri observed.

"It will be," he replied, "and when you've collected as many as possible, bring them back here and we'll organise for them to be bussed to the airport. Does anyone have any other questions?"

"Are there directions on the location of these medical facilities?" I asked.

"No, the bus drivers will know. If you want to organise help from any of your Balinese contacts, go ahead."

Right then I sighted Ellie, the son of a friend I'd known for years. Ellie had come down from Ubud to help. I knew him from the time I was managing student field study groups and I knew how reliable he was.

"Ellie!" I called. "I need some help."

He came over.

"Ellie, you know this area quite well and you speak Indonesian, Balinese and English. I need to visit these hospital and clinics." I handed him the list. "We're collecting injured Australians who can walk and bringing them back here."

"Okay, Pak Russell, sure I'll help," he said.

"*Baik, suka rela, ya?*" I smiled, saying, Fine, you like the challenge, eh? I was glad to have him on board.

There were four hospitals and clinics on our list: Kasih Ibu, Prima Medika, Surya Husadha and two others.

At the first facility, Kasih Ibu, I met an Australian

doctor. I was surprised to encounter an Australian and found it reassuring.

"Doctor," I told him, "we've come to collect Australians that are walking wounded."

He bristled, "Only Australians? There are a lot more than that affected."

"I'm sorry. I see your point, doctor, but these are my instructions from the consulate."

"All right then, come with me. There are several patients here in need of urgent attention."

He took me to those patients believed to be Australian so that we could assess their condition and determine whether they were fit for the flight. For the first time, I gained a sense of the severe injuries people had sustained.

In a small intensive care unit, a patient was being treated with burns to more than 70% of his body. I was surprised he was still alive.

Nearby was a young Canadian woman whom the Balinese nurses thought at first was an Australian. She sat, leaning forward in her hospital bed, her distraught partner beside her. They had come to Bali on their honeymoon. There was no skin left on her back. He was relatively unscathed apart from minor blast injuries. Finally we found another young couple: the woman was Australian and her partner was from New Zealand. The Australian was fit to travel but her partner wasn't. There was no way she was leaving.

It didn't take long to realise that there were no walking wounded in this place. So thanking the doctor, I gathered my Indonesian crew and we left for the next facility.

At Prima Medika, the registrar showed me into a room where there were two young Australians, both footballers. They played AFL but looked familiar just like the young men I'd been coaching at Sydney Boys High School through the previous rugby season.

Compared with the serious burns victims, I'd just seen they looked fine although clearly shaken by their experience. All I could see were superficial blast injuries – strips of flesh missing and in places their skin peppered by little pieces of shrapnel.

"It looks as though you guys aren't as badly injured as some I've seen. There's a bus downstairs and we're taking people to the airport for a flight back to Sydney."

"We'd love to get out of here," one said.

"Fine, let's go then," I replied.

"I'm sorry," interrupted the registrar with a serious lack of enthusiasm for our idea. "He has a severed Achilles' tendon," he said, indicating the man in the nearest bed "and this man has a deep abdominal wound that must be drained in the morning."

Disappointment spread across their faces.

"That's pretty definite, boys; we can't take you under those conditions. Is there anything I can do for you, apart from get you home?"

"Yes," one answered. "We've lost our mate. Could you help us find him?"

This got to me; I had difficulty not bursting into tears. They were so innocent and the most important thing to them, if they couldn't go home, was to find their mate. Having seen the list of missing Australians grow, I knew that he could well be amongst the dead.

"It's quite chaotic. There are people everywhere. There's nothing I can do immediately. Let's trust that he's fine and safe but you might like to pray if you wish."

I still feel sad when I think of their shattered innocence.

Administrative staff at Surya Husadha Hospital said they only had one Australian patient. When I found him, he proved to be a single man in his 40s from Queensland.

"I've come from the Australian Consulate," I told him. "How are you feeling?"

"Bloody dreadful. I got sprayed by all sorts of crap in that blast."

His hospital gown was open at the back so it was easy to see how extensively he was injured. His body was peppered with the same blast injuries as the younger men but the damage was far more extensive. His leg was loosely draped with a dressing and he seemed to be on a saline drip.

I told him, "I'm here to evacuate people who can walk and get them on a plane to Australia later tonight. There are no medical facilities on the flight and no guarantee of medical assistance at either airport. Can you walk?" I was a little uncertain about whether I should ask him to stand.

He stood. "I want to go home."

"Well, there's a bus downstairs. Where are your clothes?"

"This is all I have," he replied.

I decided to see how far he could walk. So dressed in a cotton gown and pulling his IV drip, he shuffled to the second floor landing.

At this point, much to my relief, a senior doctor arrived and asked, "Where is the patient going?"

"I'm going home," he replied, before I could utter a word.

"That's not possible," the doctor explained. "You have some serious burns and you are on a pethidine drip that will run out in about three hours. You will be in considerable pain on the flight."

We abandoned the attempt at that point.

After visiting the remaining private clinics and hospitals, I could only confirm the seriousness of the injuries people had sustained. In short, there were no walking wounded. We brought the buses back to Sanglah and kept them on standby, as we might have had some going out to the airport through the night.

Back at Sanglah, I made my way to the Melati Ward, which I knew had some of the most serious cases. People were crowding around the entrance to the ward and seemed to be standing, looking in.

An authoritative English voice rose over the general babble: "If you are not engaged in patient care, please leave. We'll be bringing patients out soon and it's becoming congested around the door and in the corridor."

Momentarily thinking this might mean me, I hesitated, then dismissed the self-doubt and jostled through the crowd into ward. Instantly, I was confronted with full thickness burns, yet most confronting was the smell of hospital disinfectant mixed with the familiar odour of seared human flesh. Attending countless Balinese cremations, I'd come to associate this smell with death and the orderly disposal of human remains. Here in the ward, it induced a dissonance and a profound sense of ill ease; a shocking realisation of the homicidal intent that lay behind this act of terror.

Most patients were European and conscious. I wondered about their pain management. Then glancing to my right, I caught sight of an Indonesian man. He lay motionless; his skin blackened and swollen. Unable to decide whether he was dead or alive, I moved on. Next, I saw a young man, ailing and lying face down on a bed. Tall and fit, his back was badly burned. He was about the same age as my own son, Rob, and bore a striking resemblance to him; maybe that's why I remember him so vividly.

"How are you feeling?" I asked.

He awkwardly lifted himself up onto his elbows. "Ah, not the best," he replied.

"Are you in much pain?"

"Yes, it's painful . . . somehow I'm coping."

"It won't be long. There's a plane on the way. We'll get you out of here soon."

"Good. That's a relief."

"Can I do anything for you, at the moment?"

"I'm very thirsty. Can you please get me water?"

Pushing through the crowd moments before, I'd noticed someone with bottled water. Turning, I caught sight of him still near the entrance. I moved quickly wriggling through the crowd again, grabbing a couple of bottles and moving back to the bed.

"Here, I'll open it for you," I said as the young man painfully lifted himself up on one elbow and reached out for the water.

I stayed with him as he drank, asking, "Is there anything else I can do?"

"Yes, yes, my friend. Can you please try and find him? I'm worried about him."

"Sure I can. What's his name?"

He gave me a name and I rang around without much luck. There wasn't much else he wanted, just a little more water.

Nearby was a young woman, her body largely covered by a sheet.

Approaching, I asked, "Are you Australian?"

"No, I'm Swedish."

Her face and perhaps the rest of her body were burned.

"Is there anything I can do to help you?" I enquired.

"I would like to know when we will be getting out of here."

"There's a flight to Australia in about three hours, so everyone's getting organised. Don't worry, it won't be much longer. Would you like some water?"

"No, thank you," she replied, managing a wan smile.

I took my leave and walked out to the buses. Not wanting to lose them, I kept travelling back and forth from the Melati Ward to the bus drivers, taking them food to keep up their spirits and checking in with David Chaplin by phone.

Australian military uniforms appeared. There was an Australian NCO, a non-commisioned officer, assisting with the evacuation. His Indonesian was quite good so it seemed he didn't need any back up. I felt reassured things were moving into a more official phase.

Early in the morning, I handed over my bus duty to another Australian and went back to Ubud to sleep.

In the Charnel House

Some events in life leave durable marks on memory yet, while they might have scarred me emotionally, I believe they can strengthen me spiritually. Such were the days following the Bali Bombings of 2002.

First thing Monday morning, calls came in from Australia, from Matina, my brother, Andrew, my sister, Margaret, Steve Storey, maybe others, I can't recall. Explaining the situation as I saw it was difficult. Words brought back images of suffering. I cried a lot. As the day unfolded, the magnitude of the tragedy grew more apparent.

Raw emotions were one thing and tears eased the pain, but I needed spiritual support so I rang my church in Sydney. "Good morning. This is Maximos[18]."

"Hello, Maximos." Mother Helen's voice was a delight to hear. "How are you? We haven't seen you for a while."

It was comforting to hear my Christian name, simple, enveloping and protective.

Hovering on the edge of tears, I answered, "No. I'm in Indonesia... ah... Bali actually."

"Oh!" she exclaimed. "Are you all right?"

"Well, actually, I n— I need some help. I've been working... on the relief effort... after this bombing. It's very grave. I can't contact Father Alexis, so I... was hoping I might be able to chat with Father Daniel."

"Maximos, he's not here at the moment but I can arrange for someone to call you, perhaps Father John. Would that be all right?"

"Yes, thank you. I have met him. I don't know him very well but . . . I'm happy to have the support."

---
[18] Russell's Orthodox Christian name.

Seen and Unseen

"There's important work to be done. God must want you there, Maximos. We'll pray for you."

Driving back to Sanglah Hospital with Nita and Melanie was an autopilot experience. Sanglah Hospital precinct and grounds were a place of distress.

Visitors wandered in surrounding streets and between wards, while friends and relatives of the missing crowded into a second floor meeting room designated the Family Information Centre. Nita headed off to work in the morgue, Melanie left to continue her work with victims and families, and I joined others in the information centre, a busy place but without any clear system of reception or triage.

An international mix of volunteers and distressed people emitted a steady burble of conversation with little evidence of organisation. Standing at the front of the room absorbing the scene for a while, I then asked in my clearest schoolteacher voice: "Is anyone managing this process?"

Conversation barely faltered. Then a finely dressed Indonesian woman whom I supposed was in some globalised local industry answered curtly, "What do you think?" Her tone was condescending. I thought it best to ignore her and try to find a role.

Spontaneous organisation often suffers from redundancies. Some wrote particulars of the missing on forms hastily generated elsewhere in the hospital. Names, ages, descriptions and distinguishing features were gathered. Periodically a young Balinese person collected the papers. A military chaplain arrived, taking up a spot in a quiet corner. In an annex at one end of the room, someone set up a computer with digital images of the dead: morgue workers had been busy photographing through the night. A group of Australian men arrived and looked through the images until I heard one of the say, "Yeah, that looks like him. So where is he?"

"In the morgue," answered an unseen voice. "I'll have someone show you where it is so you can make a positive identification."

I spoke aloud, "What a painful process."

"Yes, it is and I'm not sure this operation is working."

Detecting the hint of a European accent I turned to the voice. A man stood just behind me; he looked concerned.

"I think you're right," I replied. "So many loose ends; this is subdued chaos."

"I wonder where the paperwork is going. Do you have any idea?"

"I hope it's going to the morgue…"

"Well, I've followed it and I don't think it is."

"That doesn't surprise me. I'll follow the next lot and see." I dialled Nita's number and said, "I'm ringing my friend who's working there. I'll check."

Nita answered.

"Nita, I'm in the information centre. We are gathering data on missing people and sending the paperwork to the morgue. Are you receiving it?"

"What do they look like?" she asked.

"A simple form, photocopied on A4 sheets with hand written details on missing people . . . nothing more official looking."

"I haven't seen anything like that here."

After the call, I turned to my companion and introduced myself.

"Thomas." He extended his hand.

"I think you're right, Thomas. It doesn't seem to be going there. I'll do a quick check to see if I can sort this out."

"Thanks. This place will be inundated with grieving family members soon."

Following the next courier led me to a downstairs room full of tidy people peering into laptop screens, a complete contrast with the disorder upstairs. I stepped into the room.

"You can't come in here," said a woman standing by the door. I recognised her as an Australian entrepreneur.

I felt like saying, "Don't give me the shits," but restrained myself. "Who says so?" I asked.

"There is a lot of computer equipment here and monies are being received," she explained. "We have to keep the room secure."

"Fair enough, but that's of no interest to me, I'm more concerned to know where those papers are going."

"What papers? I'm just handling the money." Her tone softened. "Can you see them?"

The papers were nowhere to be seen.

Determined this was the last time I'd be frustrated in my efforts to help, I removed the Volunteer card from a name cardholder I wore and replaced it with my Red Cross first aid certificate card. Its fine print was far too small to read from a distance so now, for all intents and purposes, I was a Red Cross official.

Walking back to link up with Thomas, a man hailed me. "What's there to do? Where can I be of use?"

"Almost anything. Do you have any special skills?"

"I'm a doctor. I was on holiday in Lombok when I heard the news. I've just arrived."

"I must say, you look a bit familiar."

"I live in Balmain, in Sydney."

"Ah, I'm from Leichhardt," I said. "I'm sorry I can't tell you much; most of the seriously injured were flown out last night. You can check in with the medical superintendent. The hospital office is just over there." I pointed to the reception desk down the corridor.

"Cheers," he said with a smile and we parted company.

Without the pressure of tending to the gravely injured, I listened to stories and offered whatever support I could, that was how I met the Forbes rugby players. They were searching for three missing teammates.

Sitting with them, I listened as a remarkable account emerged. The players recounted their experiences without much emotion, through a veil of shock as if it was just part of life's routine, a challenge that we might face on a daily basis: "We ran to the back of the club. There was a wall and we lifted people over as flames grew higher and then had to climb over the wall to safety ourselves. We weren't able to get everyone out but tried until it just got too hot."

This simple revelation confronted me with my dream of the war zone the night of the bombing and the wall. What it meant still resonates for me. Certainly it prefigured elements of a story now emerging.

Such a connection, coupled with the brevity of the story told by these young heroes, led me to make contact with them twelve later.

Standing by the Bali Bombing monument on Coogee's northern headland, memories and tears flooded back as usual but this year was a little different – the Forbes Rugby boys were there. After the official commemoration, I introduced myself.

"I'm Russell Darnley. I met a number of you at Sanglah Hospital. I don't expect you'll remember me. Our conversation was short. A group of about five of you were looking for your missing mates."

Someone answered. "Yeah, it's hard to remember all the details from that time."

"I'd like to speak with some of you because I'm writing a piece on the bombing and I want to get the facts straight. This is my card."

"I'm Tony Wallace," one man said and took my card. "I'll get in touch with you."

I didn't know whether I'd hear from them again but a few weeks later Tony sent me an email and I arranged to visit Forbes. We met in the town's Vandenberg Hotel.

"We'd only arrived that day. We were just off the plane. This gave the whole event even more impact," he recalled, his eyes downcast.

"How do you think it is that most of you survived, yet three of your mates didn't?"

"Who knows?" he said, looking up at me. "The Sari Club was crowded so a few of us went over the road to the other bar."

"You mean Paddy's Bar?"

"Yeah, where the first bomb went off. I was sitting there with Greg then suddenly this massive shockwave threw me five metres across the room." He gestured with both hands to simulate his trajectory.

"Carried in a backpack by a suicide bomber, wasn't it?"

"Yeah, that one. Next thing was this huge explosion," he added, without emotion.

"We heard both of them in Ubud, 26 kilometres away. They were like thunder. What about you, were you injured?"

"No, not in the blast, but it blew off my thongs so my feet were burned quite badly."

"When you were getting out of the place?"

"No, that was okay but I went back in to pull people out. By that stage, the fire had really caught. That's when they were burned. I didn't notice it at first but they got painful later."

Tony's retelling of the story was one of understatement. At no point did he tell me he'd been awarded the Australian Bravery Medal for rescuing people from Paddy's.

Across the road in the Sari Club, his teammates faced a different challenge.

Steve and Randal were two of the Sari Club survivors I met the next day at the Vandenberg. None of us were sure whether we had talked back at Sanglah.

"So, Steve, what happened when the blast went off?"

"I was knocked back about ten metres."

"I probably went a few metres," added Randal.

"Did the building immediately burst into flames?" I asked, trying to get a sense of how the raging fire started.

"Everything was black and all of a sudden there was a glitter, a glimmer, like just from light on the roof and then within no time it was just alight," answered Randal. "It was alight, the whole thing was . . . cause it was dark to start, you couldn't even see and I remember the dust. It must have come down and collected. You could feel it in your hair for three weeks. I remember thinking . . . go straight out the front."

He stopped momentarily, as if to gather his thoughts before continuing. "We all thought it had been a gas cylinder or something. We didn't know what it was. We just all went to the front and it was in flames so quick. The roof was on fire and in the front we couldn't see any other way out."

For me, this was a terrifying image, not being able to get out onto the road, being blocked by a wall of flames.

"Then everyone was heading for this back corner because it looked as though it was a way out but there was actually no way out. It looked like a Perspex door they were trying to kick in but they couldn't."

He paused, recalling the terror that must have inhabited that moment. So Steve took up the story, "Yeah, I distinctly remember when it went off. I picked myself up off the ground and I remembered seeing a piece of tin so I pulled a bit of tin off where the thatched roof had collapsed, climbed up the timber and on top of a wall and we stopped there. I just yelled me guts out, 'Fuckin' get outta here! Fuckin' get up here!' and they just ran and by that stage, the front of the building and the thatched roof was on fire and I stood there as long as I could and my shorts got burn marks."

"From the radiant heat?" I asked.

"My shorts had a plastic badge on them and it just melted," he replied.

"It must have been pretty hot," I exclaimed.

"It was quick; it got hot so quick," Randal confirmed and said that he also made it to another section of wall. "I reckon the wall we got over was about as high as that beam over there," he said pointing to a beam in the ceiling, a little over three meters from the floor. "I just ran up and pulled myself up on top."

"It was a high wall. What would it have been, more than ten feet?" Steve pondered. "It was high. I was pulling up the people and I can remember waking up the next day and I've never been so sore in me life."

"It's amazing how you don't feel that sort of thing," I observed, thinking that these men as rugby players were well accustomed to playing on with injuries, driving themselves for the full 80 minutes of play.

"Never. I was just going, aww . . . just using muscles . . ." Steve recalled.

"There was a lot of adrenalin," said Randal. "I'm pretty sure I couldn't get over that wall now."

He's right, I thought. I could picture Steve standing on top of the wall screaming down to the people below that he'd found a safe way out of the inferno and dragging them up as they came. This is what the boys told me at the hospital.

Randal continued, "There were a couple of girls that we didn't know and they were just at the bottom of the wall bawling their eyes out so we pulled them up with us. There was a gap about the width of a shed and then there was a rooftop, which had tiles, exposed timber and electric wires. We jumped onto that roof and came over the next roof and then there was a lane. There was an aerial or something," Randal explained. "I slid down . . . no . . . Crewie went down and I was up top with the girls. They wouldn't do anything you told them. They just couldn't move."

He paused for a moment, thinking, recalling. "Yeah, I pushed them off the roof and there were people down there that caught them. Then we never saw them again," he added.

In the end, they had to abandon the wall.

Steve explained, "That emblem on my shorts melted and I was going 'Fuckin' hot! Fuckin' hot! Fuckin' hot!' and my face was burned. I had to go. I didn't look back. I just had to abandon it. So there were obviously a lot of people who didn't make it."

Twelve years after the bombing, Steve's account grounded me in that profound memory of death and the suffering. But what was the meaning of the dream? Was it only to link us so that we might heal together? I still don't know. It's a mystery.

But twelve years prior to my reunion with the rugby players in Australia, I was still in Bali, looking for ways to be useful at the hospital. There were many more conversations that followed my encounter with the rugby players, accomanpied by a growing sense that my work there wasn't substantial enough. Wanting to help in a more direct way, I decided to volunteer in the morgue. Knowing that Nita was there gave me an incentive of sorts. Slowly I made my way towards that part of the hospital.

A smell of death, of charred rotting flesh and faecal matter, were the unmistakable signs of the morgue's proximity. A policeman with an automatic weapon guarded the entrance but my Red Cross insignia immediately opened the way. I stepped inside.

Nita was seated at a computer in a small office space. Two refrigerator trucks were parked together on one side, rows of body bags were lined up under a pavilion and in another open space, Indonesian police stood guarding another collection of body bags. Here and there, bodies lay under white cotton and all the while, groups of fresh-faced young Indonesians, senior school or college students, carried ice packing it around body bags and white cloth.

There were many foreign volunteers, tourists, surfers, a collection of older women; a real mixture. Most were casually or under dressed for such confronting work, clad in shorts, singlets and T-shirts. Many of them were wearing sandals or rubber thongs. I felt comfortable that my own feet were fully enclosed and my clothing substantial. Everywhere except in Nita's office, the ground was wet from melting ice and bodily fluids. Conditions were appalling and in a one sense, I was relieved I had encountered death and images of death before, but nothing ever on this scale.

"What's there to do, Nita?" I asked.

"Ask that woman over there, Russ. I think she's doing some ID work." She gestured towards tall woman with red hair.

I approached. "Hi, I'm Russell. I've come to help. What's there to do?"

"We're trying to identify as many of these bodies as we can. I'll get you to work with someone. Would you just wait here for the moment?" said the American woman as she showed me into another room.

I waited at one end of a tiled room used for post mortems. I imagined the unseen networks of people

In the Charnel House

connected with these as yet unidentified bodies and waves of grief surging through this global array of connections.

Noticing activity at the other end of the room, my eyes fixed on an attractive young Balinese woman sitting on a high stool mounted with a lectern, a huge bound book spread open in front of her. She overlooked a large tiled trough full of pale body parts now drained of blood. Utterly macabre, the trough reminded me briefly of Hannan's Butcher Shop in Coogee during the 1950s. Back then, they corned their own meat and often had slabs of it in a tiled trough beside their chopping blocks.

Two men examined each part in turn, meticulously describing what they held while the young woman made notes. I could hear the anatomical terms as they systematically worked through the trough.

"*Tangan.*" Hand.

"*Lengan.*" Arm.

"*Tubuh tanpa perut.*" Torso without stomach, they said as they lifted part of a male torso.

A surreal jigsaw puzzle.

The young woman's focus was intense, her demeanour calm while I was in a state of buzzing hyper-vigilance.

I stepped back. Something on the floor beside me caught my attention. Beautifully manicured female feet slipped into the edge of my vision. As my gaze extended up along the length of slender legs, I was startled by the vulnerability of her nakedness, alarmed at what felt like voyeurism, then shaken by the transformation of this otherwise beautiful human form into a charred mass. Like a match that has been burned, her legs were perfectly intact, her middle exposed burnt intestines, her upper body and head a twisted charcoal form.

Standing amidst the stench of charred and uncovered bodies, my mind ran back to 1958 and the Hiroshima Panels. These remnants were the closest things I had ever seen to the destruction of human forms rendered in the panels. Searching again for abstraction, for a distraction that might offer some relief from this hell, I wondered, is this a purpose of art? In silent reverie, I answered myself. Yes, one purpose must be to trace out the edges of human experience, to provide an emotional or a spiritual map. I was grateful to the Marukis. In confronting their own tragedy, in dealing with their own trauma, they enabled me to come to the place, to sense it remotely, to be forewarned.

Though accustomed to orderly Balinese exhumations and cremations, the subdued chaos and the knowledge that this was the product of wanton violence was profoundly disturbing. I was relieved then, to hear my name.

"Russell, wasn't it?" asked the redheaded woman.

"Yes, that's me." I'd forgotten to ask her name but there was no time for niceties.

"I'll get you to work with him." She beckoned to a younger man who joined us.

"Take these tags and clipboard. Open the yellow body bags and check for anything that might help with identification. You can start over there," she said, pointing to a smaller room with a jumble of bags inside.

We began opening bags and making a rudimentary check of pockets.

"I don't have latex gloves yet," I said, "so I'll keep the clipboard and take down the details."

"Fine with me," he replied.

Although I was becoming accustomed to the pervasive stench of burned, slowly decaying flesh, each opening brought with it new confrontations. We could never be certain what state the body was in. Perversely, I thought of lucky dips as a child, what an antithesis this was.

Deftly unzipping yet another bag, we encountered the

In the Charnel House

body of a man. He was wearing jeans. His clothing was burnt in places and his body swollen. It was impossible to tell his age, but it seemed he was still young. He was remarkably intact, even when compared with some survivors I'd seen the night before. My first thought was massive respiratory damage from the fire and lack of oxygen.

"I think I've found something here," said my colleague, pulling out a hotel key and passing it up to me.

"There's a phone number on it. I'll ring them and ask who was staying in the room," I said, taking the key in one hand and dialling with the other.

"Okay, I'll keep looking," he replied, continuing the search.

Within minutes, I had a name and a British passport number. "It looks as though his name is Jonathan Ellwood," I said and took his details to the office.

Each time I made the trip back to the office, I had to pass the open door of the forensic pathology room filled with body parts. I tried not to look, but the images carved impressions in my mind.

"Hi, Nita. It looks as though we've identified someone. He's from the UK."

"Best you speak to the consular official. There is someone from the British Consulate over there, that one," she said pointing out a man who was in conversation amongst other body bags.

I walked over. "Excuse me, I think we've identified one of your citizens."

"Look, I'm busy at the moment. I can't deal with it now."

"Just call me when you're ready." I headed back to my companion who had moved on to another bag.

"Oh, there's a wallet as well," he said to me. "Here in this plastic bag." He handed me the bag.

"Okay, the keys can go with that."

We moved on, looking through several other bags before a voice interrupted.

"I can speak now."

I stood up and turned toward the man from the British Consulate. "I must apologise," he said. "I couldn't deal with everything at once back then. Where is the body?"

"I'll show you," I replied.

Within days, Jonathan's sister, Totty, and brother, Tobias, claimed his body and took him to rest in his village graveyard. Anonymous as Jonathan was at the time, his image stayed with me. I was unable to let it go.

Moments later, the redheaded American woman returned. She seemed charged with adrenalin. Handing me some additional forms for my clipboard, she asked, "Would you go out to the trucks? There is a team unloading bodies and we need to record any identifying items, watches, wallets, credit cards, passports, jewellery; anything distinctive."

"Sure," I answered, relieved at an opportunity to be further away from the body parts and outside where the air was circulating.

The trucks were parked beside the long pavilion in an area with bare earth and a little grass. A small group of foreign volunteers supercharged on adrenalin had just finished unloading one refrigerator truck. It now stood empty as they clambered over body bags stacked several deep in the other truck, searching for identifying features. The bodies were saturated and not in a good state. Some had lain beneath rubble and burned materials at the bombsites before being gathered and stored in the truck.

Conditions in the morgue and surroundings were chaotic; from a health and hygiene aspect it was dangerous and disquieting. Someone hauled a large hose into the back of the empty truck and began washing it down. The air was immediately infused with fine droplets of foul smelling mist. Small streams of brown, contaminated water meandered across the ground eventually pooling in stinking puddles.

A volunteer nurse, Kim Patra, appeared and began pouring bottles of Pine O'Clean into the stretches of pooling water between the trucks. It was strangely comforting a familiar smell one that I associated with hospitals.

"Next time you have a disaster use Pine O'Clean," she joked. "Tough on germs, gentle on your feet!"

Such a relief in this mayhem, I thought looking down at my feet as the polluted water flowed under my soles.

I heard her saying, "If we didn't laugh we'd all be . . ." I lost concentration as fine mist clouded the air.

She went on, "Stark raving bloody mad, actually."

I turned to look at her, banging my right shoulder heavily against the door of the empty truck. I had no idea what unseen dangers were in the mist that now formed a film over the truck's body or whether I had broken the skin on my shoulder but it underlined the danger in this work. I left to find a cleaner environment and examine my shoulder.

Stepping out of the morgue, my mobile phone rang. It was Father John. This too was comforting in a different sense. We chatted briefly. I felt his love. He went on, "… Maximos, there are just some parts of the world we are better off avoiding."

A strange thing to say, I thought. I've just spent the last eighteen years in this part of the world for the very reason that this vast archipelago remains largely beyond the vision and understanding of many Australians. It's our northern gateway with manifest cultural differences and there is no way it can be avoided.

"I'd certainly like to have avoided this incident, Father," I replied, "but I'm here now and it's my duty to help."

"Yes, indeed."

"There's a lot to learn here, Father, but right now, my thoughts are rather focused on this tragedy. It's hard to explain the magnitude of the suffering."

I knew he was concerned about my health and safety, so I understood what he meant in one sense but in another sense, I wanted to debate the proposition on a rational plane. Given where I had just been, it was an indisputable truth. Yes, indeed there were places where one shouldn't be. The morgue was like looking into one of Hieronymus Bosch's representations of hell, a malodorous mass of bodies and body parts slowly melting down in the tropical heat.

Walking back towards the main part of the hospital, the smell of the morgue was fading. I began looking for somewhere to wash my hands; they'd been sweating profusely. There was a painful damp lump on my left thumb. I must wash my hands, I kept thinking.

"How are you?" a voice enquired.

I looked up and was relieved to catch sight of the doctor from Balmain, apparently on his way to the morgue.

"Oh! I've been better. I'm glad to run into you. Can you help me? I've just cracked my shoulder on the heavy door of a freezer truck that was engulfed in fine hose spray mixed with body fluids. I'm worried the skin's broken."

"Of course, let me have a look."

I unbuttoned the top of my shirt and he gently examined my shoulder.

"I can't see anything. Maybe a slight bruise but the skin looks fine. There is no abrasion."

"Thanks, that's a relief. I'm off to find somewhere to wash my hands."

In the Charnel House

"If you have any problems just come and find me," he said, as he continued on his way.

Late in the afternoon, I went back to the morgue to collect Nita. It was still light and she wasn't ready to leave. I walked towards a ward building, seeking less tainted air. A very depressed Balinese family sat on a tikar, a pandanus mat outside the ward.

I looked at them and sat down beside them.

"Good afternoon" I said, in Indonesian.

"Good afternoon, sir," the older man answered.

"What are you waiting for?"

"We're waiting for news of my daughter, his wife," he answered, looking at a younger man cradling some children.

"She's not in Sanglah Hospital?"

"No, sir."

"I'm so sorry," was all I could muster. I sat, thinking momentarily, then asked if she worked in Kuta.

"Yes, sir, at the Sari Club," he murmured.

"Is this family depended on her income?"

"Yes sir. There is no other besides," he answered.

We chatted for a while. They were from Tabanan to the southwest. It was very sad. Through their experience, the wider implications for the Balinese people were becoming apparent. I felt powerless.

"I'd like to help," I said and handed him my remaining money. It was an embarrassingly small amount, just Rp 50 000, about $10 at the time. Mobile phone charges had consumed the rest.

He accepted the money without comment, his eyes conveying his thanks.

Arriving back in Ubud that night, Nita, Melanie and I went straight to Casa Luna. Proprietors, Janet DeNeefe and Ketut Suardana had transformed the restaurant into a centre of tireless support for the relief effort organising supplies for Sanglah. More to the point, it carried Australian red wine.

Reaching into my pocket for the money, I produced a green body bag tag. It was macabre and funny to me, but shocking and painful to an acquaintance standing nearby. I received an immediate and important lesson: while a bit of dark humour saves our sanity as we work inside the turmoil, people must not be exposed to the turmoil I've witnessed; they must be protected from it.

Waking on Tuesday morning was difficult. I was emotionally drained and tearful, and the slightest thing would set me off, so I decided to find some food in the village.

As I was leaving, Nita emerged and called after me, "Russell, please take Giani with you. He only had a light meal last night. He's hungry."

"Sure," I answered. "Come along with me, Giani, I'm going to the warung. We can have smoked chicken if you like."

"Oh yes, I want that," he said, running after me as we made our way along the irrigation canal, past clumps of lemon grass and beneath overhanging banana palms.

Everything was peaceful. Verdant newly planted padi, sounds of running water, a gentle breeze and the distant crowing of roosters. How could such beauty exist at the same time as such ugliness and decay? How could humans create this intricate beauty and yet show such callous disregard for their fellow beings? The reckless exercise of free will, evil, estrangement from a loving God? It was too hard to contemplate.

My gait slower than usual, Giani easily walked beside me. A fine, slight, animated boy of nine with beautiful clear skin, he was highly observant and full of life. His very presence gave me cause for hope.

"Giani, we'll go to Ibu Agung's *warung*."

"Fine, Mr Russell," he replied.

Wearing an old T-shirt and a pair of shorts, I made my way along Ubud's main street. I had never dressed so casually before anywhere in Indonesia, except on the beach. I didn't care. Every time I stopped to talk with anyone, I found myself in tears. They too were in tears. Perhaps they were beginning to realise the magnitude of the event or perhaps it was an empathetic response to my pain; perhaps it was all of this.

I bought the *Bali Pos*, spreading out the paper on a table by the window trying to read as I ate my breakfast. Its reporting on the bombing was the first I'd seen. Again I gathered a sense of the magnitude. Tears were dropping onto the paper. I couldn't read.

Far less animated now, Giani sat watching me. Later he said to his mother: "Mum, why was Mr Russell crying in the *warung*?"

Why was I crying? Was it loss of innocence, my innocence, the survivors, the volunteers, or the Balinese? Not that the Balinese were innocent. Though seldom discussed, the events of 1965 were a manifestation of evil but this new terror was such a global event.

Back at the hospital, things had settled. There were more volunteers than needed. Interpol protocols were clicking into place. Australian Federal Police were there in numbers.

Time to head for the Garuda office. I won't get out today; tomorrow will do, I reasoned.

Just outside the hospital, I picked up a lift with Kim Patra, who'd been splashing Pine O'Clean around the day before. She too was winding down now that the sick and injured had been flown out and the forensic teams were in place. We joked about the antiseptic.

The next day, Wednesday, I flew back to Sydney and arrived the following morning.

After touching base with family and my colleague, Steve Storey, everyone went off to work, and I was left alone in my rambling Lilyfield house. I couldn't bear to be alone after the crowds, intensity and the pace of the last four days and I was hungry.

Catching the light rail to Dixon Street, the normality of everything overcame me. Walking through Chinatown was like walking inside a plastic tube. Inside was the reality of Sanglah Hospital and the morgue, outside was an unchanged peaceful world.

This can't be real, I thought, there's no way these people could be going about their usual lives in the face of this great tragedy. I stumbled on along Dixon Street towards the Trades Hall.

"Russell," someone called, at least I thought I heard my name. "Russell, are you all right? Is something wrong?"

The voice sounded familiar but it was hard to break through the Perspex wall and engage.

A face in the crowd seemed familiar. An old friend was looking at me as the crowd swirled around him.

"Frank… sorry. I… um… just arrived."

"Yes, I saw you coming along the street," he said, with a look of sympathetic concern.

"Frank, I've just come from Bali. I've been working on the relief effort after the bombing. It's been very difficult work… like… like nothing I've ever encountered before."

"I'm sorry to hear that, Russell, but you're okay, aren't you?"

"Oh, I'm managing. I feel quite isolated and alone with my thoughts."

I wasn't going to start telling him what I'd been through. I didn't know where to begin and I didn't want to upset him with the graphic images that filled my mind.

He moved closer and placed a hand on my shoulder.

"There is a crisis number you can ring if you need help. I heard it on the radio this morning. The health department have set up a crisis centre for victims of the bombing."

"I'm not a victim – I've been working with them. Well ... no ... I guess I am."

"Russell, just call. I'll get the number for you now." He began dialling his phone. He spoke for a few moments pulled out a business card and wrote it on the back.

"Here's the number; put it into your pocket now, mate."

I accepted it, thinking, I do need help. I hadn't realised how much pain I was in.

"I must go but you know my number. Give me a ring if you want to talk."

"Thanks, Frank," I said. "Thanks for everything. I just need to eat." He slipped off through the crowd.

Entering a food hall, I bought some *nasi padang* for lunch. There weren't many spare seats in the food hall. I wandered around a little confused. Finally I heard someone say, "*Dia bisa duduk di sini.*" He can sit here.

I turned towards the voice. An Indonesian family of four were sitting at a table with spare seats.

"*Terimakasih,*" I thanked them and sat at one of the empty chairs.

They looked startled. The father in the group smiled and asked, "Do you speak Indonesian, Sir?"

"Yes, I do," I replied. "Are you holidaying in Australia?" I asked.

He said they had already spent a week there and were going home tomorrow.

I felt incredibly comfortable and safe, their conversation so familiar. I didn't dare tell them what I'd been doing. They were such a peaceful little group, enjoying their lunch. I felt I needed to protect them from where I'd just been and what I'd seen.

Later that day, I rang the number.

Baby Boomers and Japan

Akio was a Japanese neighbour. He was in his forties and working as consultant with a large Australian real estate company interested in selling time-share projects into Japan. We met in 2002 at a time when I was working on a project with The Learning Federation. I was engaged as a writer in a team producing Indonesian language materials. My team worked in tandem with Chinese and Japanese language teams.

The project aimed to create interactive, computer based learning materials for children. As well as teaching language, the activities explored the unseen elements in communication. We attempted to reference the concessions made when people communicated across cultures and in another language. We were encouraged to infuse our work with opportunities for recognising and responding to the third space we often enter in intercultural contacts. Our learning materials recognised and affirmed politeness as the key to successful communication.

Working in this way prompted me to take a chance in my relationship with Akio; I attempted to take it a little deeper than I might otherwise.

Several years before meeting Akio, I acquired some objects my parents inherited from Crossie, amongst these was a blood stained Japanese flag bearing an inscription. I knew that each Japanese soldier carried one during WWII. I decided to ask Akio to translate the inscription as a way of opening up a discussion about the changing relationship between our two counties.

It was a difficult decision and before making it, I thought back over my own journey from the anti-Japanese

Seen and Unseen

sentiments of Coogee in the late 1950s when the feelings were raw.

Coogee at the time was social place a network of neighbourhoods. People spoke to one another at tram stops, in shopping centres, at the beach and on the street. There was a baby boom. Expectant mothers pushing prams while hanging onto toddlers gathered on street corners chatting in informal, supportive networks. Men went off to work each day and gathered in the Oceanic or the Coogee Bay Hotels for the 'six o'clock swill' before the trek home for dinner. Saturday afternoons reverberated with the excited tones of race callers booming out from numerous radios. On the Oceanic's steps and in the Coogee Bay's beer garden, large speakers broadcasted the races for hundreds of yards against a steady drone of male voices, sometimes punctuated by the sounds of shattering beer glasses. Sundays were the day of rest and began with the tolling of the bell at St Bridget's calling the faithful to morning mass.

In this Coogee of my recollection I am a nine-year-old boy.

Merv hung over the front gate as he often did on a Sunday afternoon. The pub was closed; he'd drunk his supply of beer for the day and had moved on to the port. Sipping from a seven ounce pub glass and clutching a copy of the *Sun Herald*, he caught sight of me.

"Agh! That's done it," he said, shaking the newspaper. Often three sheets to the wind, Merv's adamance came as no surprise.

"Sorry? Done what, Merv?"

"That bloody Pig Iron Bob'n Black Jack McEwen've sold out to the Japs. They're givin' 'em what they couldn't take."

"Take? What are they taking?"

"Takin' our jobs and floodin' our market," said Merv with a severe frown.

"Paddy's market, you mean?" Market in the broader sense wasn't something I understood as a nine year old.

"Not Paddy's Market. Floodin' our country with cheap rubbish made by workers who are paid almost nothin'."

"Oh! Things from factories."

"Yep, that's it. Between the Libs'n the Groupers led by Harry Jensen they're givin' our jobs away to the Japs," he insisted.

"Things made in Japan aren't so good though; they break." I said, attempting to minimise the impact for his sake.

"They're cheap'n they can make 'em cheaper than we can because their workers don't have any rights."

I could never be certain just how realistic Merv's opinions were, though even in his cups, he seemed to be consistent in what he said, even if it was presented through an alcoholic veil.

"Merv, how do you know all of this, anyway?"

"Workin' on the wharves, mate. Ya see what's comin' in and ya see what's goin' out. Mark my words. This time next year, we'll be flooded with cheap Japanese stuff."

Merv wasn't right. Datsun appeared for the first time that year at a motor show in Melbourne but it took about three years for large volumes of Japanese imports to make an impact.

Christmas of 1960 was a watershed. Cheap Japanese toys swamped the market. Australian toy and games manufacturers protested vehemently. For me there was little cause for complaint when I was given a Japanese microscope in a neat wooden box.

Within four years, Japanese transistor radios were all the rage and getting smaller; by the late 60s Datsun, Mitsubishi, Honda, Toyota, Yamaha, Sony, National, Canon, Yashica, Nikon and Olympus had all seamlessly entered the Australian vocabulary. Made in Japan now

Seen and Unseen

assumed a different status.

Unlike Japanese goods, Japanese visitors to Australia were still uncommon. My image of the Japanese was formed secondhand through stories. Also influential was the 1952 spoils to the victor documentary series *Victory At Sea* purporting to show elements of World War II but in reality, it was an often fictional work blending reenactments and segments of training films with actual documentary footage. Both visually, and through Richard Rogers' brilliant musical score, its 26 episodes portrayed the Japanese as crafty, treacherous and intelligent demons. My exposure to the Hiroshima Panels dramatically tempered this view, though I had never met a Japanese person face to face.

One evening, several years later in 1968, I walked down a side passage into a party in Ross Street, Forest Lodge. The doorway opened straight onto a large room. Almost immediately, I noticed a beautiful woman standing on the other side of the room.

She's Asian, but not Chinese, I thought.

Our eyes met with an atypical intensity. I looked away, not wanting to press her with my obvious curiosity and interest. Drawn to look at her again, our eyes met once more and an extraordinary direct communication took place. Beyond words, it was a primal message. We both appreciated the sight of one another. I had never experienced such a direct and intense unspoken contact with an Australian woman. We both moved towards the centre of the room.

"Hi," I said almost breathlessly, cutting short the vowel.

"Yes. It means yes," she said

"Hi means yes?"

"In Japanese it means yes," she smiled.

"Are you Japanese?"

"Hai! Yes, I am," she smiled again.

"I'm Russell. What's your name?"

"Miko." She smiled again.

Until that moment, my only sense of Japanese femininity was expressed in the painted Japanese dolls on my great aunt's sideboard and the tormented beings in the panels.

Miko was short and curved with beautiful skin and long, dark hair. I felt an overwhelming urge to stroke her cheek and touched her. Her skin was very soft. Instead of slapping me back into my box as an Australian woman might have done, she moved closer.

"How did you come here?" I asked.

"My friends brought me."

"I mean to Australia. Are you studying at Sydney University?"

"No, I am doing my last year of secondary school. I finished in Japan but I must study again here."

"Your English is excellent."

"My father is the general manager of Mitsubishi. We all speak English."

"So you don't live around here?"

"No, in Rose Bay."

"Let's step outside, it's cooler."

She smiled and followed me out into the passage where several students clustered in small groups absorbed in their own discourse. Edging into a quiet corner, we chatted meaninglessly. I tried to impress her with my knowledge of Japanese student politics. She was disinterested, pressing closer. There was an irresistible energy being generated between us, beyond words. We kissed for a few moments.

"Miko, are you out there?" A woman's voice called.

"Yes," she answered.

Seen and Unseen

"Oh, there you are," said a woman appearing in the passageway. "We must go. I said I'd have you back by ten."

"Okay. Bye," said Miko as she slipped away.

I never saw her again. But amazed by the frankness of our interaction, I have held onto this incident throughout my life.

Japanese group tourism in Australia grew through the 1970s and, in 1980, a reciprocal youth working holiday program between Australia and Japan brought an influx of young, independent Japanese travellers. As Japan became the world's second largest economy, tourism from Japan boomed. Australian schools responded and Japanese became a popular Asian language. Some of my children studied it at school, and my eldest son was moved to visit Japan, but for me, now conducting business between Australia and Indonesia, Bahasa Indonesia was more relevant.

From 1987 onwards, my family occupied a large six-bedroom cottage in Sydney. There was copious space and it had the atmosphere of a grand student household with someone always coming to stay. So it was unsurprising that on my arriving home from Indonesia after an extended visit in 1992 and ascending the creaky wooden stairway in an unusually quiet house, a young man appeared from the spare room off the landing.

"I am Hiro," he said, bowing slightly as I stepped onto the landing. "I hope I may stay in your house."

"Hiro, you're welcome. I've been in Indonesia. I didn't realise you were here but you are most welcome indeed. I'm Russell." I dropped my bags and extended my hand. "Have you eaten?"

Oh, no, I thought, that's a Chinese form of address.

"Thank you, yes, I have."

"Just let me stow my bags and I'll come and introduce myself properly." Pushing my bags into my room, I resumed our conversation. "How long have you been here?"

"I just arrived yesterday."

"You flew in from Japan yesterday?"

"No, I arrive in Sydney yesterday. I'm already here three months."

"Have you been enjoying your stay?"

"Yes, thank you, I have." he smiled. Adopting a serious expression he continued. "Please accept my apology for the suffering that my country brought to Australia."

Taken aback, I replied, "There is no need to apologise, but thank you. I too must ask your forgiveness as our allies the United States of America used nuclear weapons on your people."

"Yes. Thank you," he replied, with a more neutral expression.

Impressed by his presence and happy to change the subject, I noted, "You look very fit, Hiro. Have you been working here?"

"What is fit?"

"It means healthy."

"Yes, I have cycled from Cairns to Sydney." He had an obvious sense of pride that even his rather neutral expression couldn't disguise.

"That's amazing. How far is that? It must be over 2000 kilometres."

"About 2500 kilometres. My average is about 50 kilometres each day. This gives me time to be a tourist."

"That's a remarkable achievement, Hiro. Do you plan to go further?"

"Yes. I leave for Melbourne next Tuesday."

"In four days' time?"

"Yes. I meet a friend there and we cycle to Adelaide."

"Will you cycle all the way to Perth?"

"We try."

Waiting in Yogyakarta's Adi Sutjipto Airport for a flight to Denpasar was a common enough experience. In 1993, domestic flight schedules in Indonesia were still often unreliable, affording opportunities to wait, observe and sometimes to engage with others. That day, a Japanese tour group settled into seats nearby. They were all about my own age or a little older. One man was much older. Someone's father, I thought.

Drifting in a meditative state, I watched an airport cleaner sweeping closer and closer to this quiet group. There's method in this, I reflected. Then extending a hand full of coins, the cleaner asked the old man something.

The old man replied, "*Ada berapa Yen?*" How many Yen are there?

I understood that, I thought. He speaks Malay, maybe Indonesian. I listened, cocking my ear towards the interaction. It was a familiar one. Cleaners collected foreign coins in tips or found them. Then they tried to change them for Indonesian currency with other foreigners who were departing.

The cleaner mumbled something I didn't quite catch, probably in Japanese.

The old man shook his head.

The cleaner slipped the coins into his pocket and shuffled off.

Catching old the man's eye, I said in simple Indonesian, "*Maaf Bapak. Saya rasa anda pandai Bahasa Melayu.*" Excuse me, sir. It seems you speak Malay.

He looked towards me a little bemused, and what followed I best remember in English. He told me that he could speak a little Malay.

"Where did you learn Malay?"

As I asked this question, I had an image of him as a Japanese soldier, marshaling Indonesians at gunpoint.

"In the market. I bought food in the market."

Baby Boomers and Japan

So he actually paid for his food. I know they used occupation money. It seems ordinary enough.

"How many years ago was that, sir?"

"Ah...nineteen...forty...two," he answered.

"A very long time ago then, indeed."

He was a soldier. He seemed benign enough, resolved into a harmless senescence, but I wonder what experiences he had here? Was he the archetype of the cruel Japanese infantryman in his youth?

"Long ago. This is my first time back."

"Did you enjoy staying in Indonesia, at that time?"

It will be interesting to see how he answers this I thought.

"Enjoy?" he queried.

"Did you like staying here?"

"Ah, like. Yes, I like staying here."

"Were you in the Japanese Army at that time?"

"Yes, in Japanese Army."

"So, what did you do in Indonesia?"

"I was the commander's driver."

He'd have seen a lot. I wondered what I could draw out of this opportunity.

"Were you very busy as a driver?"

"Not busy. I often went shopping in the market for the commander." He smiled.

"I suppose you met many Indonesians. Were they friendly towards you?" I asked, nudging slightly to see if he'd encountered resistance or unfriendliness. Many Indonesian acquaintances had said how they disliked the Japanese soldiers.

"Friendly," he nodded.

"And you liked the Indonesian people?"

"I liked them. Where are you from?" he asked.

"I'm from Australia." So he's changing the subject.

"Ah! Sydney?"

Seen and Unseen

I wondered if he was glossing over the realities or had acquired a mature, inner peace not wanting to disturb his own and others' equilibrium.

"Yes," I said, "Sydney. The Japanese Navy entered Sydney harbor during the war."

There was no response; merely a benign look. Perhaps he didn't understand the Indonesian. I'll try something else, I thought and said, "The Australian and Japanese armies fought in Balikpapan, Indonesia."

Ignoring my comment he said, "I've already been to Sydney." Then he asked, "When will you go back to Sydney again?"

Looks as though this is about as far as I can push it. I could ask more directly about the war but he's a friendly man, not a hint of arrogance or nationalism about. Obviously doesn't want to talk about the war.

"I'll return in a few weeks," I answered.

"I like meeting people and speaking together," he replied.

"Me too. Have you ever spoken with an Australian before?"

"No, in Australia I was with Japanese people."

He seemed as surprised as I was that we were communicating in a third language. Nothing demonic about this old bloke, I thought, then wondered if he was simply beguiling me with charm.

An announcement broke our conversation: "Attention! Flight GA250 is ready to depart. Passengers proceed to Gate Number 2."

Our conversation ended as I said, "Sorry sir. My flight has just been called. I must leave. I'm pleased to have met you. Good bye, sir."

"*Selamat jalan.*" Safe journey, he responded, smiling.

Baby Boomers and Japan

Akio's wife and children had returned to Japan for a holiday, so I invited him over for a Sunday afternoon barbecue. After several glasses of red wine, we sat in a mellow mood in the shade of a tree outside the timber yurt that served as my office and retreat.

"Akio," I began, "an old friend gave me a souvenir from the war in New Guinea."

He looked at me without any sense of concern on his face.

"It's a Japanese flag with a lot of writing on it. I think it's too difficult for my project team to translate and I wondered if I might ask you to take a look at it."

"Of course, I will," he said.

"I must apologise for asking you and must also tell you that it is blood-stained."

"Let us see. Do you have it here?"

"Yes," I said. "Excuse me, I'll go and get it."

After a few minutes, I returned with the flag, neatly stowed in a plastic bag. I placed the bag on the small garden table next to Akio's chair.

Perhaps you'd like to take it with you. I think some of the characters will be difficult to read. They're smudged."

"I will read it through the week and get back to you," he said.

After a few days he rang me and said, "I've translated what I can."

"That's great, Akio. What can you tell me?"

"The flag has the name of the soldier and his village. Communities presented such flags when a soldier went off to war."

"Hearing that, I feel that I must attempt to return this flag to this soldier's family. I hope the Japanese Embassy might help."

Seen and Unseen

"I'm sure they will if you approach them."

I hoped Akio might offer to help but instead, he went on, "It is also inscribed with a Buddhist mantra."

"What does that say?"

"This is more difficult to translate."

Perhaps it's archaic or maybe Akio is Shinto, I thought. We'd never discussed his religion.

"So you have no idea?"

"None."

"Mmm, curious. So is there anything else you can tell me?"

"I think you are right, it is probably from New Guinea. Many Japanese soldiers died there, particularly along the Kokoda Track and the north coast at places like Buna and Gona."

"Yes, it's most likely from there. Lots of artifacts were brought to Australia when our soldiers returned." I reflected on my use of the term artifact, a polite sanitising term removing any hint of the cruel reality of war. We were now in the third space, each conscious of the other's feelings.

He said, "I must go to New Guinea. Many young men lie unrecognised and unacknowledged."

"If you make that journey," I said, "I'd like to come with you."

There was no reply. A journey he must make himself, I thought and thanked him.

"You are welcome. Bye then," he replied.

Three years later, at the end of a long relationship, I found myself selling the house I'd owned for 28 years. Tragically, the flag was lost in the move, so the young man's family remains unknown and unseen.

My Second Meeting with Jonathan

For me the name Tring and my ultimate destination Aldbury evoked images of Middle Earth and The Shire. In 2009, I had no real sense of what to expect along the way, but quite soon the train broke into southern English countryside. This isn't the most beautiful part of the world, although glimpses of canal boats soon caught my attention and invoked cultural memories that survived even the antipodes.

Leaving Tring station and entering commuter countryside, village England, I noticed a sleek demountable coffee shop with an Indian crew proffering espresso coffee and Italian snacks. Back in the 1970s before the vast culinary benefits conferred by the EU, this would have been a most unlikely encounter.

I stepped up to the counter and said, "Please excuse me but I wonder if that is the way to Aldbury." I pointed in the direction I believed I should go.

"Yes, Aldbury," was the curt reply.

"Thank you," I nodded. I tightened the straps on my backpack and set off out over the railway bridge and along the road to Aldbury.

Yet to discover the beautiful track through the meadows, the journey was sometimes one of scampering up onto embankments to dodge the rural traffic. Mercifully, old world country roads and lanes are often well incised with banks that can serve as safety islands. Traffic passed swiftly and frequently and with few exceptions drivers appeared sensitive to the possibility of pedestrians.

A group of Japanese hikers appeared ahead. I had no idea where they were coming from or how far they had walked.

"Alo," one of them called as I drew near. "Is this way to Tring?"

"Yes, you're going in the right direction. It's another 1500 yards – almost a mile," I said with the assurance of a local. I guess I was a local to them.

"Thank you," they answered as we passed on the narrow verge.

I thought about how Asian connections had brought me there. An intercontinental journey from Australia via Dubai, then across Iraq, Turkey, Eastern Europe and Scandinavia and a wedding in the heart of Robbie Burns Scotland had distracted me. Now there was other business, a pressing task, the closing of a circle down south in England.

Moving with outward calm, old images from an event played on my inner screen. I saw Jonathan's body lying in that malodorous chaos. Strong images, but then, I was on the way to his village of Aldbury.

A year earlier, I had made contact with Jonathan's mother, Caroline. It was a delicate matter. While not wishing to exacerbate his family's grief, it was important for me to locate him in a place of peace and bring some resolution to the extreme memories I had of our only encounter. After some research, I rang one of Caroline's colleagues to gain whatever sense I might about the likely impact of an approach from me. With her reassurance that my contact would be appreciated, I emailed Caroline.

When we made telephone contact, I found Caroline a woman of great warmth.

"Thank you, Russell," she said. "Because of your work in helping establish his identity, we were able to bring Jonathan back home to his family and friends, most promptly."

"I'm pleased to hear that. It was a distressing encounter, made all the more so when I had to leave without knowing

My Second Meeting with Jonathan

if establishing his identity might have helped."

"We knew about the man with the key."

"When we found Jonathan's hotel key, I rang the front desk. They gave me his name and passport number, so I was able to pass this on to the man from the consulate. By the next day, Australian Federal Police forensic teams had arrived, and Interpol protocols were in place so volunteers like me went home."

"My daughter, Totty, flew in from Penang two days after the bombing and Tobias, Jonathan's brother, joined her two days later."

"I didn't know that. Hopefully they were able to expedite matters."

"Yes, they were. Tobias was part of the NATO-led group dealing with the aftermath of the war in Bosnia so he had appropriate experience."

"He'd have been better prepared than most."

Caroline had sounded so resolved and calm over the phone and I was looking forward to meeting her and bringing those memories of Jonathan to rest here in the Hertfordshire countryside.

Teaching in London years before, I'd learned that my directness wasn't always welcome. Many years living in Asia allowed time for reflecting on the nature of culture and communication, so initially I maintained the role of observer quelling a tendency to blurt out my first impulsive response to a question, when it sat beyond the bounds of appropriateness. I'd resolved that successful communication lay not in the refusal to divulge the purpose of one's travels, but in retaining a degree of initiative and providing information only when ready, maintaining some degree of control in the discourse with strangers.

Entering my Aldbury hotel I approached the counter that served as a front office. "Good morning. I'm Russell Darnley. I've booked a room for tonight."

Seen and Unseen

"Yes. Welcome, Mr Darnley," the manager said. "We've been expecting you. Do you have some identification?"

"Yes, my passport."

"Thank you, and what has brought you to Aldbury? Is it business?"

What a direct question, I thought. This feels more like the immigration officer I encountered in Glasgow last week.

"Just personal business," I replied, unwilling to say more. "Do you have a dining room?"

"Yes, it's to the rear. I'm sure you'll find it to your liking."

"Thank you. I'm ready for lunch."

I noticed on the menu that the chef's name was Ng, a common enough name back home, yet not one I expected in Hertfordshire. Enquiring, I learned that he was from Malaysia, though there was no obvious Asian influence in the menu. Lunch was an outstanding confirmation of a transformation in English cuisine. An excellent salad of small beetroots with rocket and water buffalo mozzarella tossed in a light dressing. *Bocconcini*, I mused, yet another benefit of the EU.

Mid-afternoon, Caroline arrived. Stepping out of the hotel, she pointed toward the village pond where a duck and a little clutch of ducklings cruised across the surface, while a well-fed cat stood helplessly eyeing off a potential meal now safely waterborne. "Look at that," she said.

"Puss won't be enjoying any easy meal of duck this afternoon," I said.

We both smiled. Caroline's appreciation of the natural world impressed me.

In what seemed like just a few steps, we stood at the entrance to the village graveyard, set about a beautiful flint stone church. Moments later, we stood before Jonathan's grave. I was overcome with sadness. For some reason I

My Second Meeting with Jonathan

hadn't expected him to be right here, but of course he'd be here where else?

His grave had been tended with great love and care.

"Slate," I said, touching the headstone's smooth edge.

"Yes, from an old billiard table," she replied. "Jonathan would have loved that. He enjoyed playing."

Caroline had resolved much and was well advanced in her mourning, for me this was a fresh confrontation with the reality of Jonathan's passing. Tears welled in my eyes; I felt a lump in my throat. Looking up towards the church, I searched for words.

"It's such a beautiful situation, such a beautiful church," I said, grasping for anything that would help me gain composure.

"Yes, would you like to see inside?"

"I would. Anglo-Saxon is it?"

"No, it's actually Norman or Early English style," she answered.

"I was going by the flint stone in the walls. Somewhere down south I saw an Anglo-Saxon flint stone church when I was last here."

"The stone just reflects the materials available in the area," she explained.

I looked up again. St George's flag flew from the church.

Moving through the shady churchyard, generations of headstones revealed an informal history of the village. Caroline pointed out a few of the older ones.

"It's certainly a well preserved church," I remarked.

"It was restored around 1867, so it is in good condition."

"It's not unlike St Jude's church in Randwick where I grew up."

Connections and new meanings infused the moment. This place was so far away from my home and yet so full of the familiar. How comfortable it would be to have such a close association with the church, a real benefit of village life.

Stepping through the south door, we entered a light filled space. Several women were sweeping and tending to the church, their serenity and their friendship obvious. After initial greeting and introductions we chatted.

"We've just been visiting Jonathon's grave," said Caroline.

One woman looked at me and asked, "Did you know Jonathan?"

Here in this holy place with these loving women, the moment clouded with emotion.

"I found him," I said and at this was unable to hold back my tears.

She hugged me gently and I felt such love and acceptance.

Later that evening I went for a walk. A light rain was falling, not a deterrent and not even requiring an umbrella. I looked out to see that the duck had gathered her clutch of ducklings and sheltered beside the pond in weather that was too wet for cats. I walked on down the lane through fine drizzle.

Passing the church the next morning on my way back to Tring, I was fortunate enough to find it open; I stopped. It was empty. Entering the chancel, I stood before the altar and recited the Trisagion Prayers, thanking God for the opportunity I'd been given. I spoke to Jonathan, thanking him because in his sacrifice, I saw an opportunity to grow and to come to know his beautiful village and its special people.

Singapore 43 Years on

Memories of a fetid stormwater drain spiked with a cocktail of effluent and smelling much like the Denpasar River, formed a lasting impression of the Singapore River in 1973. Another memory of the river was sitting in a hotel room looking out over several *godown* (warehouses). Painted in either white or washed out turquoise green, they sat surrounded by open land covered with a scrubby jungle of elephant grass, straggling vines, banana palms and countless other unkempt shrubs. Knowing I was to be living 300 metres from the river led me to wonder just what malodorous vapours might waft in the direction of my new residence and whether the godown still existed in 21st century Singapore.

"So what do you think of the view?" my wife, Catherine, asked.

"In a word, disorienting. I feel like I'm lost in a Lego Land, there's such a repetition of forms."

"Yes, I know, darling. It was difficult for me at first."

"I expected a change in scale but I guess I didn't anticipate the impact of all the windows, balconies and illuminated views of people in apartments. The towers also block my line of sight so and it's hard to get a sense of location."

Even from our 25th storey vantage point, I was struggling to sense where I was in relation to the Singapore of memory. Everything was different. My eyes scanned the few comforting yet random patches of green open space remaining, but they were of little help.

"It takes some getting used to," said Catherine.

"Yes. Look at that monolithic postmodern tower block opposite. For a moment, I expected a super hero to come streaking across its face but I'm not getting any of the acrophobia you mentioned."

"Go out on to the balcony then."

Opening the door, Catherine and I stepped out onto our eyrie-like balcony. Moving across the balcony, I stood back from the edge and looked out along Kim Seng Road towards some older buildings a block away.

"There's a model town down there with tiny little toy cars. They're moving at break neck speed. So this is how people drive in Singapore. My taxi from the airport went at a fair clip as well."

"It's a raceway down there, but there is a foot bridge."

"I still don't have a sense of acrophobia though."

"That's easy to arrange, darling," she smiled. "Just go to the other balcony. Over there, by the lift."

Taking a few steps through the living room and sliding open the door I peered over the railing.

"Ah yes, that does it. The Lilliputians down there are playing tennis. Confronting. I feel it now. I'm glad of the plate glass panel and the railing."

I stepped back inside looking for my iPad. I hadn't unpacked it was still in my backpack.

"Where on Earth is the Singapore I once knew? Where are the *godown*, the shop houses? Where's the diversity, the clutter and the mess? This is pristine, modern, orderly, gigantic and there isn't the slightest whiff of the river."

"Are you talking to yourself, darling?" asked Catherine.

"Yes and no; to you if you were listening but no matter," I replied. "It's certainly different. I'd like to know where I was though."

Grateful for the city-state's super fast broadband, I tapped open Sun Seeker.

"Now I see sunrise and sunset directions. I had that wrong."

"You'll get your bearings."

My challenge is to reconcile my old mental map with contemporary Singapore and build a fresh one. I wondered if there was still a buzz and diversity in the streets or had the lives of the people been entirely relocated, reassembled and transformed in this aerial world?

"Did you say something?"

"Oh! Maybe."

Apart from an occasional Lilliputian scurrying across the road below, this seemed a pedestrian free precinct.

"I was reading something from the *Straits Times* online about foreign visitors nostalgically romancing the past, yearning for a Singapore closer to the colonial era. Of course that's folly, yet finding what remains might give an insight into what's still valued and how it fits into contemporary culture."

"I guess it will, darling, but slow down; you've just arrived. Would you like a cup of tea or shall I take you out for dinner?"

"Let's go out."

Waiting, my mind leapt into nostalgia. I found myself wandering through an old family farm at Kellyville on a crisp winter's morning, a discordant dawn chorus of magpies calling as I crossed frosted fields on my way to help with morning milking. Snapping back into a contemporary realm, I confronted the urban sprawl and a four-lane highway now in place of milking sheds and cow bales. Then the mid-century Bargo of my childhood came to mind, a place with of dirt roads, poultry farms, goats wandering, local bakery, general store, nissen hut cinema, steam trains passing in the night, the glow of distant bushfires. Memories. So where were these places now?

Reaching for the iPad again, I flicked open the Facebook group "On a little street in Singapore". Long before arriving, I began taking an active interest in this heritage group it was another reference point, my digital portal to a Singapore's past?

Morning came and the Singapore River was my first port of call. With relief, I found its grey anaerobic colour had vanished replaced by a slightly turbid stream with a greenish hue. Lots of nutriernts draining into this channel – it could be worse, I reflected.

Strolling along a riverside pathway, I passed picnic spots, lawns, gardens and trees. Further upstream were gross sediment traps and artificial wetland areas providing a defensive line against the continuing problem of turbidity, clearly sourced to runoff from numerous building sites along the valley. Soon I discovered that after rain, it could still be muddy but on any day fish are easy to spot and flotsam is less common now.

Fishing was a popular pastime along the river and sometimes on my riverside strolls, I stopped to chat with a fisherman. One old man in particular was often fishing just upstream from Zion Road.

"Catching any fish?" I asked.

"None yet."

"The river is looking much cleaner than when I first saw it in 1972," I observed.

"Yes, thanks to the good government of Lee Kwan Yes, much of the mess that was old Singapore is gone."

"I read that it used to flood along here."

"It did," he answered. "In those days I lived on Kim Seng Road. Floods waters sometimes came up to the front of my house. You never knew what they might bring."

"You mean banana palms, tree branches, garbage and so forth?"

"No worse," he said with a frown of mild disgust. "Sometimes there would even be dead pigs and it wasn't just the Singapore River; Kallang River was even worse."

His final comment prompted me to chase up something I'd seen on Jerome Lim's blog *The Long and Winding Road* where I'd first read about the floods. Jerome is a resourceful commentator on change and heritage as well as the administrator of the Facebook group, 'On a little street in Singapore'. A quick search on the iPad brought up his post.

Describing a flood back in 1969 when 300mm fell in 24 hours, Jerome wrote:

> Potong Pasir would usually be one of the worst hit areas and I remember being able to see only the attap and zinc roofs of houses from the vantage of the block of flats I lived in in Toa Payoh, which overlooked the area. Vegetable farms were destroyed and much of the livestock kept in the pig and poultry farms would have drowned – another thing I remember seeing is the clean pink carcasses of pigs floating in the flood waters.

In these early days of my return to Singapore, I still obsessed about the need to reconcile my mental map of the place. I was plagued by that memory of sitting in a hotel room, looking out over several wharehouses on the opposite bank. It became imperative to find both the hotel and *godown*. I searched for the hotel with views across the river, but there are many *godown* along the river. Then one day, I had a sudden flash of recollection, it was the Miramar.

Within moments, I found its website. How could I have missed it? It's only 600 metres from home. I must have walked past a dozen times without realising.

Standing by the river looking at the Miramar Hotel, something wasn't right. There were *godown* opposite, converted into restaurants and nightspots but none the shape or the colour I recalled. Of course a coat of paint could be the issue, but the shapes were definitely wrong. A week passed before I accepted that my spatial memory was faulty. The *godown* that matched the colour and shape were on the same side as the hotel.

Some basic elements of the map now settled, it was time to extend it not just reconciling other elements, but also to begin populating it. While communication was challenging when I first arrived in Singapore, two generations of Singaporeans passing through an education system stressing English as an official language have overcome the problem. My Indonesian is also close enough to Malay to be a useful second language.

One day, I noticed a man carrying parcels of fruit and vegetables, and asked him: "Excuse me, sir. May I ask, have you been to the markets?"

"Yes, I have," he replied.

"Would you tell me where they are?"

Looking at me as if I'd come down in the last shower he answered, "Down Buffalo Road."

What a break, I thought. I've been buying all the food in shopping malls and supermarkets and paying top dollar for it. I knew there had to be markets somewhere.

Soon the new world of Tekka Market opened up. I began to meet the traders, have short conversations some in Malay, bargain a little, swap stories, meet the other patrons and find all of the ingredients I needed for cooking and making *jamu* (a traditional herbal tonic full of anti-oxidants), such a relief after the sterility of Cold Storage Supermarkets.

Some of the conversations in this new emergent Singapore were unusual by my cultural standards. Once while buying *daun padan* (screw pine leaf), one of the ingredients for *jamu*, a woman wearing a hijab asked me, "Are you going to make a cake?"

"No, not a cake. I'm making *jamu*."

"*Jamu!*" she exclaimed. "I've never known of a Caucasian making *jamu* before."

"Oh well, I'm from this region. I'm Caucasian by descent but I'm not a European. I'm Australian. Some of us learn about these things."

"Did you learn this in Bali?" she asked.

Interesting I thought, I keep encountering this. There seems to be a widespread belief that if an Australian has some knowledge of Indonesia, they must have acquired it in Bali. It was understandable but such a persistent stereotype.

"Yes, partly, but mainly from contacts in Yogyakarta and a Chinese Indonesian friend in Jakarta."

"Which *jamu* are you making?"

"One with turmeric, ginger, tamarind, pandan leaf and a little honey."

"Turmeric isn't something I use these days," she advised. "I take a combination of ingredients for women, mainly ginger and *gula melaka* (palm sugar). Turmeric dries out the uterus, so I avoid it."

This was a perfectly reasonable and useful exchange, just not the sort of conversation I'd have with a stranger at Orange Grove or Paddy's Markets in Sydney.

Soon I discovered Tiong Bahru markets and Zion Road hawker centre as well, so I had a far more economical flow of fresh food and access to excellent hawker markets where all manner of culinary delicacies were available. This was a huge leap forward since over the previous 50 years or so, I'd acquired an interest in preparing a variety of different Asian and European dishes. In some ways, this contrasted with a more typical Singaporean lifestyle involving a lot more eating out. In time, I discovered that such practices often became the subject of conversation, usually with women and often beginning with a discussion about the price of things.

Attracted by a picture hanging inside a Tanjong Pagar home accoutrements shop, I stepped inside. After

Seen and Unseen

browsing around the shop, I was drawn into yet another conversation on prices.

"How do you find the prices in Singapore?" asked the shop assistant.

"Rent is exorbitant, taxis are quite cheap, public transport is the best value for money I've ever encountered and food is a little expensive; I mean, ingredients, fruit, vegetables, red meats and fish. Chicken and eggs are reasonably priced."

"You eat at home? It's cheaper to eat out at hawker centres. Don't you like local food?"

"Oh, yes," I answered, "I often eat in hawker centres but I like to cook."

"A lot of foreigners don't seem to like hawker food or eating in local restaurants," came the reply.

So we're back in that stereotype, I thought, this being just one of several similar interactions. The implication seems to be that my real reason for cooking was an aversion to local food. Often, as on this occasion, I squashed an impulse to say something like, "I've been eating different Asian cuisines and eating in hawker centres since before you were born," and chose instead to be polite.

With social contacts now broadening, I was still absorbed in the map reconciliation process. Visits to Tekka Market took me through an area I frequented during my first visit to Singapore. Eventually I found the façade of what was once the Rendezvous Nasi Padang restaurant, yet other places in the precinct still eluded me. I guessed they had been demolished in all the progress yet nagging and obsessive doubts remained.

Later trawling through the National Archives of Singapore. I came across a rich seam of gold, images of both the Kian Hua Hotel and Bee Loh Photographics. It was easy to confirm that Bee Loh was gone; I still held hope of finding the Kian Hua Hotel. Clearly Bencoolen Street was the key.

On my next visit to Tekka Markets, I returned via Bencoolen Street. Scanning it for points of familiarity, I felt demoralised. There were some older buildings but dwarfed as they were the scale of the street was completely transformed. It was time to consult Jerome Lim's blog again to find that he had written a piece about heritage buildings along Bencoolen Street. He wrote:

> One survivor is one that is immediately recognisable – a large two storey house close to the junction of Bencoolen Street with Middle Road, No. 81 Bencoolen Street. . . . I imagined it to once have been the home of a rich merchant. . . . Like a similar house next to the former Middle Road Church, the house was one which a hotel had occupied, the Kian Hua Hotel.

Reading Jerome's words gave me hope. He continued:

> On the hotel, I have found little information. Other than several newspaper advertisements in the National Library's wonderful archives of newspapers that told me only that the hotel had occupied the building at least as far back as 1953, there isn't much on it except of an apparent suicide – a 26 year old ex-journalist had been found hanging from a ceiling fan in one of the hotel's rooms one morning in early 1988, with a nylon rope around her neck.

Relieved this was long after my time at Kian Hua, I still wondered why I hadn't I noticed it in passing. Delving further into Jerome's blog, I found the answer.

> The house is now in what has to be its fourth incarnation, having for a while after the hotel's closure, masqueraded as the gaily decorated Cleopatra Karaoke Lounge. A lot more sober looking today, it does seem to have its former glory I imagined it to have been in.

I'd often passed by without realising. When I visited the site, I was overwhelmed by the architectural genius that had transformed the old building incorporating it into a reflective 21st century showpiece.

Life changed dramatically when I started using the Mass Rapid Transit (MRT) railway system. This was the end of any systematic attempt to reconcile old and new. Now I could travel almost anywhere in Singapore within 30 minutes and soon I realised that in tandem with buses I could use the MRT to take one of the world's cheapest international journeys and visit Johore Baharu, in Malaysia. So off I went.

On the final leg of my return journey on the MRT, I discovered all the seats were occupied even those reserved for the injured, expectant mothers and the elderly.

"Would you like a seat?" asked an attractive petite Chinese woman whom I guessed was in her 50s. She motioned to the place she'd just vacated.

"Thank you, but I am really quite all right standing," I replied.

"But you are a senior and this is a senior's seat," she insisted politely.

"True, I'm already 67, but I'm quite mobile." Joking, I went on, "The senior in the sketch has a walking stick and I walked 20 kilometres last weekend."

Her expression was warm, and with a vaguely perplexed smile she resumed her seat.

I couldn't tell if she got my joke. She seemed very thoughtful but on the other hand, maybe she was just following the rules; it is hard to tell with Singaporeans.

"Are you working here?" she enquired.

"No, I've retired. Well when I say I've retired I'm actually writing a book."

"A book. What is it about?"

"It's a book of short stories. It's about many things. There are several themes but I suppose the easiest way to explain one aspect is that it reframes Australia's relationship with Asia and Melanesia. Maybe I can offer a different outlook and help people to see that they are part of the region and not just displaced from somewhere else like Europe."

"That is going to be very difficult," she replied. "When I was in Australia I found suburban Australians quite insular and racist."

I was a little taken aback by her directness even though I enjoyed that Singaporean forthrightness. I know the subculture she means. It can be very embarrassing to be associated with it when in Asia.

"Yes, some of the people in the suburbs can be insular. I worry about them. I feel sad for them and their children in the Asian century. Many seem to adopt an attitude of superiority but it's a superiority born of ignorance and there is a danger they'll become increasingly out of touch."

"I didn't like that racism," she went on. "People treated me as more primitive, as less developed. I found it very offensive."

"That can happen," I agreed. "What were you doing in Australia?"

"I was completing a Master's Degree in Management."

"It must have been so irritating for you but not everyone's like that. Which area did you live in?"

"I was staying in suburban Perth."

I wondered what I should say in a situation like this, then said, "If you'd stayed in a different city, maybe inner Sydney or Melbourne, I expect your experience would have been quite different."

"Yes, perhaps, but there was once that White Australia policy as well. It affected people's attitudes. There is a lot of racism in Australia," she emphasised.

Seen and Unseen

She was right. Things had improved, she might not have realised that, but there was always that capacity for an upwelling of racism and xenophobia. I thought of the Howard years and his failure to condemn racism in unambiguous terms.

"There's no point in me apologising for it, but I'm deeply saddened you were exposed to such racism."

The train stopped. Glancing out at the station sign I realised I was almost home. "This is my stop. It's been a pleasure chatting with you. 'Bye then."

"Good luck with your book," she replied.

Vietnam: A War Revisited

Hanoi traffic flows continuously so waiting for a break is pointless. Watching other pedestrians cross is the quickest way to acquire the technique for making safe passage. Stepping out into the jumble of fast moving vehicles is the only way forward, the crossing akin to fording a river as traffic, mainly motorbikes, swirls past like water.

After few days, I felt comfortable and could spot a new arrival in an instant. They looked troubled, standing by the side of a busy road waiting for an opportunity that never seemed to come. This was how I met Graeme Kemp.

Graeme stood beside busy Hàng Quat. He wore a Waratahs' Rugby T-shirt, his reluctance obvious as he waited for a break. Someone from my generation, I surmised, and a bit of a traveller lacking the glutton's paunch of more sedentary westerners.

I stepped up beside him. "A Brumbies' supporter'd be across the road by now."

He turned, brows raised in surprise at such an unexpected comment.

"It only takes a few days to get used to it," I explained. "Just follow me across. I've been here a week now."

"So you reckon Brumbies do it better, eh?" He smiled.

"I'll stand on this side," I said as I stepped between him and the oncoming traffic.

Out we went. Motorbikes swirled around us and in moments, we were safely across. I said, "It just flows around like water. Well, I guess that's stretching it a little. I'm Russell, by the way." I extended my hand.

"Graeme," he replied. "Thanks for that. I arrived last night. Still trying to get my head around this."

Seen and Unseen

"And keep your body safe," I joked. "Looks as though you're from Sydney."

"Good guess; Lithgow originally. I moved to Sydney in 1965 to go to Sydney University."

"Small world. I went there." By now I was used to such coincidences. "I'm about to stop for coffee at Fuk Hang Café. It's on this street. Care to join me?"

"Sure. With a name like that it's got to be worth a photo. I'm headed for the Military History Museum but it can wait."

Fuk Hang Café turned out to be called Fuk Bar, both bar and café. I'd imagined it spilling out onto the footpath like so many Hanoi restaurants and coffee shops but, instead, we entered through a small dark hallway. All was mysterious at first, but as eyes adjusted, its décor was reminiscent of a 1960s folk music venue. Set with small, round tables and straight-backed chairs, this more formal effect was softened by a random clutter of rattan armchairs covered with hand woven textiles. Its walls were hung with an eclectic array of old photos and posters.

We settled in to enjoy our coffee.

"Apart from the Military History Museum, what brings you to Hanoi, Graeme?" I asked.

"It's a pilgrimage in a sense. I was one of those anti-war people back when I was at university.

"Amazing! Me too. I'm surprised I never met you."

"I kept a very low profile and even joined the Sydney University Regiment, part of the Citizens' Military Force, for a while."

"So we're both children of the nuclear arms race," I said, inviting him to go on.

"I am. I still remember watching Bertrand Russell's arrest at a CND demonstration in Trafalgar Square. Fear of nuclear war was a constant undertone back then."

"For me, pacifism seemed the sane response to the

nuclear overkill."

Graeme nodded in agreement.

I hadn't expected to meet someone like Graeme; perhaps an Australian Vietnam Vet, but not someone who had chosen a path so similar to my own. Sharing such thoughts with him seemed quite natural.

"No doubt there was a need to defend our country," I said, "but I figured nuclear strategies offered us scorched earth and the age of the cockroaches."

Graeme's expression was impassive. He sat for a moment without responding then drew breath and said, in what seemed like a confessional tone, "When the Menzies Government introduced conscription to support their war efforts in Vietnam, I decided to join the regiment as a way of avoiding the draft."

He seemed uncomfortable but relaxed when I said, "I knew a few people who did that. I even spent a short stint working as a batman for the regiment. Just as a civilian employee mind you. I worked at a bivouac camp in the hills above Cessnock during the summer of 1965."

His expression softened. "Really, Russell?" he said. "Another coincidence. This was my first overnight activity with the regiment. It's where I first encountered the Domino Theory."

"Ah! The hoary old Domino Theory. There was a certain naive gravitational logic to it. China was up we were down. It harmonised well with primitive fears of the Yellow Peril."

"It did, but I think its historical roots were in Western European fears of Mongols and Huns. Sure the rapid Japanese advance through Indo-China, Malaya and Singapore gave it some legs as well, but I found it difficult to associate what I knew of Soviet totalitarianism with the Asian context. Communism wasn't that monolithic."

Graeme was right; China's Communist revolution was different in character to the military imposition of Communism in Eastern Europe. Apart from the war in Korea, which had been fought to a stalemate, there was no equivalent. The Malayan Emergency demonstrated the limited effectiveness of Communism in South East Asia and while there were conflicts in Laos and Vietnam, these were small in scale and complex. *Konfrontasi* (Confrontation) concerned me, yet I was benignly disposed towards Indonesia, given their non-aligned status.

"Did joining the regiment make you question your pacifism?" I asked.

"Not of itself. I didn't question it till I read Frantz Fanon's *Wretched of the Earth*. By then I'd I resigned from the regiment, which meant I was eligible for the draft."

I understood why this work might have had such an impact on Graeme's views. Fanon's treatise shaped a lot of thinking when published in 1966. It confronted many of us with the cruelty of colonisation, revealing the enormous disparities in military power between the powerful industrial countries and their colonies. It laid bare the racism inherent in colonialism and imperialism.

"Now things weren't quite adding up for me," he said, and then fell silent again.

A poster on the wall seemed to catch his attention. It showed three arms each with different skin tones representing the people of the world. They pointed down through a sky, discoloured by the smoke of battle, towards a massive B-52 bomber dropping napalm. Fire raged through groves of coconut palms. Beneath the image were the words: *Tố cáo đế quốc mỹ những xâm lược*, which had been translated as "Denouncing the US imperialist invaders".

"Iconically that poster sums up what I was just thinking," he said. "If the US was the 'defender of the free world' why were they using their military strength against smaller countries like Laos and Vietnam?"

He stopped again, staring at the poster. It was a powerful image.

We sat in silence, my mind flashing over things that influenced me at the time. Investigation confirmed something genocidal was enfolding in Vietnam. Villages were being burned, people subjected to massive bombing, crops and natural vegetation destroyed by defoliants, napalm, white phosphorous and cluster bombs maiming and terrorising. Entire villages were relocated behind barbed wire into concentration camps known as strategic hamlets. Massive amounts of armaments were being brought to bear on a small nation by the global superpower.

Graeme continued, "I began to distinguish between what I saw as the violence of the oppressor and the violence of the oppressed. Then in 1966, Private Errol Wayne Noack was killed in Vietnam. He was the first conscript to die in action. I identified with him. He could have been me."

"I was in Adelaide at the time, attending the Australian Student Labour Federation (ASLF) conference. Our response was immediate; we left the conference venue and occupied the Liberal Country League offices on North Terrace. This was a turning point for me. He was from North Adelaide, you know."

Glancing away from the poster and looking at me, he said, "I'd like to head off to the Military History Museum soon. Would you care to join me?"

"Sure. I'll get the bill."

"Thanks, that'd be great. While you're settling I'll jump onto the Wi-Fi here and Skype my wife and kids. They'll have a bit of a laugh when I tell them where I am."

Progress in the old city wasn't simple. Restaurant chairs, market stalls and motorbikes often blocked footpaths. We talked little, except when stopping to admire some of the unique streetscapes. There were streets of locks, sheet metal work, votive items, hats, bamboo, textiles and carpets, clothing, electronics and electronics repair, a well-established specialisation, street by street. Everywhere fruit and vegetable sellers plied their trade, from baskets carried on bicycles or shoulder poles, beneath festoons of spaghetti-like electrical cables.

In these streets, the strength and dignity of the Vietnamese people was obvious. Even today, in this ostensibly Communist country, there is scant evidence of groupthink or austerity. Everywhere were youthful people connected to the world through millions of handheld digital devices. An Australian Vietnamese taxi driver's recent insistence that Vietnam was just like North Korea foundered on the reality unfolding in these streets.

Back in the Australia of my youth, much of the truth about this remarkable country remained undisclosed and unseen. Not until embargoed documents from Australia's Department of Foreign Affairs and Trade were released in the 1990s, was the full extent of Australia's involvement in this pitiful affair revealed. Conservative politicians engineered an invitation to the war from the South Vietnamese regime out of some misguided construction of potential threats to Australia, a need for forward defence and their decision to use the 'Red Menace' as an electoral tool. It had nothing to do with ANZAS Treaty obligations, much less SEATO, the South East Asia Treaty Organisation. Great damage was done to Australian life and culture, but most of all to the Vietnamese.

Opposition to the war in Vietnam was characterised as unpatriotic. The Liberal Country Party coalition's success in the elections of 1966 was a testimony to their skill in capturing and transforming Australian's sense of themselves and their role as global citizens. Balanced approaches to foreign policy initiated by the Curtin and Chifley Labor Governments were thrown aside. No longer was Australia taking a leading role in initiating solutions to conflict through the United Nations, rather our foreign policy was shaped by values inherent in Prime Minister Harold Holt's demeaning words "All the way with LBJ".

Graeme and I took our time with the Military History Museum. If it conveyed one thing it was the resilience, ingenuity and the sophistication of the Vietnamese response to the war. The courtyard display of a Soviet-built MiG-21 jet fighter sitting intact amidst the wreckage of a US F-111 and French aircraft downed at Dien Bien Phu was most dramatic. Back in the 1960s, I had doubted the North Vietnamese claims about the thousands of US planes shot down. History has proven their claims correct.

After the museum, we set out in search of coffee discovering an elegant outdoor restaurant next door.

Ordering bottled water and coffee, we sat down in comfortable garden furniture beneath a portable fan. Turning the bottled water over in my hand, I read the label. Dasani, it seemed to be everywhere in Hanoi. Beneath the brand were some unexpected words The Coca-Cola Company.

"Have a look at this, Graeme." I held the bottle label towards him.

"So they won after all," he chuckled. "Ironic, isn't it. We struggled so hard against 'The American War', yet things have moved on. China's now the big problem for Vietnam."

"It sure is. If you go to the 'Hanoi Hilton', the old gaol, there's a display about the territorial struggle for control of islands and shoals in the South China Sea. The

Vietnamese call it The East Sea. They're acquiring Russian submarines to defend their territories."

"It just shows how far out of line Australian foreign policy was under Holt. Such a tragedy," he insisted. "I'm so glad I resisted the draft."

"So were you were called up in the end, Graeme?"

"Yeah. I burned my draft card as soon as I got it and tried to drag out my degree a bit doing some part time courses. By the end of 1968, I had finished both the degree and a post-graduate diploma. I was banking on Labor winning the 1969 Federal elections but they missed out by seven seats even with 50.02% of the national vote. Of course, I registered to vote and worked on the campaign."

"I remember watching that count with a big group of people. It was exciting to begin with. I had the flu so when the result was clear I was even more depressed than most. Let me get this straight though. If you registered to vote, it meant you were easy to find."

"I sure was," he exclaimed. "Within weeks of the election, there was an early morning knock at the door. Through the translucent panel, I could see a large person with a blue shirt. It was a Commonwealth cop. Without much comment, he handed me a direction to report for a medical at the Commonwealth Repatriation Department's offices in Sydney's Grace Building."

The Commonwealth Police Force was a small unit with little apparent capacity for investigative work. Given the number of draft dodgers and draft resisters at large they seemed overwhelmed.

"Do you remember Michael Matteson, Graeme?"

"Yeah, he was an Anarchist who kept making defiant appearances. On the roof at Sydney University, on a live television performance debating the Attorney General before escaping out the back of the studio. Eventually he was caught and handcuffed by two Commonwealth Cops on the Sydney University campus.

"That's the man," I said.

"I was there that day Russ. Thousands of students blockaded them and then someone produced bolt cutters and freed him. High drama but my story's less dramatic. I wasn't cut out for that type of performance."

"So what did you do once you'd been served the papers?"

"Well, I'll tell you the story. I'd rehearsed a strategy for the medical. First I went to a benign GP in Newtown. He obligingly gave me some little white pills for my stress. I didn't ever take them; I assume they were Valium or something similar. I threw a few away and kept the bottle. On advice from a medical student friend my strategy was to fake conversion symptoms, but that seemed too hard so I decided to make things up as I went along. Just before the medical I drank two schooners of beer and took a slimming tablet. In those days amphetamine based slimming tablets were available over the counter. I think this one was called Attenuate."

"Yeah, those. I knew people who used them to stay awake and study."

"They did. So anyway when I went to the Grace Building the first thing I saw was the Commonwealth Cop at the entrance.

"'I didn't expect to see you here,' he said with genuine surprise.

"'Oh, really', I answered.

A public servant called out. 'Everyone attending the medical whose name begins with A to K fall-in along this wall.'

I thought, this is starting to sound like the army already."

"I know what you mean; it was obvious even in that little stint working for the Regiment."

"Come my turn to hand in my paperwork, I happened to glance at the clerk's hand, it was missing. It didn't stop him deftly flicking open a manila folders with his stump but it was confronting. I guessed it was a war injury. Rather ironic that he was still willing to serve up another generation.

"Soon it was my turn to begin the medical. First step was an interview with the Psychologist. I reasoned that the best approach was to answer every question in the most equivocal way possible. As an exercise I decided against using the words 'yes' or 'no'.

"'Your name's Graeme Stanley Kemp?' she asked.

"'Graeme Stanley Kemp,' I repeated in as bland and non-committal manner as possible, almost like a robotic echo.

"'So you've been a student?'

"'A student,' I answered in the same tone.

"So it went on.

"When she asked me if there was any history of mental illness in my family, I answered, 'Mental illness. Mmm… not… sure… maybe. Then pausing before continuing, 'Oh, shock treatment, my mother had it.' Followed by another pause, then finally, 'I think.' I waited for a moment and said, 'Grannie, maybe?'

"Then she asked if I'd had any mental illness. 'Mental illness… mmm… not sure,' I said. 'Doctor gave me this,' producing the bottle and shaking it a little.

"I could see that the bottle wasn't the only thing that was rattled. The psychologist was becoming most uncomfortable. I thought, it's starting to work but she must realise I'm just playing around and being avoidant.

"Next it was time for the physical."

"I'm surprised they even let you go on to that stage," I said, chuckling.

Graeme continued, "I didn't say anything so it was quite straightforward up to the point of taking my blood pressure. Clearly the stress of the whole event potentiated by the slimming tablet had raised it.

"'I want you to lie down here for a while,' the doctor instructed.

"This seemed promising so I spent the next 20 minutes tensing every muscle group in my body in a type of counter yoga, beginning with my toes and working up to my forehead.

"After 20 minutes the doctor reappeared. Strapping on the sphygmomanometer again and pumping up the cuff his look of bland concentration turned to one of annoyance perhaps even disgust.

"'Get out of here,' he snapped.

"Hitting the street I was exhilarated but also mindful that the war would soon come to an end. The Commonwealth Police had been anything but efficient and the army clearly couldn't afford to be hampered by reluctant conscripts whether in the cells or in the field."

"It's an interesting story, Graeme. I must tell you mine. I'm leaving for Da Nang in the morning. Would you like to join me?"

"Great, let's do it," he smiled. "I'm glad this is my first visit."

Seen and Unseen

Headland

Climbing down the cliff by Wylie's Baths, we made our way around the rock platform. Sid wanted to see his favourite bogey hole again just for nostalgia's sake. A rising tide largely obscured the place, so we continued round to the point where the small waterfall cascades over the cliff face. Heavy rains in the past few days had transformed it from trickle to torrent.

"We can still get up here," Sid said. "Just need to take it easy. I'll give you a hand, Russ. It's slippery."

"Thanks, but I'm not a small child now. I should be helping you."

"You're my grandson. You used to call me Pa. I've noticed you've called me Sid since I first started to tell you the ANMEF story. I'm not sure why you've stopped."

"I remember. As a small child I called you Pa, but you died in 1952. You were only 58 then and I'm 67 now."

"Sure Russ, but *remember they shall grow not old as we that are left…*"[19]

"Yeah sure, the ode," I interrupted. "Even so, remember you died from a heart condition; you'd had malaria and what's more you smoked. I take your point but let's stop this Pa stuff once and for all. From now on you're Sid. OK?"

"Fair dinkum, you've become disrespectful in your old age," he retorted, his feigned gravity barely masking a smile.

We strolled back around the cliff top, past an elegant discontinuity forged and etched across the sandstone, where an ancient river once changed its course. I considered

[19] From 'For the Fallen', a poem by Robert Laurence Binyon (1869-1943), published in *The Times* newspaper on 21 September 1914.

Sydney's sandstone cliffs: seemingly intractable barriers yet only in human terms. In geological reality, they were rent by relentless abrading of surface. Their very substance was the product of countless transformations from the instant of creation when God made Heaven and Earth[20], the beginning of time and space.

Walking through the park, we headed down the hill towards Coogee Surf Club. As Sid walked beside me, he drew with him an aura like vision of Coogee as it was in his time. Behind him, buildings assumed the duller colour palette of 1952 and as we stepped out onto the promenade, outlines of great Norfolk Pines appeared as Sid passed.

I gazed seaward. By the time I turned again to speak with Sid, his image was a translucent suggestion. "Sid, I've always had difficulty with simplistic literal accounts of Creation." His image sharpened with my words.

"You don't believe in the *Genesis* account. Is this what you mean?"

"No, it isn't. *Genesis* has the sequence right; it's just the timing. Remember those early European navigators who could calculate latitude accurately but not longitude? It's a bit like that."

"So the maps they made weren't accurate," Sid asked, his image now strong and opaque.

"Exactly. St Peter says, 'Do not forget this one thing, that with the Lord one day is as a thousand years, and a thousand years as one day.'[21] He acknowledges that creation isn't on a human scale. Then much later, St Basil clarifies it even further when he points out that, 'if you say a day or an aeon, you express the same meaning'.[22] It's all in the words."

---

[20] *Genesis 1:1* Scripture taken from St. Athanasius Academy Septaguint™. Copyright © 2008 by St. Athanasius Academy of Orthodox Theology. Used by permission. All rights reserved. *Orthodox Study Bible*. Thomas Nelson.
21 NKJV. 2 Peter 3:8-9.
[22] *St Basil the Great, Hexaemeron*, Hom. II,8.

"Yeah, words," Sid reflected. "So essential and so easily misunderstood."

We continued in silence, Sid's image fading again, until we reached Coogee's northern headland: a sloping mass of sandstone grassed and graced with more recent plantings of tea tree, melaluca and banksia. During my childhood it was bare, stripped of all but grass and strands of pink flowering pig face.

"I come here often, Sid. I've thought of you a lot here but it's easy to become dwarfed by a sense of the spiritual, of eternity; so sometimes, I just retreat into geological time. I try to imagine what it must have been like in ancient Gondwana as it transitioned from Carboniferous to Permian and on into the Triassic."

"That's outside my area, Russ. I've heard of these things before except for Gond . . . what was it?"

"Gondwana."

"Gondwana. Yeah, what's that?"

"You were dead before we started using that term. It's an ancient mega continent."

By now we'd reached the white painted rails at the top of the slope with a magnificent view out to Wedding Cake Island. This is where an embodied Sid would have taken out his pipe, puffing away as he rested a leg on the bottom rung.

We remained in silence, appreciating the setting; Sid's image faded again as I drifted into thoughts on the vast Triassic sands forming the bedrock of the Sydney Basin and imagining the continent separating from Antarctica, of sea levels rising and falling of the planet warming and cooling.

I wondered how Aboriginal clans responded when the ocean began rising, the waters lapping at a steadily retreating coastal life. How did they understand the slow transformation?

A shark patrol plane flying low broke my concentration.

"What are you thinking about Russ?" Sid asked, his voice almost inaudible against the distant roar of sea and propellers.

I turned just catching his image against the afternoon sun. "I'll explain that in a moment but before I do, I've noticed changes in the way you're speaking. For example, in that last question you said 'thinking' instead of 'thinkin''. Your register's changed."

"I don't know about that, but maybe listening to you over the years, I've picked up a few habits."

"Okay, I can understand that."

"So what were you thinking about?" Sid asked.

"I was thinking of the Aboriginal clans that settled this area and wondering what it must have been like for them having to move 50 kilometres inland as the waters rose."

"Yeah, I often wondered what it must have been like for the black fella before we arrived."

"Do you think they'd have stood here, looking out like us?" I asked, not expecting an answer.

"Yeah, I reckon, maybe they would've."

"It's so clear and serene now; the rain's stopped but it can be so exposed and lonely cut by wind and salt spray. Headlands are places of such primal transformations, land and sea meeting in a realm of turbulence."

"Your great-grandmother Jane was Irish, you know. She once told me about the ruins they visited in the West Country. Old stone buildings on the headlands. She said monks used them."

"*Clochan*. I know about those, Sid."

"Yeah, it comes to mind now. *Clochan*, that's what she called them."

Celtic monks chose headlands and rocky islands as preferred places of solitude. They acknowledged their spiritual importance, recognising them as vantage points from which one is privileged to experience moments of clarity, moments in which the veil shrouding the profound mystery of creation is apt to lift.

"You've gone again, Russ," Sid interrupted.

"I was just thinking about those the ancient traditions. Sorry, but when I start to think deeply you disappear."

"Oh, so you just think me out of existence do you?"

"Something like that, but no. Coogee has special meaning for me. I see it as a place imbued with spirits, yours for one. Also it's a place of a childhood now just partly remembered."

Sid's image was strong; now I could almost smell the tobacco.

"If you think about it, my maternal ancestors' graves lie to the south of here. Some say we aren't of a place until we've buried our dead there."

Sid looked at me knowingly.

"For years, I had difficulty feeling at ease here on this headland, so most of my playtime was spent in the south. It had very positive energy." I didn't quite know how to explain this to Sid, but reasoned that I should just allow the story to unfold. "There was something heavy something outside my understanding here but in the rational postwar world, feelings were not to be valued or shared. As a young person, I put these difficult feelings down more to my own fears of the unknown or my own sense of mortality and morbid childlike fear of death."

"You could have shared those feelings with me, Russ," Sid interrupted. "I remember you being a bit scared of the dark particularly on windy nights."

"Sid, you died when I was five years old so we didn't have those conversations."

"Yeah, Russ, I was sad to go at that time but my body just wore out."

"That's okay, Sid, I was sad to lose you but life went on. I must say it was very difficult at first but childhood was exciting. It was largely free of physical boundaries. Fear wasn't a big feature of life apart from a healthy concern for sharks. I swam, surfed and dived along this coastline but I was never comfortable on this headland."

"So what was the problem with this place?"

"Well, for one, it was a suicide spot, but I'll tell you the story."

"Good, I'd like to hear it," said Sid.

"I couldn't work it out for a long time. By contrast once down in the bays to the north, Thompson's and Clovelly, it wasn't so intense then on the next headland by Waverley cemetery the intensity resumed and I felt the discomfort. So the two headlands were the problem."

"That's interesting. I can't say I've ever noticed this," Sid commented.

"In late 1966, I was working in the park by the cemetery as a groundsman. I felt very uncomfortable. I'd never had that feeling about a cemetery before; in fact, I rather enjoyed the cemetery at South Coogee where some of our immediate relatives lie. I often wandered there with my Mum and Nana as a little one."

"That's where we buried your Aunty Enid. Such a beautiful girl; such a sad loss."

"Anyway, the feeling became most acute on the day when Ronald Ryan, the last Australian to be executed, was hanged at old Pentridge Gaol. The Australian Council of Trade Unions called on workers to strike that day. I did willingly. There was no way I could to stay alone on that isolated headland on such a day."

"So they stopped hanging people in Australia? Well, that was long overdue. I didn't like the government playing God and it never did help lessen crime," Sid said.

Seen and Unseen

I hadn't thought about Sid's attitudes to such things, although judging from my mother's opinions it made sense. Australia's post-colonial history was a violent one. In attempting to solve this problem, I wondered if the headland had been the site of a mass killing of the local Gadigal people. It was possible. In my experience, mass killings leave their mark on a landscape an unseen spiritual disturbance. Later, living and working in Indonesia, I learned that some cultures were inclined to view the world this way.

In Balinese spirituality, areas had their own special energies that rendered them more or less suitable for humans. Certain places were inclined to fall under the influences of gods or demons. In this spiritual scheme higher places towards the mountains and the east were spiritually positive. Lower places towards the sea and the west were spiritually negative. I'd also wondered whether such spiritual geography might explain the headland's special energy.

"Sid, I've thought about this a lot."

He was vaguely discernible but at the mention of his name, his image began to resolve.

"There are many things that aren't easy to see. You know, it's just as well I have my Bluetooth ear piece in because people might think I was chatting with my own internal voices if they saw me standing here alone."

"What are you talking about, Russ? Bluetooth?"

"It's just a tool used in communications, another part of the unseen world."

Sid looked at me sympathetically.

"But to continue, Sid, places can have a past and I wondered whether something dreadful had happened here. I sensed something. So I researched the possibility of a massacre of Aboriginal people and all I discovered was that Aboriginal tradition might have reserved the northern end of Coogee Beach for men's activities and the southern end for women's business."

"Interesting. You know the bogey hole just below was known as Giles Baths when I lived here. It was a men's swimming place."

"Right, and over there at the southern end was McIver's women's only baths. It's still something of a Sydney landmark."

"What's this to do with your feelings about the headlands, Russ?"

"Nothing directly, it's an anecdote but I came across it trying to learn more about the headland."

I turned and began walking slowly towards the old baths, a light southeasterly breeze blowing directly into my face. It had a chilly edge to it on this early spring day.

"Just a minute, Russ. What's that tangle of metal tubes doing here? That's new."

"It's the Memorial to the Victims of the Bali Bombing. It's dedicated to people killed and injured in a terrorist attack. Just down here there's another one."

We walked down the hill towards the old portico of Giles baths. As we went, I thought about the dramatic events that have enveloped the headland in recent years. After the Bali bombings of 2002, the headland was renamed Dolphin Point in memory of the six members of the Coogee Dolphins Rugby League team killed in the blast. Within weeks of this, a local woman reported seeing an apparition on a post and rail fence line near the old baths portico. She described what she saw as the Virgin Mary.

Reaching the portico we stopped.

"See these plaques, Sid?"

"Yes, I do. What are the pictures on them?"

"They're pictures of 20 people from the Eastern Suburbs killed in the Bali bombings of 2002. We commemorate them and the others who died every year now, on this headland."

"Yes, I see. Very sad, very sad. Such a waste, war is always a sad waste."

"Yes, it is although this wasn't a war; it was an act of terrorism."

Sid looked confused. I reasoned it was a term he'd not really heard before. He waited for me to continue. "The remarkable appearance of the Virgin Mary, the Mother of God, transformed this place. Huge diverse crowds appeared, the faithful, the sceptical and the curious. The apparition could be seen everyday at a certain time in the afternoon. When I came to see it, the sceptics were the most vocal. 'It's just light and shadows' was a common response."

"Was it light and shadows, Russ?"

"Yes, it was light, shadow, post and rail, but I puzzled about what people expected. In my own mind, this was enough to mark the importance of the site."

"Yep, you've got a point there. So your feelings about the place were beginning to change?"

"They certainly were. There was still that heaviness right up on top, where we were just standing, but the energy was changing for me."

We looked out over the tiny informal shrine erected to commemorate the appearance of the Mother of God. Beyond was the commanding sweep of Coogee Beach. I thought about all that loss in Bali. I reflected on my own dramatic loss of innocence, on the pain, suffering and death I saw, on the trauma I carried with me. Tears flowed as they always did in this place. I stood with the feelings for a few moments then continued. "As you can see, this place has a new meaning for me now but I must get to the end of this story. I haven't finished."

"Go on then," said Sid, his image clear and strong despite my moment of meditation.

"I started to do some research into family history. I might add, your family history is very hard to research."

"There is a good reason for that, Russ. Ask me later."

"Okay I will. So, I thought I knew most about my father's family but there was one key element missing. Unbeknown to me my great-great-grandmother, great-grand parents and an infant great-grand uncle were all buried in the old Waverley Cemetery. What's more, my great-grandfather's brother, Samuel, and a large portion of his family were there as well. I had no idea."

"Your father didn't tell you?"

"No, and once I'd visited their graves the last piece of the puzzle fell into place. All the darkness vanished. So now both headlands are places of reflection, prayer, hope, peace and new beginnings."

Down on the beach, two fishermen pulled a small boat up onto the sand. I remembered how Sid and I often bought fish from these boats when I was a child.

Drawn to the activity, I started down the path. After a few steps, I glanced back; Sid had gone. I continued knowing that I would find him again in this place.